Embracing Travail

Embracing Travail

Retrieving the Cross Today

Cynthia S. W. Crysdale

CONTINUUM
NEW YORK

1999

The Continuum Publishing Company
370 Lexington Avenue, New York, NY 10017

Printed in the United States of America

Library of Congress Cataloging-in-Publication Data

Crysdale, Cynthia S. W., 1953–
    Embracing travail : retrieving the Cross today / Cynthia S. W.
Crysdale.
        p.   cm.
    Includes bibliographical references and index.
    ISBN 0-8264-1160-6
    1. Holy Cross.   2. Feminist theology.   I. Title.
BT453.C78   1999
234'.3'082–dc21   98-55485
                                                          CIP

To David,
who has embraced travail with me, and

To Peter and Carolyn,
who are constant reminders of resurrection

Come, ye disconsolate, where'er ye languish,
Come to the mercy seat, fervently kneel:
Here bring your wounded hearts, here tell your anguish;
Earth has no sorrow that heav'n cannot heal.

Joy of the desolate, light of the straying,
Hope of the penitent, fadeless and pure!
Here speaks the comforter, tenderly saying,
"Earth has no sorrow that heav'n cannot cure."
–Thomas Moore
From *Lift Every Voice and Sing II:*
An African American Hymnal

There is a balm in Gilead
To make the wounded whole;
There is a balm in Gilead
To heal the sin-sick soul.
–Traditional
From *Lift Every Voice and Sing II:*
An African American Hymnal

Contents

Preface

T HE CROSS HAS ALWAYS BEEN a stumbling block, for the doubtful and the pious alike. That the Good News of Christianity should have at its heart the cruel death of an innocent victim is a fact that many find hard to swallow. Many reject such "good news" as nonsense, while even those who do believe find it easier to avoid the topic than to confront it. Easter services pack the house, while Good Friday liturgies unfold to a smattering of worshipers.

In the last three decades the "bad news" of the cross has become even more apparent. Women who have been told that their suffering is either deserved or meritorious have begun raising questions. Why suffering, and why does it always seem to land on the shoulders of those already downtrodden? The ways in which a theology of the cross has been used to denigrate women and minorities have been unveiled. The perpetuation of injustice in the name of the cross has been exposed, and certain institutions and people have been called to account. Many of these critics of "redemption" have come to the conclusion that Christianity must either be rejected outright or purged of the cross altogether.

In the fall of 1996 I came to deal with these issues when I was asked to give the Glasmacher Lecture at St. Paul's University in Ottawa. My own experience of life's struggles had led me to understand viscerally the problems with valorizing suffering. Yet my religious experience also made it hard for me to reject Christian faith or adopt Christianity without the cross. My attempt to reconcile my feminism with my conviction that suffering could, indeed, be redemptive met a receptive audience in the faculty and students of St. Paul's. Over and over again, in conversations and discussions, I heard stories of ordinary people struggling for liberation from falsely imposed guilt, trying to make sense out of suffering, and wanting to incorporate their profound experiences of God into the process.

My subsequent sabbatical in the winter of 1997 then became the fertile empty place from which this book came forth. I spent a semester at the Institute for Ecumenical and Cultural Research at St. John's University in Collegeville, Minnesota. I subsequently received a Sabbatical Grant from the Christian Faith and Life Program of the Louisville Institute, which enabled me to take another twelve months away from teaching. The upshot is this book—my attempt to retrieve a Christian faith with the cross and suffering front and center, while taking stock of the very telling critiques that reveal the "pathologies" of the cross as they have often operated in Christian practice.

The book is limited in its focus. Moral philosophers make the distinction between "moral" and "physical" evils. The first have to with actions of human agents, while the second are "acts of God" in the natural world: earthquakes, flood, diseases, and the like. My preoccupation in this book is with the former, with moral evils and human actions. I deal with how people can find meaning in the suffering caused by human choices, both their own and those of others. I examine the choices that people can make to resist and transform such suffering, ways in which they can tip the balance in favor of human authenticity and hope. Though these issues are not unrelated to the question of being a creature in a web of nature beyond our control, this latter topic is a subject beyond the scope of my current project.

In this book I develop a theological model—a framework, a set of categories, an explanation of transformative processes. In presenting a model I am not trying to exhaustively describe every possible experience, or include all aspects of victimization, sin, resistance, surrender, grace, and "voice." I hope that I have not overlooked some crucial aspect of Christian theology or lived experience. But if this is the case, I stand to be corrected: a model, precisely because it arises out of the concrete, always stands to be corrected. Likewise, a model is useless unless it is applied. Bernard Lonergan likens a model to a proverb: both "he who hesitates is lost" and "look before you leap" are true depending on the situation at hand. So, "confess your sins" and "embrace your wounds" are both true. But it is the role of the individual reader in their concrete context to discern how, when, and in what manner these are best applied.

In theological discussions today there is always the issue of "particularity" versus "universality." Simply translated, this is the question of whether, since we are all inextricably bound to a particular time, place, social class, race, and gender, any one person can articulate universal truth. My work comes out of *my* particularity: it is the work of a white, middle-class Christian woman raised in a (relatively) stable home, who came of age at the end of the sixties and was inculcated with the best and the worst of liberal values. Yet what I have to offer here I offer not as an idiosyncratic project applicable to myself and a few others like me. Nor do I presume it to be the only possible model. I believe that many people will find themselves in this book, and that its main points will be applicable to a wide range of situations and people. How wide that range is will be determined not by me but by those who read the book.

The book begins by introducing the notion that some people can accept the story of cross and resurrection more readily by identifying with Jesus the Crucified. While theologies of redemption have focused most often on the betrayal of Jesus and the forgiveness of sins, many of the disempowered today find such theologies alien, if not downright harmful. To enter the story from the perspective of the victim is much more viable. Chapter 2 expands on the dynamic of discovering oneself as *both* a victim and a perpetrator of sin: I insist that the two must be held together if authentic transformation is to take place. Chapter 3 raises the further question of authentic versus dysfunctional resistance and surrender, while chapter 4 examines the importance of "voice" in interpreting redemption. Chapter 5 lays out the damage that certain interpretations of the cross have caused for people on the "underside" of political, social, and religious power. Chapter 6 puts it all together in a constructive model of sin, grace, and God's solution to the problem of evil. The epilogue suggests certain parameters within which Jesus' crucifixion might be interpreted today.

As will become obvious, the material put forward here is intimately woven into the fabric of my own life. This makes the task of acknowledging persons who have contributed to my project overwhelming, something like thanking "everyone I have ever known." Still, this work is so much the fruit of other people journeying with me, that some names must be mentioned.

The Institute for Ecumenical and Cultural Research provided an incalculable resource for my work. Dolores Schuh, the Administrative Assistant, welcomed me and my daughter to life in Minnesota with charm and efficiency; without her humor and assistance this project would never have gone forward. Patrick Henry, the Executive Director, went well beyond the call of duty in reading and editing my early drafts. His enthusiasm and confidence in my work have carried me well beyond my winter sojourn. Other colleagues and friends read, commented, and encouraged: Diane Millis, Ann Pederson, Gina Wolfe, and Frances Adeney in particular. Wendy Doyle and family befriended Carolyn and me and implicitly believed in what I was up to. For all these agents of grace I am undyingly thankful.

This work could not have been carried out without the financial support of the Louisville Institute. Likewise, I am indebted to the Catholic University of America, the chair of my department, Stephen Happel, the Dean of the School of Religious Studies, Ray Collins, and the Director of the Life Cycle Institute, Jim Youniss, for many forms of support: grants to enable my travel to Minnesota and to provide research and clerical help in bringing the manuscript to publication; leaves from teaching without which nothing would have been accomplished; and an office and support staff at the Life Cycle Institute on campus. I must acknowledge as well my wonderful colleagues in the Department of Religion and Religious Education who took up the slack while I was absent. In addition, I am especially indebted to Jason King and Ann Kasprzyk, whose research, editorial, and clerical assistance were invaluable.

Many, many people have read various versions of this book. Faculty and students of my department held a Faculty Seminar on chapter 2, offering helpful suggestions. Heidi Yoder, Donna Freitas, Theresa Torres, Elizabeth Smith, Rod Cardamon, and Mary Kenel—graduate students in my course on "Redeeming Redemption"—were tolerant, kind, and encouraging in their comments and observations on chapters 4 and 5. My ethics colleagues in the School of Religious Studies—Bill Barbieri, John Grabowski, Joe Cappizi, and John Berkman—discussed chapters 3 and 6 with me. My neighbors and friends—Kathy McAdams, Claudia Donnelly, Ann Carroll, Kathy Staudt, and Pat Loughlin—read numerous drafts and provided unfailing belief in my "voice." A wider circle of academic friends facilitated key insights into the task at hand by careful reading and lengthy discussion: Michael Vertin, Margaret O'Gara, Bill Cahoy, Ken Melchin, Bill Loewe, Michael Stoeber, and Bob Doran. Beth Johnson has had several helpful conversations with me and suggested I contact Frank Oveis, of Continuum Publishing Group, who has been a very supportive and engaging editor.

The guidance of various spiritual mentors, personal counselors, and healers of mind and body is at the root of my own appropriation of the meaning of the cross: Katherine Howard, O.S.B., Stephen Vincent, and

Jerry Wetterling in Minnesota; Karen Goldberg, Susan Goldstein, and Marilyn Merikangas in Maryland; and John Govan, S.J., in Ontario.

Last but not least I must thank my family. My mother, Dorothy H. Watkins, has always been my biggest fan; my cousin, Robyn Weaver, a constant cheering squad; and my late father, Thomas A. Watkins, an ever-present inspiration. My sister and her husband, Wendy and Ken White, as well as my brother and his wife, Ron and Sue Watkins, are an indelible part of my life and have consistently shown interest in my work, as have my in-laws, Stewart and Thelma Crysdale, and Ann Crysdale-Gourlie.

My husband, David, and children, Peter and Carolyn, have made many sacrifices for this project. David and Peter lived a bachelor life for five months in 1997 while Carolyn courageously ventured with me to an unknown world in Minnesota. Carolyn has had to put up with me telling anecdotes in public about her, while Peter has surprised and warmed me with his serendipitous queries: "So, how's your work going, Mom?" David has tolerated tirades on my part, especially when others have assumed I was "doing nothing" since I was on leave from my job. All of them have embraced the travail of living with a cranky author giving birth to an often untimely book.

1

Entering the Drama
Crucified and Crucifiers

O N A COLD, CLEAR NIGHT in February 1987 my daughter Carolyn was born. I had been waiting a full two weeks after the due date, having frantically rushed to complete the fourth chapter of my dissertation before the end of January. My mother had come and gone home again; the diapers washed, folded, and refolded, she had other obligations to return to. My father had brought Aunt Mary to replace her and to watch over two-year-old Peter when the time came. Finally, in the middle of the night, the contractions came thick and fast. I wakened my husband, David, who dressed while I alerted Aunt Mary to our departure and kissed a sleeping Peter goodbye. We walked out into a star-studded, absolutely frigid Canadian night and drove through the deserted streets of Toronto as I struggled to breathe away the now almost unbearable pains.

While I sat in a wheelchair in the admitting room I could barely give the attending nurse the requisite information. David seemed to take an interminable time parking the car (which subsequently froze so that he had to take public transit home the next morning). We were eventually ushered into a birthing room while my doctor was wakened in her Rosedale home and summoned to the hospital. I breathed and sweated and huffed and puffed, sucked ice and asked questions, tried not to push. When I could stand it no longer I said, "I just have to push!" at which point my doctor burst into the room, threw off her coat, took one look at me and said, "Okay, go ahead and push." She coached, I pushed, David breathed, and a head, then shoulders, and then a whole little person slipped into the world. After waiting and waiting, the process was over in two or three hours. David glowingly told people the next day: "Oh, it was simple: it only took a few hours." !!!

1

In all my life so far I have never been as physically vulnerable nor as close to the pulse of death and life as I was that night. I had never experienced pain so directly and so intensely. The next morning I told my husband, "Last night was the most horrible night of my life." Then I added, "Last night was the most wonderful night of my life." For days and weeks I pondered over this simultaneity of joy and suffering. For the first time I began to grasp the way in which death might not be as fearful as I had imagined. I could see, as I never had before, that death might be intensely painful and yet transformative. I pondered the notion that death and resurrection might just happen at the same time. One single insight gradually emerged: resurrection joy does not come *after* crucifixion pain, it is the same thing! This confusing yet liberating revelation has remained in the back of my mind ever since. I am still trying to make sense of it.

A few years later, I began my teaching career by using a novel by Carlos Fuentes entitled, *The Good Conscience*.[1] It is the story of Jaime, a young boy growing up in post-revolutionary, early-twentieth-century Mexico. It reveals a society imbued with every sort of social sin and describes an entirely dysfunctional family, both of which systematically destroy Jaime's self-esteem in the name of good faith. Christianity is a prime mover in all these distortions, yet Jaime's innocent faith presses him to imitate Jesus. At one point, having discovered some of the family secrets, he heads out to the edge of town, weaves some cactus fronds together, and whips himself in the hope that he can pay for the sins of his family. He is determined not to be a religious hypocrite like his mentors and so takes the imitation of Jesus literally.

I used the novel to goad my students into examining just what constitutes authentic versus inauthentic religious practice. Why, I asked them, is this *not* what the gospel is all about? I was not content with the responses in which students simply passed off suffering as inconsequential: "Oh, that was just too extreme. Jaime should have just learned how to be nice to his family." No, there was a real problem with his family and his cultural world: something needed to be changed. While beating himself accomplished nothing, I knew that pain and suffering could not be avoided. The work of Christ on the cross could neither be dismissed nor could it be repeated. Resurrection had to come with the pain, but it was neither a polyanna cheerfulness nor a reward for masochism. Just what was it?

I found the beginnings of an answer in Sebastian Moore's *The Crucified Is No Stranger*.[2] I did not so much read this book as "abide" in it for several years. Its poetic quality, paradoxical imagery, and Jungian categories would not work with undergraduates, so I transposed it into an accessible lecture format. I found that his insights combined well with models of recovery from addiction. Translating sin into the modern maladies of addiction and victimization, and recovering "forgiveness of sins" as "recovery from addictive habits" engaged the students. They could each identify some way in which they had been hurt or caught in addictions, while few of them could relate to "sin."

Woven into this journey is the ongoing saga of my struggle to gain my own "voice." I am old enough to have been raised in an era when women were not expected to be thinkers, and one apologized for being bright. In my twenties I thought I was defective because I could not undertake any of the properly feminine careers. I had questions to ask, deep and serious questions, but these always seemed to be a luxury in a world where pragmatics ruled and women were expected, above all, to be pragmatic.

During the first year of my graduate studies I attended school part-time, convinced that my primary concern should be to take care of my newly wedded husband. At school I discovered that I loved learning New Testament Greek and biblical exegesis, while my male colleagues—all headed for ordination—groused and complained about each and every assignment. The Anglican Church of Canada ordained women for the first time that year (1976) and I, being the only woman in my class, quickly became "Specimen A." Not even knowing what denomination I wanted to be, and not having any connections to a bishop, the ordination question went by the board. I got an M.A. rather than an M.Div. and then set out to find a job.

The only jobs for my kind were poorly paid part-time positions as head of Christian Education (meaning Sunday School) for one parish or another. And my questions were still coming, thick and furious. I wasn't finished yet. It only gradually dawned on me that my questions might actually be a vocation. Teaching Sunday School certainly didn't excite me and when, on a day I was feeling particularly vulnerable, a former mentor of mine—a devout Christian who was also a feminist *and* a scholar—unexpectedly walked into Sunday Morning Prayer at my church, I took it as a sign. I enrolled in a doctoral program and, without knowing it, decided to take "voice lessons."

Such lessons involved a host of tools and teachers. There were those who, schooled in the critical realism of Bernard Lonergan, believed that education was a matter of following one's questions. There were non-academic women who were themselves survivors of a variety of false expectations, who encouraged me to look at family life with a new lens. Carol Gilligan came out with *In a Different Voice* just as I was searching for a dissertation topic. She provided me with a new language as well as a new set of questions. Somewhere in there I discovered silence and the joys of solitude, embarking on retreats at a variety of religious houses where no one needed to know my business. Ironically, such silence contributed to my learning to speak. Finally, with the encouragement of a very support-ive dissertation director and a host of other mentors, all of whom believed implicitly that I had something to say, I managed the bearing of two chil-dren, the writing of a dissertation, and the trauma of an oral defense. In spite of the many voices—literal and figurative—that told me I was ruining my children, that I wasn't paying my way, that I ought to be doing some-thing useful, I had at least learned to sing a few scales.

If my doctoral program served as an initial set of voice lessons, the sub-sequent job interviews (eight in two years, from southern California to Vancouver to Toronto and Washington, D.C.) developed my repertoire. Each one different, some involving sensitive political controversies, I had to learn how to say what I was, who I was, and what I could and could not do. Most of all I learned not to play to the crowd but just to be very sure about what it was that I wanted (besides a job!). In the end I arrived at the Catholic University of America as *Dr.* Crysdale, one step closer to being a real person with something to say. I sang scales as well as more complex oratories to my undergrads, working Jaime, suffering, and the Crucified into my repertoire.

A job, an office, a departmental secretary, even a phone number to give to the daycare center—all seemed like luxuries after the transitory life of a graduate student haunting library corridors, a daycare mother with no fixed worksite, and then an unemployed theologian (explain *that* to your hairdresser!). It didn't take long, however, to discover that I still was not a "real boy." I was Pinocchio practicing at singing or dancing. And though I did think I had something to say, I had to get it into the right language—I had to convince others I had something to say; my "something" had to find a public forum. Amidst baseball practice, Brownies, groceries, and all the academic domestic work—grading papers, seeing students, sitting on com-mittees—I managed to find an audience. In my sixth year I gradually gained some fleshly substance: approved first by my department (I gained an arm or two) then by the School of Religious Studies (now I had two legs), the Academic Senate (a torso began to take shape) and finally the Board of Trustees (I got a real head with a brain in it), at the age of forty-one I finally became a real boy who could sing and dance on her own.

In the middle of all of this, for a variety of reasons, I had entered into group therapy. The group was led by an extremely skilled woman and made up of highly talented, articulate, well-educated, middle- and upper-middle-class women. We were all very confident and well spoken, women of the nineties who had long since shed our naive assumptions about a woman's place in the world. Yet we all had some difficult situation to deal with, current dilemmas that, inevitably, had roots in our families of origin. For each there was an objective dilemma over which we had little control: a handicapped child, a child who had died, a husband who turned out to be gay, childhood sexual abuse, the biochemistry of manic depression or clinical depression, an ex-husband who refused to let old battles die. Yet for each of us there emerged an Achilles' heel, some way in which we contributed to our own demise, capitulated to the demands of our friends and relatives in spite of our great competence in other areas of life.

Slowly I began to see that we were all there with Jaime in the desert. There we were, making our whips out of cactus thongs, allowing ourselves to feel pain as if this were a means of grace, a road to salvation. We each had real dilemmas in our lives: cheerful acceptance would not do. Yet our many "solutions" only compensated for others' dysfunctions, and we were all struggling to embrace the pain of our situations while learning how to resist them and change old patterns.

It became clear, to me at least, that we were dealing here with spiritual and religious issues, not just psychological or social ones. Each person had both her demons to deal with and her ways of finding spiritual strength. The therapist was a practicing Jew; most of the other women had Roman Catholic backgrounds, coming from large, pre–Vatican II families in which standards of behavior were high and alcohol was not spared. Two of us had inherited a stoic Protestant work ethic. Many of us continued to be involved in religious institutions, but even those who didn't had some rituals of meaning that gave them strength beyond their current dilemmas. The need to explain an authentic alternative to Jaime's option, and my memory of the melding of pain and joy in childbirth, took on new significance. Over and over again, true healing seemed to come with grief, "good grief" that touched us where we needed to be touched and brought relief rather than agony.

Then I was invited to visit St. Paul's University in Ottawa to give the 1996 Glasmacher Lecture. They particularly wanted me to do something on feminist theology, not only in the lecture but in sessions with graduate students and faculty. When pressed for a title I swallowed hard and jumped in: I agreed to speak on "Feminist Theology: Ideology, Authenticity, and The Cross."[3] I returned to my synthesis of Sebastian Moore and added some work on resistance from Walter Wink. I illustrated my points with stories of my own and stories of African American slave women,[4] ending with a piece from Maya Angelou's autobiography.[5] The audience was most responsive, and several days of discussion ensued, including long talks about "sass" and "gossip."[6] Most significantly, Angelou's story includes a poignant moment when a young boy defies the stereotype of ignorance laid upon black students by spontaneously singing "Lift Every Voice and Sing" before his graduating class. There was nothing to do but actually sing the verses as I told the story. There I was, giving a lecture full of my own ideas and literally singing in public!

In preparation for this lecture I came upon *Christianity, Patriarchy, and Abuse*, an anthology edited by Joanne Carlson Brown and Carole Bohn, which documents ways in which Christian theologies of redemption and suffering have wreaked havoc in the lives of women.[7] Here my sense of needing to provide an alternative to Jaime became concrete. Here were the stories of women who had taken on suffering as some sort of holy action, being told that their suffering was either deserved or meritorious. The women from my group were in this book, I was in this book, Jaime was there too. Painfully, the Christian gospel was recounted, not as a narrative of good news but as the tool of infinite and indescribable pain. Though many of the contributors concluded, implicitly or explicitly, that the cross simply had to go, my own experience wouldn't allow me to accept this. Somehow death and resurrection had to go together or hope had no substance.

Shortly after the lecture in Ottawa I had a sabbatical leave from teaching. Though I had had another project planned for this time, I was so taken with these issues that I laid it aside and worked out an alternate plan: I would spend the time working out these mysteries that had been woven into my life for so long. I spent five months at the Institute of Ecumenical and Cultural Research at St. John's University in Collegeville, Minnesota. The lack of chaos, the reverence for the aesthetic, the life of Benedictine prayer, the quiet solitude of an office in the bowels of the library, the deep, deep cold and mounds of snow, the befriending by farmers and scholars alike, the eventual, long-suffering entrance of spring, all provided a kind of womb in which my own questions, pain, struggles, and voice could further unfold.

As I began to write, I was one day given a copy of Roberta Bondi's *Memories of God*, also written under the encouraging midwifery of the Ecumenical Institute. I opened to her chapter on the crucifixion, entitled "Out of the Green Tiled Bathroom." It tells about how one day she simply lost the meaning of the crucifixion. Though she was a scholar of Christian history and doctrine, though she herself was a devout believer, she suddenly found the crucified to *be* a stranger. She prayed to understand what this was all about and then, a week later, had a terrible nightmare. In it she is in her great aunt's farmhouse in Kentucky, standing in a darkened hallway looking into the familiar green tiled bathroom. There, to her horror, is her beloved husband kneeling in the bathtub while a man with a sharpened knife prepares to slaughter him. Roberta knows immediately that this knife is meant for her, that her husband is dying in her place. She tries to scream, to stop the horror, but is helpless and unheard as the bloodletting ensues. She wakened from the dream terrified and in a cold sweat, but as she woke she realized clearly: "This is what you have always thought the crucifixion was all about, but that's not it."[8]

The remainder of the chapter tells how she gradually "unpacked" everything she had been taught and had experienced: the assumption that women will sacrifice themselves for husband and children, the lack of sympathy, the blame for a neighboring mother who killed herself, the summer revivals in Kentucky, where being a wretched sinner was the prerequisite for salvation, the "doing without" of the Depression and the Second World War. The chapter ends with her rediscovery of meaning in the cross through grief rather than guilt. By living through one Holy Week accompanied by Mary, the mother of Jesus, she comes on Good Friday to suddenly see God as a grieving mother, pained at the suffering of her son, longing to bring healing to a broken world. She comes to see the issue of her own salvation, not as that of forgiveness but as that of healing, healing the false shame that had so crippled her life.

This new vision is what my work here is all about. My purpose is to provide a framework for interpreting the kind of new integration that many people, like Bondi, stumble into of their own accord. Others not as fortunate as Bondi continue to struggle with a disjunction between their faith and their own experience. I hope to offer a fresh model for understanding redemption that will open up new ways of integrating life and faith.

The cross and resurrection have traditionally been interpreted as redeeming humankind from sin as arrogant ambition. The problem that is solved by the cross is our direct or indirect destruction of those we love —including God—and the solution is God's forgiveness, manifested in the resurrection. Redemption involves a transaction whereby Jesus died for us, standing in our place to pay the penalty that we owe to God for sin. While this approach retains its prominence today, another side of the story is now being told.

The difficulties with understanding sin primarily as pride, especially for women and those on the "underside" of history, have been recognized for several decades.[9] For those who approach the cross with an already beleaguered sense of self, what is to be discovered in the cross and resurrection is not—initially—forgiveness but healing. The wounded victims of the world, in contemplating Jesus on the cross, discover themselves not primarily as crucifiers of a sinless one but as victims who have been slain. Jesus the crucified becomes ally and friend; God the Father becomes grieving parent; and the Risen Lord signifies healing and empowerment.

In this chapter I will begin to explore an understanding of redemption that incorporates this alternative approach. The story of betrayal, repentance, and forgiveness continues to elicit profound transformation for many today. It needs to be balanced with a clearer recognition of the other side of sin, the acceptance of denigration that equally undermines relations with God and neighbor. This drama of identifying with the Crucified and discovering the healing of a Risen Lord needs further exploration.

THE CRUCIFIED IS NO STRANGER

Sebastian Moore, in his book of this title, provides a modern interpretation of salvation as a personal drama that unfolds in believers' lives. His key insight is that Jesus represents for us our own potential Self—the deep and hidden person that we are before God—which we crucify rather than allow to live. "What if Jesus were the representative, the symbol, the embodiment, of this dreaded yet desired self of each of us, this destiny of being human ... ? The crucifixion of Jesus then becomes the central drama of man's refusal of his true self."[10]

This drama works itself out in two successive situations. First, there is the actual historical drama from the first century, in which the resentment of the powerful toward a holy man leads to the destruction of the work of God in Jesus. Second, there is the drama as it plays itself out in the life of the Christian, who, "confronted with Jesus crucified, finds all the evil in his life becoming *explicit* as the wilful destruction of his true self now concrete for him in the man on the cross."[11] As the historical situation resolved itself in the bodily resurrection of Jesus, so, in the life of the believer, does the making explicit of one's Self-destruction become the occasion for transformation.

A key here is the way in which the cross makes explicit what otherwise remains an obscure tendency to destroy that which we could (and at some level want to) become. The crucifixion of Jesus is not just the death of the Holy One; it is his *murder,* and in it is revealed the final outcome of the generic evil that otherwise remains diffuse. Because of Jesus' purity, because there is no evil in him, all the evil is revealed on the side of those who will his death. "The evil thus restricted to the crucifiers becomes an *act,* arising in the human heart and proceeding to its destructive conclusion: an *act,* don't you see, and no longer an *atmosphere.*"[12] Evil thus taken to its final extreme, the death of the sinless one, the death of the pure Self, is revealed to be ultimately powerless, to exist *within* the purview of God's love.

In this approach sin becomes not disobedience to a divine command but an innate conflict between who we are and who we can become. The human secret is that, finally, we do not believe in ourselves.[13] Operative in all our desires and aspirations is the "death wish." Sin, then, becomes the "alienation between the conscious ego of man and a total self in which he has his place in God's world." Salvation is the "overcoming of this protean alienation."[14] And its overcoming consists not in its demise but in its rise to power: evil taken to its full extent is revealed as ultimately powerless.

The full extent of evil, of this death wish, this desire not to be one's Self, is manifested not only in the refusal to be oneself but in the destruction of any evidence that one might be called beyond the ordinary world of daily life at all:

> Evil is the inability of the death-wish to be simply a death-wish: its necessity to justify itself by removing the very *grounds* for requiring of us a more intensely personal life. This shows itself in the resentment that is sometimes felt in the presence of an exceptionally good and courageous man. The desire to remove him is the desire to remove an unusually eloquent piece of evidence for the fact that we are called to full personhood. The most passionately protected thing in us is our mediocrity, our fundamental indecision in respect of life. Its protection will require, and will not stop at, murder.[15]

Furthermore, this process of acknowledging our own Self-destruction, mediated through the crucified Jesus, leads to insights into how we are not only crucifiers but also the crucified. The more we can see the ways in which we sabotage our own flourishing, the more we are able to see how we ourselves are victims, are objects of crucifixion.

Moore explains this process, yet continues to emphasize the dilemma of evil and sin as an issue of *hubris.* Sin as pride is now translated into the ego needing to be in control, the ego refusing to yield to the Self. Jesus stands as the symbol of this Self and, as crucified, makes explicit the results of the ego alienated from its source: pride taken to its full extreme.

For some—perhaps mainly women, but any who are designated non-persons in this world—the path to salvation may begin from the other side. Many persons are socialized into believing that their identity lies solely in their usefulness to others. Economic, social, cultural, and political forces contribute to this message. For these persons, the Self—the full extent of their human flourishing in communion with the Divine—has not been revealed or offered to them. This is not to say that a deeper, whole Self, independent of the demands of social interaction, does not exist. Nor is it to say that the rejection of such a Self is not at the heart of sin. It is to say that the call to be the Self needs to be issued before it can be rejected. It is to say that the rejection of Self comes in a different form, not as the ego taking charge but as the ego capitulating to others' definition of full human flourishing.[16]

For those who *begin* thinking of themselves as non-Selves, salvation has to do with the discovery of integral dignity and the choosing of this mystery of Self by a *strengthened* ego. From this angle one discovers something altogether different in entering the cross and resurrection story. Indeed, one discovers the full extent of evil's power, run to its full extreme. But in contemplating Jesus on the cross, one discovers oneself, not as the crucifier who willed this death, but as the victim who has been slain. Jesus as our true Self is slaughtered, not in the first instance by our own death wish but by the definition of others, of the powers that think they can define being: who is and isn't a valid human person.

In this case, transformation works in the opposite direction. By identifying with Jesus the Crucified, one is able to name one's own victimization, to face the wounds that have hampered one's full human flourishing. Detrimental assumptions that one is constitutionally *unable* to be in communion with God are unveiled as false presuppositions that destroy one's potential Self. Resurrection is the revelation of God's loving embrace in spite of such oppressive powers. Eventually, one may come to see one's complicity in such oppression and denial of Self. But in the first instance the Crucified becomes friend instead of stranger, and resurrection is God's raising of one's belief in Self in the face of powerful messages to the contrary.

The point is that while some people discover themselves in the crucified Jesus as *crucifiers,* others will come to the challenge of new life through discovering themselves in Jesus as the *crucified.* And while tradi-

tional interpretations have emphasized the former movement, the rising
voices of those on the underside of cultural, economic, and relational
power highlight the latter route as important and viable. While resurrection continues to convey forgiveness, the experience of resurrection as
empowerment is becoming a forceful transformative moment for many
today.

THE BIBLICAL DRAMA:
BETRAYAL AND POWERLESSNESS

This new angle on Moore's insight can be sharpened by reflecting on biblical characters as they are portrayed in the drama of Jesus' death and resurrection. Betrayal is the theme of the drama as it unfolds in the Gospels.[17]
There is Judas, whose betrayal is explicit, devious, and clearly misguided.
There is the crowd who—once having sung "Hosanna" and welcomed Jesus
—shouts "Crucify him" before Pilate. And then there is the great tragedy
of Peter, whose betrayal is more subtle yet all the more anguished because
of his disclaimers ahead of time. He who would be loyal to the end turns
out to tell the worst lies of all. When he denies any knowledge of Jesus,
Peter's culpability in condoning Jesus' death is poignantly signaled by the
crowing of the cock. Peter's ambitions and promises crumble miserably,
his "death wish" made explicit in his public betrayal, leading to his own—
eventually salvific—dissolution.

The fruit of this dissolution, for believers, is forgiveness. Those who
allow themselves to see themselves as crucifiers, discover that *even* here,
even in allowing and willing the death of God's Son, there is forgiveness.
The powerful postresurrection testimony of those who had fled when confronted with Jesus' arrest is a witness to new life. Not only had Jesus' project not been a failure after all; more importantly, desertion of Jesus does
not result in God's rejection. In failing to defend Jesus, and thus willing his
death, the disciples' false ambitions were exposed so that they could discover and live out of new, Spirit-filled Selves.

So where are the women in this story? As the tragedy unfolds through
its various venues and encounters, the women who had supported, nur-
tured, fed, listened to, and anointed Jesus are not mentioned. Finally, at
the end of the crucifixion, there is a single sentence or two mentioning
them: "There were also women looking on from a distance. Among them
were Mary Magdalene, Mary the mother of the younger James and of

Joses, and Salome. These women had followed him when he was in Galilee and ministered to him. There were also many other women who had come up with him to Jerusalem" (Mark 15:40–41; cf. Luke 23:48; Matt. 27:55–56).[18] They are mentioned also at the end of the story of Jesus' burial: "They watched where he was laid" (Mark 15:47; cf. Luke 23:55; Matt. 27:61). Then, of course, ensues the story of their arrival at the tomb on the first of the week, ready to anoint the body, only to discover that it is gone.

Where is the salvation here? What is the theme of death and resurrection for these women? Certainly it is not that of betrayal and subsequent forgiveness. They do not seem to be discovering themselves as culpable murderers. On the contrary, they are "looking on from a distance," present (they haven't run away) yet unable to be players in the drama, powerless to stop what is clearly heartbreaking and a travesty. What do they do in response? They do what they have always done: they take concrete caretaking action. One woman anoints Jesus before the drama begins; the others make and carry out plans to anoint him afterwards.

What these women confront in Jesus' death is their powerlessness. They suffer evil, not as perpetrators of murder but through grief, as onlookers to a whole system of evil they are powerless to affect. The choice of betrayal is not theirs. They are not actors enough in the drama even to choose to run away. They watch in powerless agony from afar and then prepare to minister to Jesus' concrete bodily needs, even in death.

The moment of truth for these women, when they must confront the dissolution of themselves, of their false assumptions, comes in their discovery of the empty tomb. Whereas for Peter and the other disciples it was the threat of conflict that brought them to the brink of chaos and fear, for these women it is the confrontation with resurrection. Compare Mark 14:50 "And they all [the disciples] forsook him and fled," or Mark 14:72 when Peter breaks down and weeps at the crowing of the cock, with Mark 16:8:

> Then they [the women at the tomb] went out and fled from the tomb, seized with trembling and bewilderment. They said nothing to anyone, for they were afraid.

This terse ending has baffled many for years, and, indeed, someone early on in the tradition added a more extensive ending. Still, it reveals how shocking this encounter must have been for these women.

The possibility of resurrection challenged these women's powerlessness, as well as their traditional ways of coping. In watching the crucifixion these women had to come to terms with their own impotence in the face of evil. In the resurrection of Jesus this lack of power could be transformed. What also had to be transformed, however, was the women's traditional roles as "copers" with evil (they were not able, after all, to anoint Jesus). They were confronted with the possibility of being true Selves, and this possibility was both exhilarating and terrifying. Whatever their response, new life was offered to these women not as a forgiveness of sins but as a freedom from powerlessness.

This admittedly free reading of the Gospel story serves to illustrate an important point. The essence of sin may indeed be our propensity to not become our true Selves, may be the tendency toward mediocrity that constitutes a death wish. And salvation can indeed be understood as the overcoming of the protean alienation between ego and Self. Finding ourselves in Jesus on the cross and experiencing resurrection may in fact be the means by which this alienation is transcended. But the process of this discovery may be very different for those on the underside of history than it is for those who are traditionally positioned as agents of their own destinies.

THE CAIN AND ABEL SYNDROME

The story of Cain and Abel can further illustrate the cycle of destruction that results from sin as the death wish unacknowledged. Chapters 2, 3, and 4 of Genesis capture the drama of both God's good creation and the human inability to live as a Self in communion with that creation and with God. Made in the image of God with a natural desire to *see* God, Adam and Eve nevertheless mistake this desire for a desire to be *like* God. The innate longing to be a Self in relation with the Transcendent gets reduced to a simple formula: "If we eat of the fruit of the tree of knowledge we will be like God, knowing good and evil." This mis-conceived ambition ends in destroying both Self and relationship with the Divine. The effects on interpersonal relations and interaction with creation are graphically pictured in Adam and Eve's suddenly revealed nakedness.

With the next generation the drama gets more complex. Cain has the gift of tilling the soil while Abel is a keeper of flocks. The deep desire to be in relation with the Creator along with the visceral recognition of creaturely insecurity leads both to present thank-offerings to God. God acknowledges Abel's offering but, for a reason untold in the story, does not respond to Cain's gift. Sin now takes another turn: it is not only misbegotten ambition but the begrudging attitude that disdains the very values one had hoped to achieve.[19] Cain is not only angry at God but hates Abel himself, hates him for having entered the kind of relation that Cain wished he himself might have. He coaxes his brother out into the field, attacks him, and murders him. Rather than being the Self-in-divine-communion that he might be, Cain opts for the victory of the ego. He allows resentment to reign and destroys the very evidence of his call to transcendence. Rather than moving out to the "other"–his brother, God, the earth itself–he chooses to conquer the "other," his brother most directly but also his relation to God and to creation.

Cain, once confronted with his deed, eventually repents. He initially skirts God's query regarding Abel: "Am I my brother's keeper?" But the consequences of Cain's actions speak for themselves: "Your brother's blood cries out to me from the soil!" Cain's pride, combined with his option to avoid the challenge of being a Self-in-relation, leaves him transparent to God and alienated from the soil itself. The Lord proclaims: "Therefore you shall be banned from the soil that opened its mouth to receive your brother's blood from your hand. If you till the soil, it shall no longer give you its produce. You shall become a restless wanderer on the earth" (Gen. 4:11–12). Cain is devastated by the course of events and bemoans his fate. God relents and protects Cain from his vulnerability, putting a mark on his forehead lest anyone try to kill him.

What about Abel? He disappears from the drama altogether since he has been murdered. Still, his blood cries out, eliciting a response from the Lord. Abel represents for us the victims of sin, the recipients of the projected death wish, who are murdered rather than allowed to maintain their Selves before God. It is not what they *do* that offends but who they *are*. Thus it is not their deeds that must be addressed but their very existence: they must be murdered. Rather than face the ambiguity of being both finite and oriented toward the infinite, the Cains of the world destroy the evidence of both. They "murder" anyone who is "other," hoping to protect themselves from both the vicissitudes of being a creature and the awesomeness of facing the divine. In the process, they murder their own Selves.

Such "murdering" can take myriad forms. There are obvious hate crimes in which particular persons are beaten simply for being different. There is the witness of the Holocaust in Europe, in which millions of Jews were systematically killed in order to free the Aryan race from "contamination." But there are also the more subtle and indirect ways in which poverty, discrimination, language, religious practices, marital customs, educational curricula, generational bias, and mass media succeed in killing aspirations to Self-hood.

Abel can be found murdered in those assumed to be "niggers," "witches," "kikes," "micks," "bitches," and "retards." The heart of this murder is not simply threatened or actual death but spiritual demise. The possibility of being a whole Self in communion with a divine community of Selves is not rejected by these but denied to them altogether. They are cut down before they even have an opportunity to come before God with an offering. They are told that they are not even human persons, are not, like the rest of mankind, created in the image of God. Desmond Tutu captures this travesty in reference to the apartheid system in South Africa: "For my part, its most vicious, indeed its most blasphemous aspect, is not the great suffering it causes its victims, but that it can make a child of God doubt that he is a child of God. For that alone, it deserves to be condemned as a heresy."[20]

In sum, the murder of Self—the refusal to be a creature in communion with a trinity of divine Selves—works itself out through murdering the "other." And this occurs both directly in dyadic relations and systematically through structures of oppression. The Cain and Abel syndrome is the cycle of alienation whereby the failure to embrace the challenge of Self leads to the conviction that certain others don't deserve recognition as Selves and/or deserve death.

BLOOD CRYING OUT FROM THE GROUND

The murder of Abel foreshadows the crucifixion of Jesus. The interpretation of both stories over time has focused on the redemption of the perpetrators of sin: on Cain's redemption through his repentance and God's compassion, and on the forgiveness of Jesus' betrayers through new resurrection life. I am trying to highlight the other side of the story: What does it mean to be Abel? To be "murdered" unjustly because you represent the "other" feared by those with power? What does it mean to enter the crucifixion story as one of the crucified? And what is the nature of resurrection under such circumstances?

The road to salvation for "Abel" is not repentance, is not recognizing how he has murdered others in his effort to destroy the call to transcendence. Indeed, Abel was the one who *had* established a creaturely communion with the Divine. For Abel, as the victim of murder, of someone else's rejection of Self, salvation lies in *crying out from the ground.* His blood cries out and refuses to be silenced. God hears the cry and responds.

So, for the crucified of the world salvation involves finding a voice to declare their humanity in the face of powerful messages to the contrary. Humility and repentance only silence the "blood" that, however mutely, serves as evidence of human life. Victims need to listen to this blood, to recognize in themselves and their communities the life-blood of their human aspirations. Rather than accepting limitations and assuming they are unworthy of relation with the Divine, the crucified must learn, and have learned, that they too are made in the image of God. They cry out and listen, discovering God's presence in spite of their demise. The very speaking out becomes evidence that such designated non-Selves are in fact capable of thinking, reasoning, speaking, deciding, acting, reaching out toward that which lies beyond.

The good news of the resurrection is that no murder, however vicious or final, stands as an obstacle to the discovery of one's Self as a creature oriented to communion with others and with the Divine. No murder—physical, psychological, or spiritual—can remove the possibility of resurrected life even from the least of the earth. *Everyone* is created as a Self in the embrace of God's triune love. Discovering this truth, encountering the God of the universe even in bloody death, and proclaiming oneself a child of God, are part of the process of redemption for the crucified. African-American slaves in the United States, the poor in the base communities of Latin America, blacks in South Africa, battered women and abused children, all join a cloud of witnesses stemming back to the earliest persecuted Christians, witnesses who have discovered and proclaimed resurrection in the midst of "murder."

While this process of redemption may not involve *repentance,* it does involve *conversion.*[21] A woman who had been afflicted by hemorrhages for twelve years and had suffered greatly at the hands of many physicians reached out from the midst of the crowd to touch the hem of Jesus' garment (Mark 5:25–34). She was seeking not forgiveness but healing. Yet this gesture—her way of speaking out—was a gesture of great courage that involved choosing to radically change her position in the world. The gesture defied all the protocol that "clean" and "unclean" designations had prescribed.[22] Like Abel's blood crying out, this woman's gesture signified an about-face in the accepted order of the world. She believed in her own potential wholeness and refused to be deprived of abundant life in the face of Jesus' life-giving power. The reaching out was itself a pivotal and converting moment.[23]

Still, gaining a voice and speaking out, in whatever way, are only the beginning of a long process. It is a process that will eventually involve taking responsibility for oneself. Jesus, not content to let the moment pass, asked that the woman make her gesture known. "The woman, realizing what had happened to her, approached in fear and trembling. She fell down before Jesus and told him the whole truth" (v. 33). This cryptic verse reveals little about what exactly transpired between the two, and gives few hints as to what "the whole truth" might have been. At the very least we can surmise that *simply* reaching out is not enough. Salvation/healing involves taking responsibility for the consequences of one's conversion and following through on whatever public changes may be necessary in one's life.

This is why the bleeding woman's gesture is a conversion and not just an idle movement. It is why the confrontation at the empty tomb is so threatening to the women involved. To claim a Self means taking responsibility for one's actions in a new way. It catapults one into a fresh examination of just who is responsible for what. It forces one to face the ways in which one might have perpetuated the systems under which one has been voiceless. The underclasses of social power gain a certain kind of comfort from the status quo. To subvert this is also to realize just how one has been hiding behind the false freedom of not having to be a Self.

Resurrection life for the crucified means claiming a voice, naming victimization, claiming human dignity and then discerning responsibility. Passive compliance is a sin as much as is pride. Discerning complicity, recognizing the role one plays in one's own demise, realizing how one has actually destroyed one's own "lord of glory" by accepting the denigration of others, is a complex and difficult road to follow. The pitfalls are numerous, especially since a great host of accusers are more than willing to blame the victim. But taking responsibility for one's contribution to a symbiotic relationship of submission and domination is radically different from accepting the blame of the oppressor. Naming victimization and declaring an alternative truth—the power of one's dynamic human spirit in relation to God—goes hand in hand with encountering Jesus' life-giving Spirit and confessing "the whole truth."

2

Embracing Travail

Victims and Perpetrators

ONE SATURDAY AFTERNOON WHEN I was nine or ten I was rattling around the house with nothing to do. Suddenly I remembered the brilliant fall leaves I had carefully gathered and stored, weeks earlier, in a volume of the *Encyclopedia Britannica*. It was time to retrieve them and make a beautiful piece of art. I carefully removed the leaves from the giant tome and headed down to the basement with a roll of waxed paper under my arm. Surely I was old enough to master the iron myself. I laid out the leaves between two sheets of waxed paper and started to iron. The waxed paper stuck to the iron, the leaves fell on the floor at just the crucial moment—my work of art disintegrated into bad smells and singed fingers. I grabbed my precious pile of leaves and crushed them to smithereens in the palm of my hand. The moment I did it I burst into tears in shock and grief: I had destroyed the very beauty I had wanted to preserve. The violence of that moment, the unexplainable destruction of the very thing I held precious, and the unfathomable grief that accompanied it have stayed with me all my life.

Many years later I had managed to get the summer job I had always wanted. Working at a Christian camp in the Adirondacks, I was part of a staff that assisted groups going trekking in the mountains, a kind of Outward Bound for Christian high school students. I had a cycle of jobs, sometimes in camp repairing equipment, sometimes taking day hikes to replenish supplies to hikers, sometimes meeting them with a rack of canoes to set them off on the next stage of their journey. The highlight of the summer for me came when I got to be part of a pair that would establish and "man" a base camp in the wilderness while the campers did their three-day solos. My turn to go set up base camp with Larry arrived. The night before we were to go my boss called me into his office. He informed me that, through prayer and discussion, he and the rest of the staff had decided that having a co-ed couple at the base camp would constitute too much of a stumbling block for the young trekkers. He was rearranging the schedule so that two young men would supervise all the solos while I stayed in camp mending sleeping bags. I left his office with dignity but then tore up to my room above the kitchen and sobbed uncontrollably at this injustice. It was a very minor injustice, given the wide scope of evils in the world, but at the time it felt like the ruination of all my hopes and dreams.

Neither of these stories illustrates the work of sin in any dramatic way. But they do show how the struggles of life and the thwarting of deepest yearnings may come either through self-sabotage or through the actions of others. The confidence and pride with which I undertook mastery of an art work disintegrated into an inner violence of which I had been totally unaware. Like Cain, once I lost control of the situation and things were not going as I had planned, destroying my creation proved more appealing than failing. In the process I ended up sabotaging my own deep attraction to beauty, the longing to create something of value, which lies at the heart of human flourishing.

In my experience at camp, my equally good intentions were once again circumvented, this time through the choices of others. My own longing for solitude and communion with nature and my capability to exercise numerous gifts were both thwarted by those in authority over me. The decision stifled my personal flourishing on grounds that carried a lot of "baggage" but no real "weight." Gender and the suspicion of immorality, rather than competence and moral integrity, served as criteria for a choice in which I had no say. An entire system of biblical injunctions, hierarchical leadership, and paternalism toward women supported both the decision and my exclusion from it.

In the previous chapter we explored a new approach to the redemptive process of cross and resurrection, through identifying with the crucified and discovering healing. We also examined sin as Self-destruction, the negation of oneself as a finite creature called to wholeness in relationship with God. This primordial choice to reject Self can arise from a pride that seeks self-aggrandizement. It can manifest itself in a resentment that destroys the very values one longs for. But some persons are socialized into believing that they cannot be Selves, that they are less than human and are unworthy of God's love. In this case, salvation is not primarily a matter of repentance, humility, and forgiveness. Instead, it involves claiming a voice and proclaiming one's transcendently oriented humanity. It involves a conversion that challenges false messages about Self, yet also takes responsibility for one's fundamental choices.

The dynamics of healing, repentance, and responsibility must be further explored. Dividing the world simplistically into victims and perpetrators of sin is inaccurate and misleading. In fact, each person is, at some level, both a victim and a perpetrator of Self-destruction. Whatever the nature of the transformation, and whichever direction it takes, beginning with the crucified or with the crucifier, neither pole is dispensable. Sooner or later, in some form or other, one must discover oneself as both a crucifier and a victim. The failure to do this can lead to self-righteousness on the one hand or self-immolation on the other. Both leave one vulnerable to destructive ideologies and inauthentic religious practice. The alternative leads to true redemption but not without embracing the pain of new birth.

The objective of this chapter is to explore the dynamics of being both a victim and a perpetrator. First, we will examine the process of "embracing travail," of seeking healing and taking responsibility on the route to transformation. We will then consider the implications of this new approach for several classic topics in theology: the meaning of Jesus, who he was and what he did; God and the problem of evil; and the nature of grace.

DISCOVERING SINS, EMBRACING WOUNDS

Though it may be very subtle, everyone is both a perpetrator and a victim of sin.[1] The messages of our communities may make it very hard to confront or name either. And while communities are structured in a way that socializes some to have a sense of power and pride while others consider themselves meek and malleable, both sides of sin must be discerned and repudiated. For those trained into a subordinate mentality, confronting their own sabotage of Self may mean recognizing complicity and codependence. For those reared to expect choice and success, facing the demise of Self by others may mean seeing how they are boxed in and unable to flourish by the very power they have inherited.[2]

Let us begin exploring this dynamic interaction by examining several case studies. Helen is a thirty-eight-year-old mother of five whose marriage went through a period of great chaos. Her husband, though a brilliant computer programer, lost his job at IBM just before Helen gave birth to twins. Helen herself had continued to work as a registered nurse in order to keep her training up to date. Lack of communication between Helen and her husband added to the difficulties. In the end, Helen was exhausted and barely able to function, seeking the help of a counselor in order to hold herself and her family together.

With counseling, Helen learned how to make some changes in her life. She insisted that her husband recognize her need for regular childcare assistance: it became part of the family budget. She planned dates with friends so that she could develop her own relationships outside of the home. She realized that she needed to take care of her own needs as well as the needs of those around her. But just when things were beginning to settle down she happened to watch a public television special on childhood sexual abuse. By the end of the hour she was sobbing hysterically, unable to control her shame and grief. Her own history as a child in relation to her father came flooding back and opened a whole new horizon of pain. In the days and weeks that followed she spoke with each of her sisters. One of them had been accusing her father of sexual abuse for years, but Helen had dismissed her as unreliable, wild, and crazy. Now she, too, had to confront the dark places of her childhood.

In order to take charge of the chaos in her life, Helen had to come to terms with her own victimization. This involved naming her pain, recognizing that her father's behavior had demeaned her, had taken away her dignity. She had been used as an object of someone else's needs instead of respected as a whole person. Healing in her case had to begin with naming this victimization, with embracing the pain of the past and living with it in the present.

Still, even as Helen courageously faced these issues, her life continued to be out of control. She got into disputes with her supervisor at work. She took on a second job to earn extra money so that her husband wouldn't complain about her spending. That conflicted with the children's needs, so she took on an on-call job with more flexible hours. This didn't work out so she decided to do a further degree in nursing. The tuition was so high that she took on yet another part time job, but then had to arrange after-school care for the children. Eventually, she came to see that she herself perpetuated a life of chaos. She kept sabotaging her own decisions, her own needs, her own voice. In fact, she preferred a life of chaos. It was what she had known as a child and it felt comfortable. Having discovered her great grief, she then had to come to terms with her complicity, her "sins" as they contributed to the situation.

To have told Helen, in the first instance, that she had to take more responsibility for her life, that she had to face the ways in which she was "crucifying" her Self, would simply have reinforced old patterns, would not have led to healing. Encountering the "crucified Lord" in the form of her own broken child was also, in itself, not transformative. She needed to come to see her own role in the dysfunctional pattern, to confess her "sin," as it were, and "do penance," that is, to make the changes necessary to yield new life.

John is an orthopedic surgeon. He is financially secure with an income that allows his wife to stay at home taking care of their two children. He works long hours but relaxes on the golf course on weekends when not participating in his children's sports activities.

One day about seven years ago John had a splitting headache at work. In what seemed to be the simplest of solutions he wrote himself a prescription for a narcotic drug and had it filled at the hospital pharmacy. In the ensuing weeks, whenever he had a headache, he would take some of these narcotics to feel better. Then he got into the habit of taking some pills at his mid-afternoon break, just in case a headache would set in. He began to use different pharmacies around town and to write bogus prescriptions for people who never existed. As a physician he had the authority to do this without being questioned It never occurred to him that he was an addict since, as he put it, "addicts are people in ditches with needles in their arms."

John could have gone on like this for decades had he not been caught. One pharmacist began asking questions; John's colleagues recognized a pattern of poor judgment, silly errors, sometimes bizarre and questionable behavior. When confronted, the threat of losing his license to practice medicine forced John into treatment.

John, in a position of power, could deceive himself and others. He persuaded himself that he was enhancing his ability to perform his job. Healing for John meant facing the ways in which actions he thought were helping him were actually destroying him. He was sabotaging his "lord of glory," his own potential Self. He was also harming others through deception and deceit. When he was unable to take responsibility for his actions, others had to call him to account, ask him to take stock of his "sins" and "do penance."

John's entry into treatment, his taking responsibility for his addiction and its consequences, was only the beginning. He came to see the perpetual loneliness he had suffered as a child of older parents, his father a violinist with the Philadelphia Symphony Orchestra, his mother engrossed with philanthropic projects as part of the cultural elite of the city. John was dispensed with at the best boarding schools in the country, seeing his parents only on holidays and summer vacations.

John came to a point of great grief. He got to know himself as the forgotten child that he was, a victim of others' benign neglect and simple incompetence. As he embraced this lonely child, he began to see how his addiction had been a way of numbing pain. By always having an out, a tangible way of making himself feel energized and alive, he could avoid the constant, nagging emptiness. It was only in embracing the pain of this rejection that he could actually take charge of his life and find other ways of redressing the old wounds.

The point of these stories is to illustrate that perpetrators of Self-destruction (leading to harm toward others) are often also victims of Self-destruction (from harm done to them). Likewise, those socialized into serving the purposes of others can at times perpetuate their own Self-destruction, sabotaging their own flourishing because it is comfortable and familiar. This is not to say that every person of dominating power ought to be exonerated for his sins because he is in fact a victim. Nor is it to say that victims of systemic maltreatment need to take the blame for their denigration. It is to say that, while the entry into transformation may come from different directions, true transformation means completing the circle: victims discovering responsibility and perpetrators embracing wounds.

Notice the cyclical nature of this process. The Cain and Abel syndrome, in its ongoing influence, means that victims seeking resolution of their pain become perpetrators who, in turn, create more victims. These latter persons, in an effort to be healed, often turn their energy in all the wrong directions, using whatever power they have destructively toward those with yet less power. I, having destroyed my work of beauty, deal with my grief by mocking the creative talents of my younger sister. She, in her turn, develops an insecurity that manifests itself through regular cheating and deceit. Having been caught lying on one occasion, she turns her shame into blame and insists that her best friend had framed her. The best friend, unable to elicit truth out of the situation, begins mistrusting friendship and pushes away all who come close. And so on, and so on.[3]

Turning the cycle around involves one person, at least, refusing to perpetuate it. The wounded person, rather than passing on the pain, embraces the pain and seeks healing. Such healing enables him to forgive, and such forgiveness frees his perpetrator from defensive living. This person, in turn, is freed to face her own pain and seek forgiveness for her harmful actions. So the cycle becomes not victim—perpetrator—victim, but healed—forgiven—healed.[4]

One more story provides an example of such reversal. Monty Roberts, in his memoir, *The Man Who Listens to Horses*, reveals how traditional means of breaking horses promotes violence. By "listening" to horses and learning their language, Monty began to devise a new way to tame horses without violence. This also became the medium of his own healing. As a child he himself was a victim of his father's volatile temper. His father believed he had the right to control both children and animals through force. In turn, he had no patience for Monty's new way of treating horses with dignity.[5]

> One day, at the age of fifteen, Monty was explaining his new methods to his mother when he realized his father had entered the room and was listening:
> He stepped forward wearing a hard, unforgiving look. I knew what that meant. He stepped in front of us, his color heightened by his terrible fury. The veins stood out in his neck as he shouted, "I don't want to hear any more of this sort of talk."
> "Dad—"
> He shouted louder, one of his hands curling into a fist, the other jabbing at my chest. "You are ungrateful to me."
> "I'm not."
> "You are too stupid to do anything without my help." I swallowed hard, knowing what was coming, as my mother pleaded, "Marvin, please . . ."
> "You owe everything to me!" With that, he raised his fist to his opposite ear and brought it back across my face, knocking my jaw hard. On this day, finally, I was not going to take it. I advanced on him, my hands on his arms, and backed him against a wall. I looked him in the eye, and he seemed to grow a little smaller. I had anger now to match his, and I came within a hair of unleashing it.
> I felt then what I have occasionally felt since but always resisted: an urge to strike. But at that moment the chain of violence was broken. I would not be like him—either with other humans, or with animals.[6]

Monty did not strike his father, and Monty was able, however briefly, to sit and explain his views to his father. While his father never changed his methods, this event became the beginning of Monty's freedom from his father's domination.[7]

Needless to say, such a reversal involves nothing less than a radical transformation of individual heart, mind, and psyche, as well as of communal habits of meaning and value. Monty's decision to alter the cycle of violence in relation to his father was only the beginning of an upward battle in changing accepted procedures for training horses. But such a reversal is precisely at the core of the Christian gospel, at the heart of the claim that resurrection life can and does invade the suffering and pain of the cross. The nature of such a reversal, and the Christian contribution to it, we will continue to explore. The point here is that liberation from cycles of alienation cannot take place unless *both* sides of the cycle are confronted; wounds as well as sins, healing as well as forgiveness.

EMBRACING TRAVAIL

This new double-sided approach to redemption yields several important implications. First, note how destructive a lopsided teaching on healing and forgiveness could be (and has been). To assume that salvation is only about the forgiveness of sins—taking responsibility for one's failures and one's Self-destruction—will overpower those who have a broken sense of agency in the first place. At the individual level, to counsel someone who is in desperate need of relief from victimization that they need to confess their sins and clean up their act is to further destroy what is already fragile. At the social level it is the script that has been written into the socialization of so many oppressed persons. There are the battered women who have been told that disobedience is the cause of their beatings. There is the slave child who is told that her "lying" will be the cause of her damnation, so any speaking out is prohibited.[8] This produces the double bind where those who don't wield power are held responsible for the behavior of those who oppress them. And it creates the double bind where any effort to be freed from oppression is countered with the call to repentance.

The opposite can be just as destructive. Whereas the former lopsidedness has infiltrated many explanations of redemption over the centuries, the discovery of victims can also have its destructive overemphasis. In the individual case, pastoral care in its integration of modern psychology has tended to reinterpret sin to the point of ignoring the responsibility of the agent altogether.[9] The reaction to the Victorian preoccupation with vice has been to unmask the many destructive repressions for which "sin" has been a cover story. This has led to a theology and pastoral care in which, at times, persons are not called to account for their roles in various dysfunctional life patterns. At the social level, the backlash to the unveiling of victimization is becoming apparent in popular complaints about the excesses of feminist or antiracist movements. While these backlash complaints are not without their own difficulties (involving the facile dismissal of these important issues in favor of the status quo), they do indicate the need to retrieve again the central role of the agent in creating his or her own liberation.[10]

Second, note the great difficulty of allowing transformation to unfold on its own course. In Moore's language, our death-wish, our tendency to reject full flourishing and to destroy even the evidence that such flourishing is possible, is so strong as to warp even resurrection when it occurs. Therapeutic insights into pain become a formula to avoid pain. The confessing of our sins becomes a recipe for salvation, easily at hand should we lose sight of salvation at any point. The very entrance into the process of healing becomes a quick fix, so that the arduous journey of true healing can be stealthily bypassed altogether.

The glimpse of new life, of resurrection, is both freeing and terrifying; we claim it yet also claim control over it. While the Gospel of Mark recounts the fleeing of the women in the face of resurrection, there is also the tale of Mary Magdalene clinging to the risen Jesus (John 20:17). As Jesus had rebuked Peter earlier (Mark 8), he here rebukes Mary and tells her to let go. She needs to live with her new life in all its ambiguous tension rather than clinging to her newfound resurrected love.

Third, the negotiating of this transformation is nothing less than a conversion. Whether it is sudden or gradual, facing sabotage and embracing pain involve a radical shift in horizon. What we thought was true turns out to be false. What we assumed to be good behavior is now seen as unhealthy, dysfunctional, evil. Even God needs to die—and the dark night of God's absence endured—so that God can be rediscovered.[11] This process takes time, and we need to abide in ambiguity and darkness while resurrection emerges.

What language can we use for this "center," this place where one simultaneously accepts new life (both its pain and its responsibility) and does not cling to it too tightly? "Embracing" is better than "clinging." When one clings, one is desperate. Like the child suffering from separation anxiety who will not let go of his mother as she leaves him with a sitter, we cling to the new life, wanting to hold onto the good, the beloved. Yet "embracing" is a hold that is also gentle, that holds and lets go without fear of loss.

"Travail" is the other image I have chosen to characterize this process. While what we embrace is a tension, a balancing, it is not always focused, as in the balancing of a book on one's head. It is a dialectic, a constant shifting between principles of change.[12] Sometimes we need to abide in grief and simply be present to our pain. Other times we need to dry the tears and work on what needs changing. So also is the travail of the mother in the birth process. At times there is great pain and all one can do to control it is to breathe rhythmically. At other times one needs to push, to engage actively in bringing about the new life that is emerging. Were one only to push, or to push at the wrong time, new life will not emerge. Were one only to engage in breathing exercises, the birth process will be prolonged. Embracing travail means *allowing* the process to take place without manipulating it, accepting the moments in the process of birth, working with them without denying the difficulties involved.

So transformation takes place through abiding in this center, the center which isn't really a center at all but an ever-fluctuating process that is nevertheless whole and not divided. Like the Self, which is real, the center of who we are, but which we can never quite grasp, the travail of conversion is concrete, real, yet beyond our control.

Given the pain and difficulty of negotiating this travail, of sustaining the Self, what can possibly be the incentive for accepting the pain and working on the birth? Given our basic death-wish and the innumerable subtle ways in which we and powerful forces beyond us sabotage our flourishing, what can hold our attention, keep our loyalty, grant us hope, engage us in this tenuous and self-dissolving (while Self-creating) process?

The only answer can be an encounter with resurrection power and the God who restores life out of death. It was an encounter with the Risen Lord that sustained the early disciples, and it is a glimpse, however fleeting, of union with God, of God's whole-making love, that sustains believers today. It is only through "being grasped by ultimate concern," through an "other-worldly falling in love,"[13] that one can even consider negotiating the pitfalls of travail. And the travail image itself breaks down, because resurrection hope is altogether different from the expectation of results.[14] It is not that one simply puts up with labor pains because one looks forward to a baby. Instead, one embraces travail because one is in the embrace of God.[15] And though one's glimpse of this resurrection reality, one's sense of being divinely embraced, is not always immediately present, the undertow of one's deepest desire for God nevertheless carries one forward in what we have usually called the life of *faith*.

This is where the psychological process yields to a spiritual one. "Incorporates" is perhaps better than "yields" since the two cannot be separated. The point is that the psychological process of healing can lead to adaptation to one's reality, but it only succeeds in making people whole Selves to the degree that there is some transcendent Other, the love for which holds one in hope amidst the pain. Alcoholics Anonymous has recognized this since the beginning and incorporated it into the Twelve Step program. Viktor Frankl discovered this in a Nazi concentration camp one day when the beauty of a violet sunset called him forth into claiming meaning amidst hunger, brutality, and murder.[16]

Though the Other to whom one is committed or by which one is grasped is not necessarily designated in religious language or given the name "God," without some ultimately world-transcending object of one's love and desire the healing process easily gets derailed. From the Christian perspective, this derailment is not only a sidelining of the healing process but a kind of idolatry in which we fail to recognize God's ultimate transcendence. And, according to Christian experience and doctrine, this ultimately transcendent Other is itself a community of Selves in relation: Father, Son, and Holy Spirit.[17]

A RENEWED UNDERSTANDING OF JESUS

This model of embracing travail while in the embrace of God can contribute to our understanding of Jesus. Jesus signifies the Self, the wholeness that each of us is called to in God's embrace but which evil, manifest in our complicity, has crucified. But the Christian faith proclaims Jesus as more than just a symbol, an archetype with psychological benefits. Jesus was also a historical figure, a concrete living, breathing human being with all the particularity in which each of us lives. Christianity claims that this historical person, Jesus, was the *incarnation* of God in the human world. What can this incarnation mean in light of the victim/perpetrator model?

First, Christians of the first four centuries struggled with the meaning of Jesus' relation to God and to us, deriving answers in language that spoke of "nature" and "persons." These were terms that resonated with the generations that sought to turn biblical faith into clear categories within a Hellenistic world. But in the modern world these categories have diminishing relevance, and merely to repeat them obscures the question rather than clarifies it.[18]

Instead, let us take Moore's lead and think of Jesus as the one person who did indeed live a human life without succumbing to the fear that is at the heart of Self-destruction. This is not to say that Jesus was some sort of Cosmic Self without an ego. Rather, it is to say that Jesus was the one person in history who lived out of a communion with God integral to his identity, such that his ego ambitions did not interfere with or destroy his deepest Self-in-divine-relation. Because of his unique and preexisting communion with the Creator and the Spirit, Jesus embodied the perfect integration of ego (that executes action), persona (the roles we play in relation to others), and Self. Christianity claims that this perfect integration of wholeness and holiness has concretely occurred in history, in the person of Jesus of Nazareth. Further, Christians believe that God willed such a life in order to free human persons from the Self-destruction that is sin. "Like us in all things except sin" now comes to mean "Like us without the terrible alienation between ego and Self, between the human and the divine."[19]

The presence of such a person was designated by the earliest believers (using the images available to them at the time) as the inbreaking of the kingdom of God. The extraordinary (yet quite ordinary) quality of Jesus, as living wholly in the embrace of God, led them to identify him as "Messiah," "Son of God," "Son of Man," "Savior." But the presence of such a person elicited quite dramatic responses from different quarters. While for some Jesus became the object of love and worship, for others this embodiment of (w)holiness had the opposite effect, eliciting fear and resentment of the greatest (and "holiest") sort. Given the protean alienation of humankind, such a sinless person could not long exist without drawing the worst of evil to act against him. And even those who did follow him could not abide until the end: either they lacked the will to sustain solidarity with such a (w)holy emissary, or they lacked the power to intervene, or both.

But here the mystery deepens. The alienation that is sin was overcome, not only by the birth of such a sinless one but also by his death. His death, like his life and person, was unique in all of history. He not only lived an integrated life in the embrace of God, but he did so *even in the face of evil*, manifested in the injustice of his trial and crucifixion. Just at the moment when he, of all people, could have justifiably pulled out all the stops on his ego defenses, when he could have used the power of his (w)holy psychic energy to expose the un(w)holiness of his persecutors, he chose to stop the cycle of revenge and violence by suffering evil rather than doing evil.[20] It is not that he chose suffering as an end in itself, but that he willingly accepted it as the inevitable consequence of deciding to maintain his integrity and communion with God in the face of evil and injustice.[21]

And here the supreme contradiction of the entire story takes place. Jesus, the only one in history to live out the reality that each of us is called to be, the concretely historical representative of God as a (w)holy human Self, is destroyed. Evil is taken to its ultimate extreme. The one least worthy of death is killed, in the name of righteousness, law, and order. The

ever-continuing cycle of the victim who destroys others, making new victims who seek healing in all the wrong ways, creating tragic heroes who in
their very attempts to settle justice only seek revenge: this cycle of evil
stops dead in its tracks at the one pure victim in history. Jesus' refusal to
continue the cycle leads to the most concrete and graphic manifestation
of the root and result of evil: the murder of God's beloved Son.

Then, after all is said and done, a few meager players in the story discover a different truth: that such ultimate evil, the death of the one incarnate God-presence, is *itself* within the embrace of God. Even evil taken to
its worst extreme cannot destroy divine communion nor kill human
integrity. The one destroyed by evil continues to live, through death and
beyond. The Risen Lord makes himself known in the gathering of believers, to those who had betrayed him and to those who had been loyal but
powerless.

The implications of this—even today—are tremendous. Jesus' resurrection means, quite simply, two things: (1) there is no evil on earth that we
might *suffer* which is beyond the scope of God's healing and (2) there is no
evil on earth that we might *commit* that is beyond the reach of God's forgiveness. These are profound and, for some, unbelievable claims, yet they
signify the heart of the Christian gospel and are the source of hope for the
likes of Helen, John, and countless others.

Note several things that are theologically important here, if not essential. One is that Jesus was indeed a real living fulfillment of our desire for
wholeness and for God.[22] The contemplation of a symbol, the cross as
merely an archetype that is instrumental to rather than intrinsic to transformation, will not sustain us. If we are to abide in the darkness of conversion, in the ambiguity and pain of travail, of seeing glimpses here and
there of our victimization and healing, of our sin and its forgiveness, there
must be One who has, in fact, *been there.* There must be One who has suffered as we have, who has borne the brunt of our Self-hatred and yet
lived.[23]

Second, we see the intimate and indispensable connection between the
doctrines of *incarnation* and of *justification*, of who Jesus was and what he
did. The life or death of a good man or woman, no matter how exemplary,
could not do the trick. The fathers of the church recognized this in the
debates of the early centuries. Though they were preoccupied with Jesus'
identity, the visceral and volatile way in which they argued made it clear
that they felt their very *salvation* was at stake.[24] If Jesus was not indeed a
pure victim, an embodied fulfillment of the desire we all have to be a Self

in God's embrace, then he is simply one more example of a victim who is also, at some level, a perpetrator of evil. The cycle does not stop; it only repeats itself. Jesus, as the actualization of an ego/persona/Self in divine relation, who suffered evil rather than doing evil, marks the possibility of the end of the cycle, represented concretely in Christian imagery as the kenosis of God that brings about the end of death (1 Cor. 15:51-57).

GOD AND EVIL

While questions about who Jesus was have preoccupied most of Christian history, the average believer is often more stymied by the *theodicy* question: How can belief in a good God be reconciled with the existence of evil and suffering? My approach will not solve this quandary but may yield some new angles on it. Rather than beginning with a distant all-powerful God and insisting that he act with logic and righteousness, if we begin with our deepest desire for God and discover how it is thwarted, both by our victimization and by our choices, we run into the explicitation of evil in the cross, and *thereby* discover the limits of evil and the power of God. We don't begin with God and then make sense of suffering and sin, rather we begin with our experience of pain and alienation and, in making sense of it, discover God and the infinite breadth of her embrace.

Moore highlights, as did St. Paul, the paradox involved here. There is a reversal of the expected order, and it is such a reversal that poses the stumbling block to Jew and Greek alike (1 Cor. 1:17-25). Moore emphasizes that what we discover in the crucified Jesus is not the solution to evil but evil taken to its ultimate extreme:

> In the ultimate order the ultimate sin, of crucifying the Just One, reverses itself, the victim giving life to the crucifiers. Sin, in our deep, necessary, negative power, has no being. The only kind of "being" it can have is the sight of itself in its ultimate effect, the crucified. . . . The ultimate truth, which is God's unique embrace, is that the essential *effect* of sin—the crucified—is, identically, the healing. What sin ultimately is, is seen in the crucified. What sin ultimately is, is forgiven [and healed].[25]

If the question of God and evil is some version of "What was God thinking?" Moore's answer is that God recognized that the only final solution to evil was to allow it to be made explicit and thereby expose its lack of ultimacy. To be in the embrace of God is to be within the embrace of a God so good that evil, with its ultimate non-being, is not outside of God but transformed within God:

> Finally, it is impossible to live with this mystery of the crucified as the symbol that transforms evil into sin and sin into forgiveness [and healing], without coming to see that this crucified embrace of God *anticipates* all evil, and the conscious creation that must carry the potential for evil, as well as *embracing* evil after it has become a fact. . . . It is trivial to regard the creation of potentially sinful man as a "risk that God took," with the cross of Jesus as the remedy God applied when the risk became disaster. Such an account fails to see the difference between saying that God is able to draw good out of evil and the more radical statement that God's love *embraces* evil. This is not to say that there is evil in God. It is to say that God is a reality in which evil is mysteriously transmuted.[26]

This expression of the paradox does not solve the logical question, nor does it explain why a good God allowed evil in the first place. It does, however, reveal the character of a God so omnipotent and so good that no sin can separate us from her and no suffering can so destroy us as to make her inaccessible. While this does not exonerate God, perhaps it reveals a different kind of God and a different approach to the questions.

This was brought home to me several years ago when I read the volume edited by Emilie Townes, *A Troubling in My Soul,* which includes the subtitle *Womanist Perspectives on Evil and Suffering.*[27] I enjoyed the articles and the wonderful retrieval of resources from African-American slavery: songs, stories, narratives, autobiographies. I could not help but feel, however, that the issue of theodicy—how can we get God "off the hook" when so much suffering surrounds us?—was not really addressed. When I dared to express such misgivings at "Breakfast with an Author" at the annual meeting of the Society of Christian Ethics, at which the editor and several contributing authors were present, the revealing response I received was, "We've always known *God* was good, it is *people* we have trouble with." This generated a new insight for me, which was that theodicy questions, as I have known them, may be questions arising from privilege: when we are raised to expect the natural order to serve our needs, we are indignant when our expectations are thwarted, and call God to account.[28] Theodicy from the underside may be quite a different set of questions; *given* the reality of lives of suffering, how can we find hope and make sense of our experience, especially in light of our faith in God?[29]

A corollary of this approach regards the meaning of suffering. In common parlance we often assume a difference between suffering that is redemptive—leading to a further good—and suffering that is unredemptive —with no positive outcome. We need to look more closely at this distinction. In fact, there is no suffering that simply exists "out there," whose meaning and value are somehow determined apart from the person experiencing the suffering. Suffering is always an *interpreted* event. And while some theologians insist on distinguishing salvific suffering from oppressive suffering, the difference here is in the way in which certain events are interpreted and evaluated, not in the events themselves.[30] This is an essential point because it grounds the claim, made earlier, that there is no evil that one can suffer that is beyond the scope of God's healing. There is, to be sure, oppressive suffering, and I am not claiming in any way that such suffering is good for people; only that such suffering *can be* the locus of God's presence, *can be* the medium through which we encounter God.

At the same time, redemption is not an entirely subjective event. Just as Jesus is more than simply an archetype that can be a catalyst for transformation, so there is a historical and, in this sense, objective moment in salvation history. Jesus' life, death, and resurrection radically shifted the potential meaning and value of human history. The cycle of sin—revenge—further violence was broken and the full possibility of human flourishing in union with God was met. The efficacy of this new reality continues to be worked out in human communities over time. The objective fact of God's entrance into our world in a new way opens transformative possibilities that continue to unfold. Thus, Christians stress the "already but not yet" meaning of salvation and the need to "work out our salvation in fear and trembling."

GRACE

In discussing the process of discovering sins and embracing wounds I spoke of the possibility of reversing the cycles of evil, of turning the victim—perpetrator—victim repetition into a transformed cycle of healing and forgiveness. Still, the radical courage and choices involved in such a transformation are well beyond the power of any one person to elicit. We noted how tenuous any movement toward salvation can become, since even glimpses of God's healing and forgiveness can be co-opted into a quick fix over which we retain control. For this reason, Christians have always insisted on the utter helplessness of human persons before the enormity of sin: to insist that one can reverse the cycles of alienation, can solve the problem of evil with one's own abilities, is simply to perpetuate the distortion that is at the heart of sin.

The Christian answer, then, to this dilemma of alienation, suffering, and evil, is to insist that *God* is the agent of salvation. It is God who initiates the reversal, who brings about the necessary transformation of hearts, minds, and psyches, who thus facilitates the renewal of cultural meanings, social values, political and economic systems. Just as Jesus did not raise himself from the dead but *was raised by* God from the grave, so we too must depend on God to free us from both our sins and our wounds.

This initiative of God, this gift of renewal that God offers, is what Christians have referred to as *grace*. The witnesses to the resurrection experienced the presence of the Risen Lord—and the new life it brought to their beleaguered souls—as a pure gift from God. Both the betrayers and the powerless knew that an entirely new world was opening for them and that they had done nothing to bring it about. Indeed, many of them had fled —in one way or another—from the very possibility. St. Paul emphasized grace and defended this gift of resurrection over against those who would return to the dead letter of the law, of salvation by obedience.

While the biblical literature graphically describes the power of this serendipitous union with God in peoples' lives and explores the implications of it for living, later patristic and medieval scholars sought to explain grace in theoretical categories. Questions of how God could be just yet forgive sins arose. Issues about the very nature of God and of Jesus' work in redemption were approached not in narrative and sermonic fashion but in categories that abstracted from any one person's experience. The purpose was to devise a theology of grace, a metaphysical theory that would describe the nature of reality (metaphysics) in a way that would apply universally (theory).[31]

In the modern era we have rediscovered the role of the concrete person in knowing, doing, and believing.[32] Thus, while theories of justification—how the sinner is made righteous in God's sight—continue to be important, the process by which grace transforms people's inner and outer lives needs further exploration in an age after Kant (who questioned not the nature of reality but the nature of the human mind) and Freud (who uncovered the role of the unconscious in human living). Sebastian Moore undertakes this project in his work, and I have tried to develop it by exploring the dynamic relation between being a victim and being a perpetrator of sin.

So how can we explain the operation of grace today? The deep longing to be a whole human person, we have seen, is often truncated, both by our own sabotage and by the actions of others. Our socialization into fear of others and accommodation to their needs damage this deepest Desire, which is a yearning to be a whole Self that is met fully only in union with the Divine. Such a union is frightening as well as enticing, and we manage to circumvent it even when opportunities offer themselves. The cycles of alienation begin to be transformed when something outside the system shifts what the fathers of the church called our "appetites." A taste of fulfillment of this deep Desire stirs up power, courage, deeper yearnings, willingness to pursue fulfillment of Self at all costs. Hunger overtakes fear.[33]

Such grace—the glimpses of union with God, the experience of resurrection here and now, the taste of ultimate Desire fulfilled—comes in many and varied forms. It does not necessarily appear in mystical visions but most often occurs in concretely embodied ways. It is communicated through neighbors, friends, music, dance, liturgy, nature, even death, loss, and pain. Whatever its incarnate form, and however fleeting its vision, the effect of such grace is to change the criteria of our deciding and acting. Where we had previously run from the pain of transformation, from facing our wounds as well as our violence, we now want to be cleansed of these so that greater light, more joy can be uncovered. Something stops the ordinary course of events short and taps a deeper need, grief, longing, hunger, that calls us into repentance and healing.

Further, this shift of appetites, this touching of our deepest Desire for Self in communion with God, is complemented by grace as insight. The tapping of our Desire opens us to insights we had previously avoided, while new insights are instrumental in shifting the ground of our feelings and decisions. The cock crowed, Peter remembered his vow, saw his clear failure to keep it, and dissolved into grief and shame, opening the way to new life. Mary of Magdala, bewildered before the empty tomb, queries a gardener and then, hearing her name, recognizes him as "Rabbouni" (John 20:11-18). In our story of Helen, watching a documentary on childhood sexual abuse was the occasion for a great "Aha!", in her case one in which she discovered memories and feelings that had been long repressed. For John there was likewise a revelation about himself, a discovery about a pattern of behavior he had never considered addictive. God's gift of grace manifests itself concretely in us through (often unsolicited) insights; insights into facts, into feelings, into past behavior and future possibilities.

An example of how the grace of Desire and revelations of truth can be both unexpected and transformative is provided by Monty Roberts's work with horses. In an epilogue to Roberts's memoir, Lawrence Scanlan tells how, in working with difficult horses, Roberts is able to disclose damaged human relationships. On many occasions, revealing the history of abuse toward a horse becomes the catalyst for unveiling familial abuse. Scanlan recounts the following:

> But the most compelling incident took place in Dublin. Monty was working in a round pen with a so-called mad horse before a throng of people. The horse's owner, a handsome, agitated woman, had previously explained how impossible it was even to catch the horse in the paddock. "My husband," she told Monty, "is a good horseman, a tough horseman, and he says this horse is a maniac."
>
> In the ring, Monty used hand motions to prove to his satisfaction that the horse had been beaten. "I am going to tell you what the horse is saying," he told the audience through his lapel microphone. . . . "He's saying he's been kicked in the belly and head, and had a whip across the hocks. This horse is full of stories."
>
> At that point Monty looked over to the woman, who was frozen in her aspect, her mouth open. He face betrayed her sudden doubts about the wisdom of letting this man tell all about her horse—and more. "She was looking across the ring at her husband, and when I spotted him I knew the horse was telling the truth. Horses, in fact, never lie, and this horse was no exception. The horse comes to me, I saddle him, and get a rider on, and the horse is moving around like a million dollars. By now both the man and his wife are extremely distraught."
>
> "Someone," Monty said into the microphone, "has to apologize to this horse."
>
> The demonstration over, the crowd began to leave the arena. The woman approached Monty in the ring.
>
> "You're in danger," he told her.
>
> "I can't talk about that," she replied, "I'd rather give up my life."
>
> When her husband joined them, Monty told them that their lives would be a shambles until they got a handle on the violence. Monty had cut to the quick, and the response was immediate and emotional. The man threw his arms around Monty, and pleaded, "I need help, I need help." It must have been a riveting scene: in the ring where a mad horse had been proven sane, three people, their arms entwined, linked by a common history of pain.[34]

The unveiling of the truth stirred up in this man his deep Desire to be different, to be whole. The grace in this situation was not overtly religious, nor was it a set of pleasant feelings. Nevertheless it was a gift that offered both healing and forgiveness.

Still, the gift had to be accepted. "Cooperative grace" came in the choice of the man to seek help. In fact, this man did get the help he needed and now conducts seminars for other men who use their fists on people they say they love. Likewise, in our earlier story, Helen made changes in her life, read books on sexual abuse, began writing a journal, found her own therapist. John, confronted by his colleagues, sought treatment and apologized to his family and friends.

Further, the process spirals back on itself, since such actions, while not *creating* grace, increase the likelihood of the needed insights and appetites to emerge. Helen, by reading books on sexual abuse and by discussing these things with her counselor, opened herself up to further feelings and discoveries, though she knew that they might be painful. The horseman, by seeking help, is now able to open up new possibilities to others like him. Monty Roberts's demonstrations, group therapy, books, counseling, prayer, sacraments; these cannot *produce* grace—the understanding and willingness needed for transformation—but they can increase the likelihood of such grace occurring.[35]

Let us examine this gift and response further. In any insight, any discovery, there is a certain lack of control, a certain patience required. We have all had the experience of trying to remember a name or solve a puzzle, when the solution is "on the tip of my tongue," or "not getting it" when someone has told a joke and everyone else is laughing. Once you've got it you've got it; if you don't get it, you don't get it. And "getting it" involves a change, not only in your mind, but in your whole person; your face flushes, your heart rate changes, you relax, or laugh or, in Archimedes' case, jump out of the bath and run naked through the streets shouting "Eureka!" While not all insights are as dramatic as this, the point is that (1) insights come to us and are not always under our control, and (2) once we have an insight, our consciousness shifts in some irreversible way.

Transformative insights, indeed all insights, are instances of *operative* grace: they are *given to* us, not *created by* us. Still, this shift, this gift, requires a response. We need to test each insight to ensure that it is correct: as Bernard Lonergan noted, insights are a dime a dozen and not all of them pan out. Archimedes could have run down the street naked only to discover the next day that he was wrong. John rightly needs to challenge his colleagues' assessment of his behavior as addictive, just as Helen needs to check her response to the TV show with all her sisters, with the facts of her childhood. Insights lead to judgments, and judgments often require "research": confirming the bright idea with the evidence at hand, comparing notes with other inquirers, examining one's own presuppositions. In addition, judgments lead to further questions for action: What are the implications of these new truths for living? How do we need to change our behavior in order to honor the grace/insight that has been given? The gift requires a choice: *cooperative* grace.[36]

The same is true of grace as a shift of Desire. We cannot force experiences of deep union with the Transcendent; we cannot contrive to make God present to us in any given moment. Patience is required. The gift of new love, the stirring up of longing, the shift of appetites—while communicated concretely through persons and events—has a serendipity to it that we cannot control. Yet once we have been touched, a response is demanded. We can ignore such glimpses, rejecting them as mere fantasy and silliness. Or we can assent to the movement initiated, seek to discern its meaning, follow the inclinations of the Spirit, pursue the new values and choices required of our living.

As St. Paul labored to explain, efforts to manufacture love, disciplines of obedience to moral strictures, in themselves only lead to spiritual death. Freedom to choose new life, power to face pain and persecution, love that abounds, all come as gifts. Still, the gift is freely given and leaves our ability to choose intact: we must respond with cooperative grace in cultivating Desire and fostering its influence on our decisions and actions.

Though our actions cannot commandeer grace, the importance of certain disciplines cannot be overstated. Often the insights necessary for transformation are not forthcoming because the dominant culture circumscribes them, setting up parameters of meaning and value within which only certain insights and judgments are allowed. Attending to our deep Desire may be considered taboo, and silenced yearnings remain suppressed, even in the service of religious piety. The powerful role of consciousness-raising groups was and is to create a safe place in which to allow new insights and recovered yearnings to emerge.[37] The term "consciousness-raising" is apt, since new insights shift our entire awareness and protected environments lead to the emergence of Desire long imprisoned. What self-help groups, therapy, spiritual direction, retreats, alternative liturgies, and other such activities do is simply increase the likelihood that transformative insights and appetites, with their subsequent judgments and decisions, will occur. They are essential for those who have not been traditionally designated as knowers or actors in our world.[38]

In sum, the transformation of sin and suffering is a transformation of meaning and value, which has occurred already in history but which continues to take place in concretely embodied subjects living in the here and now. Such transformation involves grace as a liberation of Desire and a series of insights that are given and not achieved. We do not merit salvation by our works but are dependent on the grace of God to reveal salvation to us. Still, we can do "that which is in us" to foster such transformative desires and insights, that which is in us often requiring great courage and resilience.[39]

3

Embracing Travail

Surrender and Resistance

I SPENT MOST OF MY CHILDHOOD, as siblings do, battling with my older sister. In the earliest years the encounters were physical: literally rolling about on the floor in one sort of tussle or another. I remember when this shifted: around age nine or ten the rough-housing stopped and the engagement became psychological. We exchanged blows by insult and innuendo. In both types of conflict I ran up against an obstacle that baffled me. With great logical reasoning I would return her pinches with my own. When she insulted me I would respond in kind. The motto for such retaliation was, "Now you know what it feels like." The objective was not to inflict suffering but to reduce it; if only she knew what it felt like she would stop being so cruel. But she didn't get it. Instead, she would use my tit-for-tat as further ammunition against me. If I was unlucky enough to exercise my logic of retaliation in the presence of my parents, the backlash was immediate: "Why would you do that to your sister?" My claims to justice went unheard, my objectives were unmet, the battles continued unabated and as ugly as ever.

On other occasions I responded to suffering with bravado. I was known in the neighborhood as a tomboy and prided myself on climbing trees and throwing baseballs with the best of the boys. One day I decided to prove my "boyhood" by offering myself as a target. A neighbor boy had a new bow and arrow and I volunteered to be tied to a tree so that others could take pot shots at me. I was sure that this act of courageously accepted sacrifice would prove my worthiness once and for all. As the arrows were flung at me I discovered that this was a painful endeavor and, sure that I had now proven my willingness, I asked to be released. To my surprise my pleas were not heeded. Instead my cries were taken as further reasons to

40

continue the assault. In the end the attackers simply lost interest, and I was left to untangle myself and go home. Once again my objective had failed. My willingness to sacrifice was supposed to have yielded respect and relief, but my attackers didn't get it and I was left hurt and unvindicated.

My yearning for vindication went beyond just my own interests. As a sensitive child I was keenly aware that all was not right in the universe. In an empathetic way I presumed that I could and should do something to change the course of evil in the world. I was bright enough to envision solutions to various dilemmas and determined enough to think I could make a difference. My intentions were altruistic, and thus I was demoralized whenever I hit a dead end: why couldn't I contain the chaos and change the world by my good will?

The profound limits on my moral intentionality came home to me one day when I was in my mid-twenties. I was driving through an especially nice residential section of Toronto, imagining that I would one day live the life of peace and tranquillity embodied there. Suddenly I noticed a commotion: kids yelling and chasing a large dog. I stopped the car to see what was wrong and discovered, to my horror, that the dog had a cat by the throat. The cat was bleeding profusely, clearly on the edge of death. Our efforts to free the feline victim failed miserably: the dog would not let go and tore off into the neighboring yards with its prey. I returned home shocked and defeated. As I tried to calm down with a cool drink on my back porch, the horror and purposelessness of the scene overwhelmed me. The burden of responsibility—I should have been able to do something—and my moral impotence not only grieved but enraged me. Suddenly and violently, I threw my glass against the brick wall of the house, shattering it into a million pieces.

In the preceding chapter I insisted that redemption must involve embracing ourselves as both perpetrators of evil and victims of it. This chapter takes up a further question: Can one just accept victimization or sin without a clear and determined effort to change them? Embracing travail must include resistance to evil. But the nature of this resistance remains to be explored. Does resistance involve retaliation or, at least, retribution? In what way can sacrifice yield concrete change, if ever? A theology of the cross embodies the paradox that surrender to the effects of evil somehow yields resurrection. But what makes that surrender an authentic resistance rather than a capitulation to the forces of oppression?

I will first develop the notion of an "ethic of risk" as a way of subverting domination. I will illustrate this with contemporary examples as well as apply it to Jesus' life. Then, as in the last chapter, I will draw out the implications of my approach for various theological topics: good, evil, and God's omnipotence; the final fulfillment of hope; and solidarity and compassion.

AN ETHIC OF RISK IN A WORLD OF DOMINATION

In response to middle-class cynicism, Sharon Welch develops an ethic of risk.[1] She relies on the literature of African American women to illustrate this ethic, an ethic that shows resilience, hope, and persistence in the face of ongoing oppression. It involves "persistent defiance and resistance in the face of repeated defeats." An ethic of risk is "responsible action within the limits of bounded power."[2] This stance toward life not only recognizes that we cannot guarantee decisive changes in the future, it is undertaken because *not* to risk would mean death. "The death that accompanies acquiescence to overwhelming problems is multidimensional: the threat of physical death, the death of the imagination, the death of the ability to care."[3] An ethic of risk is characterized by three elements: (1) a redefinition of responsible action (as risk-taking rather than controlling), (2) a grounding in community, and (3) strategic risk-taking.

The first key element is the distinction between an ethic of control and an ethic of risk. An ethic of control assumes that moral action produces clear results. It leaves little room for ambiguity and involves "controlling events and receiving a quick and predictable response."[4] This decisive action renders one invulnerable to evil: one has a clear plan, a strategy, that will not only rid the world of (this current) evil but protect one from further threats.[5] In contrast, an ethic of risk shifts the understanding of moral action to that which may yield only partial results. The goal of moral action is not complete success but the creation of new conditions whereby transformation may take place. It accepts vulnerability but undertakes risks in the name of life-affirming dignity.

Second, if one is to undertake action that challenges the structures of oppression, one needs a community of meaning to sustain such action. "Responsible action as the creation of a matrix for further resistance is sustained and enabled by participation in an extensive community."[6] An aspect of this community is its historic narrative: by telling and retelling stories of earlier resistance and hope, or by retelling dominant history in new forms, one sustains a vision of change. One is empowered by the retrieval of a "dangerous memory."[7]

Third, an ethic of risk is not to be mistaken for throwing oneself away in sacrifice. One does not put oneself in total jeopardy, for this would simply sabotage the good that might come of resisting. One must calculate not the likelihood of a positive outcome as in an ethic of control but the degree of risk that will yield hope rather than further destruction. "Martyrdom is not encouraged, yet the willingness to risk physical harm, and even death, is acknowledged as sometimes necessary. The measure of an action's worth is not, however, the willingness of someone to risk their life but the contribution such an action will make to the imagination and courage of the resisting community."[8]

With this redefinition of moral action as strategic risk taking, it becomes clear that the objectives of resistance are as much to maintain the dignity of the actors and their community as they are to solve problems:

> The aims of an ethic of risk may appear modest, yet it offers the potential of sustained resistance against overwhelming odds. The aim is simple— given that we cannot guarantee an end to racism nor the prevention of nuclear war, we can prevent our own capitulation to structural evil. We can participate in a long heritage of resistance, standing with those who have worked for change in the past. We can also take risks, trying to create the conditions that will evoke and sustain further resistance. We can help create the conditions necessary for peace and justice, realizing that the choices of others can only be influenced and responded to, never controlled.[9]

Welch's work can be expanded in relation to Walter Wink's analysis of the powers of domination.[10] Wink's project is explicitly Christian and specifically biblical: his task over three decades has been to interpret the meaning of "principalities and powers" in the New Testament. He takes a position midway between those who see "powers" as other-worldly entities and those who attach this biblical category to current sociopolitical structures. He asserts, instead, an integral worldview: the powers of evil are embodied very concretely in the material world but have a spirituality as well. The powers are not essentially evil but are "fallen" and the key to this fall is capitulation to a system of domination, acceptance of the "myth of redemptive violence."[11]

The myth of redemptive violence goes back to the ancient Babylonian empire, where the *Enuma Elish* depicts the creation of the world through conflict, combat, and violence.[12] More important than its religious history is the way in which this myth continues today. Wink reviews modern media, especially cartoon dramas, to show that this myth perdures: Olive Oyl is abducted by Bluto, Popeye comes to her rescue but is beaten to a pulp by the villain until, at the last moment (when Bluto is, in effect, raping Olive Oyl) a can of spinach pops out of Popeye's pocket and into his mouth. Transformed by this quick fix, Popeye rescues his beloved and vanquishes the villain. "The format never varies. Neither party ever gains insight or learns from these encounters. Violence does not teach Bluto to honor Olive Oyl's humanity, and repeated pummelings do not teach Popeye to swallow his spinach *before* the fight."[13]

The basic structure is that clearly designated good guys combat and ultimately conquer the evil villain. The good guys must always win; the evil characters are unredeemably evil; and the unredeemability of these villains justifies the violence used against them. "Cartoon and comic heroes cast no shadows."[14] There is no ambiguity; there are no tragic decisions to be made; no one ever repents or confesses. Most important, evil is projected outward onto another.

> The myth of redemptive violence is the simplest, laziest, most exciting, uncomplicated, irrational, and primitive depiction of evil the world has ever known. Furthermore, its orientation toward evil is one into which virtually all modern children (boys especially) are socialized in the process of maturation. . . . Once children have been indoctrinated into the expectations of a dominator society, they may never outgrow the need to locate all evil outside themselves.[15]

In what Wink calls the "Domination System," Welch's ethic of control is clearly operative. The domination system presumes that evil, when encountered, can be overcome through direct action. The most powerful of direct actions is violence, so that violence becomes the *modus operandi* of the domination system. The myth is that violence and control will be redemptive. The danger is that, ultimately, violence and control become ends in themselves, and must be preserved at all costs.[16]

What is the appeal of such a myth? It is salvation through identification with the powerful elite and the avoidance of true responsibility. Welch uses Harriet—a white philanthropist working for the poor on a Caribbean island, in Paule Marshall's *The Chosen Place, The Timeless People*—to illustrate this.[17] Harriet's generosity came along with her refusal to deal with the source of her fortune: the slave trade itself. She denies any responsibility for her family's complicity and fights the enemy as she perceives it, her notion of poverty. When her help is misunderstood and not received as she had hoped, she retreats rather than gain insight into the dynamics of her fortune and her charity.[18] Wink's comment about the appeal of the myth of redemptive violence applies:

Everything depends on victory, success, the thrill of belonging to a nation capable of imposing its will in the heavenly council and among the nations. For the alternative—ownership of one's own evil and acknowledgment of God in the enemy—is for many simply too high a price to pay.[19]

Wink goes on to explore the dialectic that exists within the biblical tradition: a dialectic between a system of domination and the notion of a partnership community. Some parts of the Hebrew Scriptures reinforce a powerful Yahweh who orders his chosen people "to destroy, plunder, and kill all but the virgin daughters of their enemies, and to take these as sexual slaves, concubines, and involuntary wives."[20] Over against this assumption of control and domination is the tradition of the Hebrew prophets, some of whom directly chastised Israel for its dependence on military power. Wink cites Abraham Heschel's remark that the prophets were the first people in history to regard a nation's reliance on force as evil.[21]

Jesus followed a long line of such prophets and preached the liberation of all peoples through partnership values rather than domination. The New Testament calls this the "kingdom of God"; Sharon Welch prefers the less hierarchical designation the "Beloved Community."[22] But whatever the label, it is clear that Jesus acted against the mores of his time. Through his preaching, his concern for the marginalized, his treatment of women, his breaking of ritual practices, his insistence on love of enemies, culminating in his death on a Roman cross, Jesus embodied an alternative to domination.[23]

It was not long before this alternative gave way once again to a Domination System. Thus, sin quickly became defined in an exclusionary way; women were forced out of leadership; and, once Christianity gained the sanction of a state religion, the ethic of control and the myth of redemptive violence once again held sway. In the modern era "the dream of the New Reality of Jesus has long since turned into a nightmare, first of Christendom, then of our more recent secular totalitarianisms. In all this, the conquest of women went hand in hand with the exploitation of the poor, the conquest of weaker nations, and the rape of the environment."[24]

Either Christianity must be rejected outright or the gospel must be retrieved, a gospel that includes an ethic of risk rather than an ethic of control, a gospel that incorporates a narrative not of redemptive violence but of redemption in some other form. How can we interpret the work of Christ in a way that empowers transformation and promotes resistance to injustice? Can we envision a theology of the cross that emerges out of *risk* rather than *control*?

To answer this question adequately let me develop Wink's analysis of domination a bit further. His categories of domination and redemptive violence presume overt power to be the culprit. But just as the category of "victim" needs to be added to a theology of sin as pride, so also the "power of capitulation" needs to be added to the analysis of domination. The flip side of the myth of redemptive violence is the myth of redemptive suffering. While some participate in the domination system through overt power, others participate through socialization into being the objects of redemptive violence. Rather than projecting evil onto others, these introject it onto themselves. The solution to evil is thus seen as self-denigration, sacrifice, and suffering. While the myth of redemptive violence relies on the projection of evil and then its destruction, the myth of redemptive suffering depends on the introjection of evil and its deserved punishment.[25]

The most important point here is that suffering, though in some senses the opposite of domination, is not its antidote. The two simply form a symbiosis that perpetuates evil. The solution demanded here is to break the cycle altogether. What is needed is some "third" way that embraces yet goes beyond the cycle.

To clearly grasp this alternative, both resistance and surrender need to be defined within an ethic of risk rather than an ethic of control. Resistance within an ethic of control is action that directly combats domination and uses its tools. It *feels* just and righteous, just as my attempts to hurt my sister in return for her cruelty *seemed* obvious and logical. But this kind of resistance takes up the tools of those one is resisting, and such tactics rarely, if ever, work.

Likewise, surrender can seem like a means of liberation from oppressive harm. But this surrender is fueled by the fear that energizes domination and uses its tools, in this case deceitfulness and manipulation. This kind of surrender is not action designed to overcome the system but an astute way of learning to work within the system. It adopts the assumptions of the system, and it is just as ineffective as my attempts to gain worth in the eyes of the boys who shot arrows at me. This myth of sacrificial worthiness has at times led Christianity astray and must be rejected if the gospel is to be truly redemptive.

Resistance and surrender within an ethic of risk have a very different quality. Four such qualities can be delineated: (1) a *restructuring of meaning,* involving the creation of a new set of choices and values emerging out of love rather than fear, (2) *embracing oneself as an agent of action* (responsible for sins) as well as *naming the ways in which one has been victimized* or socialized into a system of oppression, (3) *recognizing the limitations and risks of moral action* rather than determining expected outcomes, and (4) *reclaiming the liberating elements of the communal past* and creating new communities of meaning. Let us explore these qualities in relation to some contemporary examples before applying these dimensions of risk to Jesus.

RESISTANCE AND SURRENDER TODAY: ILLUSTRATIONS

Discerning Dignity

Linda is forty-three years old. She comes from the middle class and is bright and spunky with a quick wit and active sense of humor. She always looks well kept, if not distinguished, and has a high sense of moral standards. She is a devout Methodist, with a progressive theology committed to social action. She has had a host of jobs in her life, of the managerial sort; she is good at organizing others and is a catalyst for networking people and skills. She has a strong family background and is particularly close to her one sister, who lives near Linda's home in Boston.

Linda is in the process of ending her marriage of seven years. This is her second marriage; she has a fifteen-year-old daughter from a first marriage and two sons from this current relationship. Billy is two years old and Danny is six years old. Danny suffers from a rare respiratory disease whose prognosis is ambiguous. He is one of the oldest surviving victims of this disease, and, though he lives a relatively normal life, he is under regular medical surveillance and is subject to a host of experimental treatments. Harry, the boys' father, left the household a year ago after a long period of tumultuous negotiations. He now lives around the corner and takes the boys for three nights at a time, in a rotation with Linda.

Since the marriage began to fall apart, Harry has systematically denigrated Linda, accusing her of stealing his belongings, of trying to raid his assets, and of pitting the children against him. He consistently insults Linda in front of the children and uses the boys to bait her into rescinding the custody arrangement. He will not let the boys return to Linda's house with clothes that he has purchased for them, insisting that Linda bring "her" clothes to his house for the boys to wear home.

Most destructively, Harry takes very few precautions regarding Danny's health, allowing him to overexert himself, keeping him up until all hours, and insisting that he should be able to play soccer just as well as his cousins. Whenever Linda institutes any restrictions on Danny's activities, his father tells him it is because she does not love him. Though Danny would love to get a cat, having one in the house would jeopardize his breathing. Harry tells Danny that Linda is lying about this and is simply being mean. Harry has also mobilized his own family around his cause: none of them will speak to Linda and they reinforce the negative image of her to the children.

Linda has done everything in her power to make this difficult situation easier for the boys. She deals in good faith with their father, making plans and keeping promises so as not to jeopardize the boys' well-being. She refuses to speak ill of Harry in front of the children, trying to instill respect and love in them. But she is up against a system of domination that presumes an ethic of control. Harry assumes that this is a win/lose relationship, and he is pitting all his forces against her, most notably against her character and integrity.

Linda is caught in a double bind. If she takes up Harry's tactics against him, it only confirms his suspicions. A power struggle ensues in which she is always second-guessing his attacks, for example, checking the children's overnight bags every time they come home to reclaim "her" clothes. On the other hand, if she attempts to cooperate, she is merely taken advantage of. For example, if Danny gets sick on a day that Harry has him, Harry will ask Linda to take Danny so that he can go to work. Linda usually agrees to such situations, sometimes rearranging her own schedule, because (1) she is concerned for Danny's well-being and (2) she wants to act in good faith. But her good faith is rarely reciprocated. Harry hardly ever accommodates Linda's schedule and often lies about his own whereabouts.

What do resistance and surrender mean in Linda's situation? To resist surely does not mean fighting Harry back on his own terms; such battles would further victimize the children. But, at the same time, surrender does not mean accepting Harry's negative caricature and verbal abuse, nor his deceitful tactics. How can Linda embrace travail and wrest some "redemption" out of this situation?

First, authentic resistance involves *restructuring meaning*. Linda does not have to accept the domination rules by which Harry operates. Most important, Linda needs to claim herself as a Self, as someone with integrity regardless of how Harry portrays her. This means she will have to let go of whatever residual investments she has in Harry's opinion of her. Most painfully, she will have to let go of her need for her children to vindicate her worth. She will need to enter into the death of old meanings, hoping in resurrection, not as a controlled outcome but as a present claim on her reality.

Second, this refusal to accept Harry's framework of meaning will require Linda to both *embrace pain* and *take responsibility* in a new way. She

will have to embrace pain in many ways: the pain of being wrongly portrayed to her children and others, the pain of a broken relationship, most
of all the pain of loneliness and the insecurity of Danny's future. At the
same time, Linda needs to take responsibility for her own contribution to
the situation. She does rescue Harry from his responsibilities when he
complains. She bears the financial burden of Danny's health care and is
the one who takes him to all his doctors' appointments, allowing Harry to
deny the entire dilemma. Linda must learn what she is responsible for and
let Harry—and the boys—bear their own burdens.

Third, authentic resistance and surrender mean *accepting limitations*
and *taking risks*. Precisely because Linda is conscientious she expects to be
able to fix something. Her own moral and psychological integrity enables
her to see how destructive Harry's ploys are. But she faces clear limits in
her efforts to change the situation. If she denies these limits she will, in
one sense, maintain hope. But if her hope lies in expecting the situation
to change, or in her own power to alter Harry's attacks, she will be
doomed to disappointment. Instead, she must adopt an ethic of risk, one
that accepts the fact that the best she can hope for is to create conditions
of possibility for change. She can create an atmosphere of love and confidence that will serve, in the long run, as resources for her children's transformation. But she cannot guarantee that they will ever understand, will
ever see her point of view.

Fourth, Linda will never be able to live within yet against the domination worldview unless she has a *community of meaning* that supports her
resistance and helps her to discern surrender. This community cannot be
entirely new: it will build upon Linda's past and rewrite the story of her
life. She, with the help of others, will need to review her own narrative:
How did she get into this situation? Was she a fool or is she a victim of
Harry's deceitful charm? What can her journey and her mission mean *now,*
over against what she thought she was creating in partnership with a
spouse? Most important, she will need to create a coherent and meaningful story to tell her children; honestly admitting the pain of their life situation and giving them some tools by which to interpret their lives in
purposeful ways.

Authentic resistance demands the creation of intentional communities.
Whereas we all grow up in taken-for-granted communities of meaning,
recognition of oppression entails an attentive critique of these meanings
and a purposeful creation of alternatives. One changes friends, hangs out
in different venues, eats new foods, stops drinking the old cocktails.
Whether the new community is a therapeutic, a religious, an aesthetic, an

educational, or a geographical one, or all of the above, the intention to create new relationships and sets of values and meanings is the key.

"Community" here refers to a multifaceted and many-layered reality. It is not just "the friends one keeps" but the entire matrix of economic, political, social, religious, and cultural values in which one stands. Linda comes to understand how she is at a disadvantage economically because of her reliance on Harry as "the Good Provider" (which, in fact, he wasn't: he squandered their savings on a car business that never turned a profit). She sees the power of patriarchal assumptions, particularly strong in the ethnic origins (Greek) of Harry's family. She discovers class bias: Harry comes from working-class stock, which has made him both defensive and jealous. Linda, for her part, has assumed that life would be stable and secure and is shocked to find herself on the edge of poverty. Linda begins to see how her religious training has reinforced all the distortions she is now working against. Still, she depends on such resources to give her a new vision.

Having illustrated what resistance and surrender might entail for Linda, let me add two caveats, namely: (1) the stakes are high and (2) the task is not easy. First, the risks are particularly difficult in Linda's case because of Danny's health. In any marriage breakup one must come to terms with the undesirable influence that an ex-spouse will have on the children. In Linda's case Harry's unreliability could cost Danny his life. The temptation for Linda to intervene—to take on more than her share of the responsibility—is tremendous. She constantly has to weigh the surrender aspect of her resistance with the stakes at hand.

Second, this is no easy task. The center place of travail, the surrender that is not capitulation and the resistance that is not violence, is never found once and for all. It can only be discerned over and over again, in each new situation. This is why it demands faith and why being embraced by the Divine and a community of love is so essential. The task of discernment will, over time, yield habits of discernment, but the struggle is never without pain, ambivalence, and ambiguity.

Fierce Ambiguity

Another illustration may be instructive here. In this case it involves someone learning resistance and surrender on another's behalf. The story told by Sister Helen Prejean in *Dead Man Walking*, now made into an award-winning film, illustrates all the tensions that embracing travail involves.[26] In this case, there *appears* to be a clear villain—the perpetrator of a horrific rape and murder of innocent teenagers—and clear victims—the teens themselves and their families. But as the story unfolds the categories get confused: the families of the victims are the persecutors of a convict who also has a family and who proclaims his innocence. He now becomes the victim of systemic violence, and capital punishment becomes the issue. Sister Helen, without ever planning to, becomes the agent of resistance, resistance to a whole system of legalized death. But this resistance requires grappling with precisely that tension between victim and perpetrator which redemption is all about. Her role becomes to enable the murderer to take responsibility for his actions even though he is a victim of state violence, and to help the victims' families come to see that they are now perpetrating the violence of which they have been victims.

Sister Helen's journey is an imitation of Jesus. She gratuitously entangles herself in the travail of Matthew's struggle as both victim and perpetrator. Near the end of the film, on the day that Matthew is scheduled to be executed, he says: "I want to thank you, sister, for helping to get me saved. But I want you to know, me and God, we got all things squared away. When I stand before God on judgment day, Jesus, he's going to be there to speak for me." Sister Helen responds, with horror and conviction: "Oh no, Matthew, redemption isn't some free ticket that you get because Jesus paid the price for it. You got to *work* on your salvation." The remainder of the film is a vignette of this work, and Sister Helen bears Matthew's sins in the sense that she allows herself to participate in the pain of his journey, both the pain of his sin and the agony of his impending death.

Perhaps the most difficult aspect of Sister Helen's resistance involved visiting the families of the victims. Unwilling to side simplistically with Matthew as victim, she knows that she must embrace the pain of his crime. The people she visits do not comprehend. There is a poignant scene in their kitchen when they discover that she continues her activity against the death penalty. They, working out of a domination worldview, had assumed that her visit meant she had changed her mind, that she had come over to "their" side. When they discover this is not the case, they are shocked and indignant. They literally force her out of their house with insults and verbal abuse.

In the end it is not clear to what degree Sister Helen's resistance has been "successful," but she testifies to the transformation it has made in her own life. In the preface to the book she states:

There is much pain in these pages. There are, to begin with, crimes that defy description. Then there is the ensuing rage, horror, grief, and fierce ambivalence. But also courage and incredible human spirit. I have been changed forever by the experiences that I describe here.[27]

Sass and Other Tools

The stories of African American slave women provide another set of examples of resistance, surrender, and hope. Shawn Copeland, in her article "'Wading Through Many Sorrows': Toward a Theology of Suffering in Womanist Perspective," recounts the stories of African American slave women who suffered every type of sexual and physical abuse imaginable.[28] Yet she also recounts how memory, the telling of stories, and the singing of spirituals all aided the recovery of identity, culture, and self as a means of resistance. She appeals to the sass of black women as a form of resistance. The dictionary definition of "sass" is "impudent or disrespectful back talk." Yet, as Copeland says, slave women used sass to "guard, regain, and secure self-esteem; to obtain and hold psychological distance; to speak truth; to challenge 'the atmosphere of moral ambiguity that surrounds them.'"[29]

She recounts how a slave woman, Linda Brent, stood up to the master who sexually abused her:

> When the physician mocks her marriage plans, calling her fiancé a "puppy," Brent sasses: "If he is a puppy, I am a puppy, for we are both of the negro race. . . . The man you call a puppy never insulted me." Infuriated, Flint strikes her. Brent sasses again: "You have struck me for answering you honestly. How I despise you!" "Do you know," Flint demands, "that I have a right to do as I like with you—that I can kill you, if I please?" Unbowed, Brent sasses yet again: "You have tried to kill me, and I wish you had; but you have no right to do as you like with me." At this, Flint is enraged, "By heavens, girl, you forget yourself too far! Are you mad?" Indeed, sass is Linda Brent's means of physical and psychological resistance. Brent is not mad. Of course, thinking that Brent may be mad makes it is easier for Flint to dismiss her behavior—and salvage his ego. Rather, Brent and her sassing sisters are naming their own standards, claiming their own bodies, their own selves.[30]

The function of sass is to restructure meaning and, in so doing, to redefine the situation and question domination assumptions. Though Brent has little hope that her sass will change anything, she engages in an ethic of risk, the most important part of which is her claiming of her own identity. She accepts the limitation of her context and surrenders to the suffering that her sass might bring. Yet she knows that not to resist would mean death of another kind, the death of self-meaning.

Sass is one of many tools for resistance: humor, wit, poetry, songs, civil disobedience, nonviolent protest, ridicule, liturgies, and rituals can all have a liberating effect. Walter Wink tells of the time Desmond Tutu was walking by a construction site where only one person could pass at a time. He confronted a white man coming toward him who, recognizing Tutu, stood firmly in his tracks and said, "I do not give way to gorillas." To this Tutu stepped aside and said, "Ah, yes, but I do."[31] Maya Angelou attests to the power of song and poetry when she tells of the time a white bureaucrat humiliated her all-black eighth grade graduating class. Their self-esteem was recovered when the class valedictorian stood and, instead of presenting his speech, simply began singing "Lift Every Voice and Sing," the hymn that serves as the "negro national anthem."[32]

All these cases, in different ways, illustrate authentic resistance and the struggle to discern surrender. They all involve a restructuring of meaning—most notably, claiming dignity and self-identity—as well as embracing pain and taking responsibility, accepting limits yet taking risks, and reliance on (with simultaneous revision of) one's community of meaning.

Surrender and Resistance in the Crucified

Jesus and the Restructuring of Meaning

The death and resurrection of Jesus is a narrative that suggests multiple meanings. It has, in many manifestations of Christianity, been understood within the framework of Welch's "ethic of control" and Wink's "system of domination." Under such a lens, God becomes an agent of decisive action who rescued sinners by redemptive violence, in this case the violence of willing his own son's death. The resurrection is evidence of the success of this plan. Jesus becomes the sacrificial scapegoat who takes on the violence of our sins and is rewarded for his willingness to do so.[33] This transaction, in spite of theological efforts to the contrary, ultimately makes of God a bloodthirsty deity and perpetuates the myth of redemptive violence (on God's part) and redemptive suffering (on our part).[34]

It is possible to understand Jesus' life, death, and resurrection in a very different light, one that illustrates resistance and surrender within an ethic of risk. In this approach, Jesus' manner of living becomes central to the meaning of his death. It is not that Jesus chose to die, as if his death itself would constitute a solution to sin. Instead, he simply lived with a new set of values on a daily basis, recognizing the dignity of all and using power in a transformative, healing way.[35] He thus surrendered to suffering only as the risk he knew he was taking in choosing to live life the way he did. Likewise, he resisted the religious and political distortions of his day by living and declaring an alternative set of meanings.[36]

The most important aspect of Jesus' claim to new meaning involves the intersection between who Jesus was and what he did. The New Testament makes it clear that Jesus' actions and preaching arose out of his unclouded sense of identity as a son in relationship to his Abba-Father-God. Thus, what Jesus chose to live was not only a radical set of meanings and values, a "program for happiness" of some sort. More centrally, Jesus chose *himself* as a child of God. The most radical element of his resistance is that he defined his life's meaning according to his identity, as a beloved Son empowered by divine relationship. Using the language of the previous chapter, by living out of the center of his Self, by abiding within God's embrace, he chose a radically alternative embodiment of resistance to the evil forces of his day.

Jesus' death, then, becomes the logical conclusion of the radical way he lived. It also serves as the ultimate unveiling (apocalyptic) event. In one sense his mission failed, his resistance did not work, and one could rightly question whether he can serve as an adequate model of resistance. But, as Sebastian Moore claims, there is a dénouement here, an ironic reversal, and it is this reversal that provides the alternative, the opting out of the cycle.[37] By refusing to succumb, even in the face of death, to the Powers' definition of him, Jesus exposed the Powers for what they were. Wink puts it as follows:

> Here was a person able to live out to the fullest what he felt was God's will. He chose to die rather than compromise with violence. The Powers threw at him every weapon in their arsenal. But they could not deflect him from the trail that he and God were blazing. Because he lived thus, we too can find our own path.
>
> Because they could not kill what was alive in him, the cross also revealed the impotence of death. Death is the Powers' final sanction. Jesus at his crucifixion neither fights the darkness nor flees under cover of it, but goes with it, goes into it. He enters the darkness, freely, voluntarily. The darkness is not dispelled or illuminated. It remains vast, untamed, void. But he somehow encompasses it. It becomes the darkness of God. It is now possible to enter any darkness and trust God to wrest from it meaning, coherence, resurrection.[38]

In accepting death as the expected consequence of claiming his (w)holy identity, Jesus revealed the character of God as well as the nature of human identity. God, it turns out, is not like the Powers, is not a wrathful God demanding justice at all costs. God refused to battle with the Powers on their own terms. He would not use violence to promote his cause. Instead, in allowing Jesus' death, and in raising him from the dead, God revealed that there is a permanence and transcendence to human identity that evil cannot destroy. Authentic resistance is the claiming of that identity and a refusal to damage it through capitulating to power tactics. Authentic resistance thus becomes a statement of faith in eternal life, meaning confidence that one's identity perdures in God's embrace in spite of the oppressive definition of others.

> Jesus' death on the cross was like a black hole in space that sucked into its collapsing vortex the very meaning of the universe, until in the intensity of its compaction there was an explosive reversal, and the stuff of which galaxies are made was blown out into the universe. So Jesus as the cosmic Christ became universal, the truly Human One, and, as such, the bearer of our utmost possibilities for living.[39]

Note, finally, that the restructuring of meaning involved here is not a benign activity that unfolds easily around afternoon tea. It is a "black hole" that sucks in the "very meaning of the universe." The transformation required can, in fact, involve the death of God—in this case, whatever "god" it is that stands in the way of God's work in us. Everything that one had known of God may disintegrate. This is the dark night of the soul, the experience of the absence of God so clearly described by St. John of the Cross.[40] It is reflected in Jesus' own experience, graphically portrayed in his desperate plea on the cross: My God, my God, why hast Thou forsaken me? Authentic resistance will involve the death of (certain) meanings and values. Authentic resistance involves surrender to such a death, so that new meanings and values may arise.

Embracing Victim and Sinner

This is where the hints of Moore and of Wink come together. Jesus' suffering, death, and resurrection are models of resistance for people of all races and classes who are oppressed. But unless one discovers oneself in Jesus, discovers oneself as both victim and crucifier, this resistance runs the risk of either succumbing to suffering and yielding to the Powers, or of turning into a vengeful violence that never establishes justice. Either

way one becomes a part of the system of domination; one perpetrates
rather than ends the cycle of redemptive violence and suffering.

One of the key features of the domination system is the projection of
evil out onto another, justifying this Other's defeat. The flip side of this
projection is introjection, so that the supposed Other—the scapegoat or
deviant in society—accepts evil onto herself as deserved. The end of these
cycles demands that both sides be *acknowledged* and *reversed*. Redemptive
healing and resistance involve the withdrawal of projections and acceptance of the evil within. They also demand rejection of falsely introjected
sin and the naming and healing of injustice. This reversal, and the restructuring of meaning, the renaming of oneself that it involves, is not a pre-
cursor to authentic resistance but is integrally woven into it. As structures
are changed and cultural values redefined, wounds can be embraced and
sins confessed. As one takes responsibility for oneself and embraces pain,
one is empowered to discover new meanings and to take action to change
oppressive structures.

Jesus both historically enacted this reversal and symbolically embodies
this reversal. He did not project evil onto others, but neither did he mince
words in assigning culpability. He did not falsely introject evil onto himself
—he did not, in this sense, "take our sins upon him"—but knew exactly what
he was responsible for, and lived this to its conclusion. Yet, ironically, his
refusal to project or introject evil meant that Jesus bore the *effects* of evil in
their extreme. In this sense he *did* take our sins upon him, embracing suffering as the necessary outcome of his refusal to distort evil through blame
or self-denigration.

Accepting Limitations, Taking Risks

The Jesus story reveals a key aspect of an ethic of risk in that Jesus
accepted the limitations of his creatureliness. An ethic of control presumes that the moral actor has more capability than he really has, presuming a kind of omnicompetence in solving problems of evil. The New
Testament reports several occasions on which Jesus confronted this sort of
supposedly easy solution. The temptations in the wilderness and the struggle in Gethsemane were conflicts over Jesus' moral agency. Would he, who
of all people might resort to power tactics, accept his human limitations
and suffer the risks that his identity and mission entailed? Or would he,
with one fell swoop, use his authority to fight or flee from the Powers?

Jesus accepted the fact that, as a human being, he was a creature with limitations. He flatly refused to mistake his divine identity and mission with a lack of finitude. He recognized that whatever choices he made would have limited results. Rather than fall into the myth of moral action yielding a decisive outcome he engaged in "strategic risk-taking." He took what action he could, realizing that its objective was not a final solution but the setting up of the conditions of possibility for transformation.[41]

This approach required, and still requires, surrender to suffering. But this surrender is quite different from the myth of redemptive suffering. It is the acceptance of suffering not as an end in itself, nor as a means to an end—redemption. Rather, it is surrender as recognition of both finitude—one cannot by fiat erase moral evils—and the law of the cross—that the cycle of victim and perpetrator can only be reversed through someone suffering rather than retaliating. This is the surrender that opts out of the cycle rather than the surrender that is part of the cycle. It is the surrender that is a necessary part of resistance if resistance is to maintain *risk* rather than succumb to presumptions of *control*.[42]

This kind of surrender is neither discerned nor embraced easily. As with the travail of the previous chapter, discovering the middle place that accepts the suffering necessary for resistance yet maintains integrity is a difficult task. This is the "strategic" part of risk taking, and it is illustrated by Jesus' struggle in Gethsemane. This struggle I take to involve both a dilemma of discernment—figuring out if this is the best way to resist—and a battle over acceptance. In the end, Jesus resolved, "Not my will but thine be done." This needs to be interpreted not as an obedience that contravened Jesus' integrity but as a plea to be embraced. No one, including Jesus, can undertake such risks, and the surrender to suffering entailed, unless one abides in Divine Love, in this case designated as the communion of wills.

Not only does Jesus undertake an ethic of risk; he reveals a God who takes risks. Rather than solve the problem of sin by eradicating its source in us, God chose to take the risk of becoming human. Refusing to act on an ethic of control, God allows moral evil to spin itself out. The cross and resurrection stand as events and symbols that set up a matrix of new meanings that are *potentially*, not *necessarily*, transformative. They forgo control to leave the risk intact. Though they raise questions relevant to oppressors and victims alike, they do not answer such questions a priori. And, just as the players in the historical drama did not all get the point, so many today do not comprehend. But the potential for transformation is there, if one is willing to enter the risk, embracing travail and embraced by God.

Remembering Community,
Creating Community

Authentic resistance and surrender, the transformation of suffering, do not
come full-blown out of nowhere. We are all embodied and enculturated,
socialized into sets of values, economic structures, religious systems, political processes. To speak of resistance and surrender, then, presumes concrete praxis, and this praxis will take different forms depending on the
personal, social, and historical situation. We have inherited traditions, and
all of these traditions are a mixture of values and disvalues, insights and
oversights, clear-headedness and bias, authenticity and alienation. Discovering ourselves as sinners and victims will go hand in hand with discerning
authenticity and oppression in our communities of meaning. There are no
shortcuts, and, though there are aids to facilitate such tasks, each person
and community must muddle through in its own self-correcting process of
learning.[43]

Jesus lived in a concrete matrix of cultural, social, religious, and economic structures. His resistance involved discerning and retrieving, in
communion with God and God's people, the best of his heritage. His interpretations were not acceptable to all, but he did insist that he was fulfilling the law and living out what the prophets had intended. His Jewish
upbringing was part and parcel of the good news that he lived and
preached. He engendered a dangerous memory of the best of his religious
and cultural upbringing by transforming it. Resistance as Jesus lived it and
surrender as he accepted it had to be sustained by a matrix of communal
meanings and values. Even Jesus was not exempt from such enculturation
and needed its resources for resistance.

Jesus was not alone in retrieving and restructuring his tradition. In the
Gospel of Luke, the women who discover the empty tomb are confronted
by two dazzling men who tell them to *remember* what Jesus had told them
about his betrayal, death, and resurrection. The turning point for these
women comes when they do remember his words and return to announce
these wonders to the other disciples (24:6–9). In this case, the earliest witnesses to the resurrection had to reinterpret the life and words of Jesus
himself in order to craft new meaning out of old presuppositions.

In the first century the early Christians covered immense ground in
retrieving the meaning of Jesus' life and teaching, first orally, then in missionary correspondence, and finally in gospel form. Most profoundly, they
had to retrench with regard to the meaning of God's reign and the Messiah's role in history. Jesus' death on a Roman cross challenged every

expectation possible and up-ended many conceptions of God. Then, as these Christians encountered non-Jewish contexts and cultures, the gospel had to be adapted and revised to meet new audiences. Resistance and surrender took on further meanings as conversion to Christianity took its toll on familial relationships and issued into the era of martyrdom. Inevitably differences in interpreting the meaning of Jesus led to factions within Christianity and then discernment of authenticity took another turn: orthodoxy versus heresy. The cultural matrix shifted to encompass state sanctioning, and the era of Christendom ensued. The dialectic of interpretation and reform thus spins itself out through Christian history.

Jesus used the best of his tradition to offer resources for the resistance and surrender that break the cycle of domination. His restructuring of meaning was not ahistorical, and the ongoing work of the church remains embedded in evolving contexts. Authentic resistance and surrender demand communal support and rely on communities of shared meaning and value. But these are ever subject to distortion and demand constant renewal themselves. Thus resistance and surrender, in order to be authentic, must always be open to critique and renewal. Authentic resistance and surrender cannot, of their very nature, be controlled but demand the risk of ambiguity and the work of constant discernment. In other words, authentic resistance and surrender involve embracing travail.

GOOD, EVIL, AND GOD'S OMNIPOTENCE

My development of redemption as an ethic of risk leads to several important theological implications. A first task is to clarify the nature of the relationship between good and evil. Within the system of domination it seems clear that there is an opposition between good and evil. This polarity is obvious and simple and demands a quick and decisive solution: eradicate evil. The problem, of course, is that evil is often projected outward or introjected inward, so that such solutions rarely get to the heart of basic sin. Indeed, they tend to perpetuate the system that needs correcting. Welch and Wink have correctly discerned that there is a flaw here. The opposition of good and evil that the domination system and the ethic of control presume needs reexamination.

The temptation is to deal with the myths of redemptive violence and redemptive suffering by reducing the polarity of good and evil. By heightening the ambiguity in good and evil and celebrating a diversity of viewpoints, the hierarchy of presumptions about who is good and who is evil can be unmasked. The rigid polarity, which is at the heart of domination and which has been so destructive, is dissolved in favor of ambiguity and tragedy. The harmful consequences of assuming that good needs to overcome evil are addressed by recognizing the mixture of good and evil in all human experience, and highlighting the complementary unfolding of good and evil as part of God's presence in history.[44]

While the need to emphasize the ambiguity involved in discerning good and evil is important, I believe that reducing the complete opposition between good and evil to a complementary process is problematic. The *flaw* in the domination system is not in presuming that good and evil are radically opposed. This latter insight is sound and fundamental to the Judeo-Christian tradition. Rather, the problem with an ethic of control is the idea that evil will be overcome through domination and conquest. In fact, the way out of the cycle of violence and sin is not to *reduce* the opposition of good and evil to a complementary tension. It is, rather, to move to a higher set of meanings and values, one that *sublates* the tension of victim and perpetrator, suffering and domination, into a new integration. This new integration *is* a victory over and negation of evil and has been designated in various ways: "being saved by grace," an "other-worldly falling in love," or (my version) "embracing travail while in the embrace of God." The higher integration it yields has a host of images to describe it: resurrection, the promised land, heaven, and so on.[45]

The flaw in an ethic of control lies in designating good and evil *within* the domination system, as if domination were good and suffering were evil, or vice versa. There is an opposition here, but it is a *distorted* polarity and its reversal involves its transformation. It is not that one pole needs to eliminate the other. It is, rather, that the cycle needs to be converted to one of healing and forgiveness rather than suffering and domination.[46] And *this* polarity—between a *distorted* cycle and an *empowering* one—*is* a genuine contradiction, two alternatives with an *excluded* middle (in contrast to the "middle" of "travail" which is embraced). Healing/forgiveness and domination/suffering form a polarity that involves a clear opposition: one is good and the other is evil and the one needs to overcome or, better, transform the other.[47] To solve the domination problem by declaring good and evil to be somehow complementary is to undercut the very salvation that one is trying to discover and create.

A second and related insight has to do with the nature of God. If it is true that good issues from evil through its negation and transformation, that the solution to cycles of domination is not within such cycles but beyond them, then God, if she is involved at all in the process, must herself be outside the system. There is no question that images of God as an all-powerful and all-knowing patriarch have contributed to centuries of cultural and practical domination. The omnipotent God of the Jewish and Christian traditions has often been used to legitimate great atrocities and severe oppression down through the ages. The temptation is to make this God the enemy, and to declare that any restructuring of meaning must deny the existence of such a God. One, then, either becomes an atheist or emphasizes God's immanence, God's presence in the mire of our finitude and sin.[48]

This move, like the denial of the opposition of good and evil, will ultimately sabotage the possibility of freedom from domination. While I certainly would claim that God is present in the mire, in the struggle of resistance, and while I myself hold to a very immanent God, this immanence cannot mean that God exists in the same way that I do, within a finite system that is forever tainted by evil. Unless God transcends the system, unless God has the "higher viewpoint" that can yield transformation of suffering, there is no way out of the system. God must be omnipotent in a way that is diametrically opposed to the "potence" that domination thinks it has.[49] This divine power is a power to transform the cycles of evil within which we live and, in so doing, negate and conquer evil. This is the God of the Psalms and prophets whom we must retrieve.[50] He is a God who is omnipotent yet overcomes evil not by domination but by transformation and, in Christian terms, this transformation occurs precisely because God was and is willing to risk entrance into a finite world tainted with evil.[51]

A FINAL RESOLUTION?
HOPE VERSUS EXPECTATION

Just as the redemption I have outlined demands an omnipotent God, the resistance and surrender that transform suffering and evil require hope in a future resolution of injustice. The nature of such hope, what scholars discuss as different forms of *eschatology*, needs to be carefully delineated. There is religious faith that expects salvation in some future heaven, in such a way that current injustices are overlooked. Tyrants, masters, the political status quo, all hope for such fervor to catch the hearts and minds of their citizens. This is eschatology as the "opium of the people" and it curtails rather than energizes resistance. It supports the surrender that is capitulation. On the other hand, revolutionary movements, including religious ones, can endorse hope in heaven on earth. Such faith can promise or even demand results here and now and criticize faith in a distant future.

Both Wink and Welch point to the hazards here by showing the shadow side of "utopia." Welch discusses this in the context of U.S. nuclear armament policies, claiming that the utopian imagination has several, ultimately self-defeating qualities. Utopian ideals include no acceptance of long-term struggle but expect immediate and decisive results. The future is envisioned as one of complete security and invulnerability in which all conflict is eliminated. This lack of conflict gets translated into ideals of uniformity, so that difference per se is seen to be problematic. Concretely, U.S. military policy is oriented toward spreading the "success of the American system" to all.[52] Ironically, these ideals end up promoting the danger of a nuclear holocaust:

> The aim of a final defeat of all evil forces, or the aim of finally meeting all human needs, does not appear as anything but praiseworthy on the surface. It is indeed surprising to find that such utopian goals as the defeat of evil and meeting of all needs can have, and often do have, highly dangerous consequences and that these constructions make peace less likely and justice seem less likely.[53]

Wink sees the same danger operative in work for social justice. "Dreams of perfection are fatal to social change movements."[54] Reformers themselves are socialized into their own set of distorted hopes and aspirations. Utopian dreams only serve to promote a sense of failure:

> Driven by their ideals, they denigrate their own accomplishments as inadequate, as if they should have been able to do more. Or they change the goal just as they are close to realizing it so that they never get to celebrate victories along the way. They burn themselves out trying to live in utopian fashion with all their old socialization intact. . . . Rather than recognizing that we are all racist or sexist or undemocratic as a result of our social upbringing, and developing ways to assist people gently in the needed transformation, the movement declares that anyone with these attitudes is a traitor or deviant.[55]

This cautionary tone has been adopted by some theologians as the "eschatological reservation." This is simply the reminder that all our victories are partial, that our work for justice cannot be "directly identified with the work of God nor identified as the kingdom of God."[56] Both conservative and liberal theologians have criticized liberation theology on

this account, the liberation theologians responding that such an eschatological reservation can serve to curtail work for reform, as if the kingdom
of God never made inroads into the world of domination.[57]

Just what kind of eschatology and hope are needed for authentic resistance and surrender? Some hope *is* needed. Utopian ideals may be dangerous, but without some vision of a new future, change will never come
about and cynicism will reign. I have proposed that moving out of the
cycle of domination and suffering by transforming it involves faith in
God's power, healing, and love. This alternative horizon carries with it a
new vision of the future as already present, in our own transformation, yet
still to be accomplished. This is not "utopia" but the "already but not yet"
of St. Paul's mature theology. It is a "realized" eschatology in that resurrection is experienced *in* the cross, not as a reward or success that follows
suffering. It is also a future eschatology in that one clearly sees and accepts
the unfinished work of redemption yet trusts God to wrest it out of history. The task of envisioning this future is the work of imagining the
unimaginable, recognizing the unimaginability of this future to be the necessary eschatological reservation. This is a mysterious future, recognized
as a known unknown as well as an unknown unknown, not tackled as a
problem to be solved.

Such an eschatology has at its core hope rather than expectation. Gerald May describes the difference between expectation and hope:

> Efficiency breeds expectation: love nurtures hope. . . . In the abstract, hope
> is a wish for something; expectation is assuming it is going to happen. . . .
>
> Expectation refuses to permit wondering or doubt, and so it is closed off,
> final, frozen. When an expectation is not met, it dies. Sometimes, with
> grace, hope is born from the rubble of dashed expectations. More often, the
> death is simply denied, reality is ignored, and another expectation—just as
> rigid and just as impossible—is forged. Without some birth of hope, each
> remanufactured expectation is covered with a thicker coat of cynicism and
> paranoia. Expectation is brittle and can only be shored up by delusion, but
> hope is soft and willing to suffer pain.[58]

Hope is flexible and willing to change its goals, while expectation
grasps at solutions; it has attachments which easily become addictions.
Hope *embraces* the future, while expectation *clings* to it. In hope the imagination flourishes, concretely embodying images of new possibilities yet
never turning such images into idols. The transformation of expectation
into hope involves nothing less than conversion, just as the shift from dom-
ination/suffering to resistance/surrender is a type of death and resurrection. The old visions must die (and continue to die in an ongoing process),

and often the new visions are not forthcoming. Then one abides in faith as the conviction of things not seen, waiting upon hope and carried by an undercurrent of Desire.

A whole host of issues remains to be addressed in constructing a contemporary eschatology. These include personal immortality, history as linear versus cyclical, and the meaning of "communion of saints," especially in a nonandrocentric worldview.[59] My point here is to insist that (1) some vision of a hopeful future (individual and collective) is necessary to sustain authentic resistance and surrender; (2) such a vision will not be utopian as under an ethic of control; (3) authentic resistance and surrender require *hope* and—in the absence of an imaginable future—*faith* rather than expectation.

SOLIDARITY AND COMPASSION

The need for genuine hope returns us again to the question of community, since visions of a new heaven and a new earth are made out of the stuff of the past, of inherited traditions of meaning. Still, we have become acutely aware in recent decades of the multiplicity of communities that exist, even under the banner of Christianity. The complex nexus of race, gender, social class, sexual orientation, and other variables has raised questions about the possibility of a universal story of faith, hope, and love. Can there be solidarity and compassion between and among persons of radically different social locations?

To put the question more concretely, can Linda, a Methodist, middle-class divorcée living in Boston, have solidarity with a Roman Catholic nun in Louisiana and with the man on death row whom she has befriended? Can these people find anything in common with Linda Brent and her sassing sisters, African American slave women of the nineteenth century? Can they find themselves in the story of Maya Angelou, growing up poor and black in Arkansas in the 1940s? Can they stand in solidarity with a proud, black Anglican archbishop living in South Africa? Most important, can any of these people discover themselves in a Jewish rabbi living in the Mediterranean basin two thousand years ago?

"Solidarity" comes from the French reflexive verb, *se solidariser*, which means "to join together in liability; to be mutually dependent [upon], to make common cause [with]."[60] It involves a relation or connection among communities of people, but the nature of this connection needs to be made clear. Solidarity requires not just facile similarities, such as sharing racial, gender, or social class designations. Nor does it mean supporting a cause, as if in a pep rally, taking on someone else's issues as if backing a team in the World Series. Shawn Copeland goes beyond these simplistic meanings to describe genuine solidarity:

> Solidarity, as a defining quality or characteristic of a group or community, emerges from a common and/or complementary field of experience, of understanding, of judgments, of decisions, and of commitments. Solidarity emerges from the concrete unity of interests, sympathies, aspirations; common scrutiny, appraisal, and questioning; shared beliefs, values, and judgments; common decisions, commitments, and loves.[61]

How do these shared experiences, judgments, and commitments arise? I believe that they must have at their core the paradox of embracing travail. Certainly, honest communication is at the heart of solidarity: telling our stories, listening to others, finding common ground, even if it entails courage and hard work. But unless one is also facing oneself, open to discovering the nature of one's wounds and to taking responsibility for one's oppressive actions, such conversations can backfire. If one group is simplistically designated as "oppressors" while another is assumed to be "the oppressed," the false polarity of the domination system rears its ugly head. This polarity needs to be transformed by the honest sharing of the ways in which each of us, all of us, are both victims and sinners. The dominance/ suffering polarity of an ethic of control is transformed into a complementary dialectic of resistance and surrender only through the travail of confessing sins and embracing wounds. An ethic of risk becomes an ethic of solidarity when such travail is both courageously entered into and honestly shared between persons of differing cultural, social, and historical locations.

Compassion is "passion with" and has to be at the heart of solidarity. If people simply share causes and movements together, they are bound to fail. Authentic resistance involves solidarity, and this requires "suffering with." This "suffering with" cannot be either a projection or an introjection of others' pain into our own lives: this simply mimics the tactics of the domination/suffering cycle. The compassion required for solidarity must begin with owning one's own pain and recognizing one's complicity in it. *Out* of such pain and recognition of sin one can then genuinely enter into the passion of another.

For example, Walter Wink tells about the four months he spent in Latin America in 1982, observing dictatorships and visiting slums, talking to peasants and those who had been tortured. For months after this he slipped into a spiritual darkness, a deep despair. He began having repeated dreams about being detained in a Somoza concentration camp in pre-revolutionary Nicaragua. Gradually he began to identify his own experience of detention. As a child he had been caught lying, and had then been humiliated by his parents and sent to the "brig," a garage storeroom, for the night. He comments: "That night in a very profound sense I 'died' emotionally. And now, decades later, amidst the general hopelessness of the situation of the oppressed in Latin America, I found myself sinking back into that old despair I had myself first known as a detainee in my own house."[62] He goes on to tell another story of a woman whose social justice work brought her in touch with her childhood experience of abuse and helplessness.

Wink tells these as cautionary tales, evidence that we can be tempted into social activism through introjection and projection of our own wounds. But they also illustrate that, freed of an ethic of control, the connection between our suffering and that of others can be a catalyst for solidarity and healthy resistance. In fact, *unless* we make such connections, our solidarity can be terribly misguided.

A corollary of this position is that *grief* rather than *guilt* is the route to solidarity. "Liberal white guilt" has run its course and discovered its limits.[63] Feeling guilty for one's privilege only drives one further into a defensive ethic of (controlled) charity. Guilt may drive one to "risk," but the risk will be a false imitation of Jesus, a *mea culpa* looking for absolution. If one genuinely enters into not ascribed sin but real ways in which one has— knowingly or not—been complicit in the bias of one's community, and if one faces the damage that this has done to oneself as well as to others, one cannot help but *grieve*. Such grief may require concrete recompense or retribution, but these actions will emerge from honestly standing with another rather than as a way of dismissing the other's claims.

This adds another dimension to the surrender that is the counterpart of resistance. While each person must come to terms with surrendering to his or her own realities of suffering, solidarity involves surrender to *others'* pain in a way that may be entirely gratuitous. While one often has little choice over one's own painful realities, one can choose to either avoid or enter into the passion of others, particularly others who live in very different worlds of meaning. While our own passion is often the *reason why* and the *route by which* we enter others' worlds, one can intentionally choose to enter these different horizons. In fact, such deliberate acts of solidarity may reveal new angles on one's own journey of travail.[64] This direct choice to embrace gratuitously another's travail, is precisely what Jesus and his *kenōsis* were all about. *This* kind of imitation of Jesus is well worth emulating.

Still, the power dynamics of communication cannot be overlooked. When we choose to enter another's world, we must do it with the savvy knowledge that all things are not equal, that we are, most likely, not on a level playing field. Some of us come to the encounter with socially designated voices and the unwritten power to define the conversation. Others come disempowered, never having been taught the socially acceptable skills of being heard. Most of us are some composite of such power and its absence, speaking with confidence in one conversation and cowering in others. For those with relative "speaking privileges," surrender for the sake of solidarity involves learning to listen attentively. For those who have been traditionally silenced, learning to speak may be the risk they need to take. Shawn Copeland discusses this as follows:

> On the part of white women, such active listening will require them to reject postures and stances of guilt. For white women such listening constitutes half of the condition of possibility of authentic social praxis. To negotiate the borders of race and social class, ears, minds, and hearts must become attuned to vocabularies, grammars, syntaxes, scales and tones. It is obvious that attuning oneself to the distinctiveness of these several voices calls for practice; equally obvious is an understanding that practice calls for a new and bold expression of the virtue of humility. . . .
>
> As for red, brown, yellow, and black women, speaking will require us to reject postures and stances of manipulation. For us such speaking constitutes half of the condition of the possibility of social praxis. To negotiate the boundaries of race, gender, and social class, our voices must mediate the experiences, understandings, meanings, values, and worlds of our peoples authentically. It is obvious that such negotiation summons us to attune ourselves to the differentiated voices within our own communities; here also practice and the virtue of honesty are necessary.[65]

Copeland goes on to say, "This distinction between speaking and listening is heuristic rather than determinative; these roles may be exchanged."[66] Her point—and mine—is twofold. On the one hand, categories such as victim and perpetrator, oppressor and oppressed, speaker and listener ought not to be associated exclusively with one social location.

At the same time, one cannot enter into compassion and engage in solidarity without wide-eyed awareness of—or at least a willingness to discover—the power differentials at work in all social exchanges. My contribution to the notion of solidarity is to insist that, like authentic resistance and surrender, it requires embracing the travail of both woundedness and sinfulness. This, in turn, does not come easily or naturally and itself involves a conversion, a transformation that will both yield solidarity and be brought about by it.

4

Gaining a Voice

The Discovery of Discovery

THE DRAMATIC STORY OF HELEN KELLER'S struggle to communicate culminates in her profound discovery of meaning. Helen, deaf and blind since birth, had been unruly and unreachable until her teacher came to live with her. The "miracle worker" devised a symbol system by which she could spell words into Helen's hand. For months Helen enjoyed this game without making any connection between the finger movements and the objects they designated. Finally, after a particularly bad tantrum, Miss Sullivan chases Helen to the outdoor water pump. There, with water pouring over her one hand, Miss Sullivan spells w-a-t-e-r into Helen's other hand. The penny drops: Helen excitedly spells the word back again while splashing her teacher with water.

Helen's single insight became the discovery of a whole new world of meaning. Having grasped the concept "water," Helen dragged her teacher excitedly from one object to another, all around the yard. One simple "Aha!" led to a million more, culminating in the poignant moment when she seeks out her father and eagerly waits while Miss Sullivan spells out P-a-p-a. To grasp that words *mean* something is to open up whole new worlds of exploration. What Helen discovered was not just "water" but her own capacity to think. It was a discovery of the power of discovery.[1]

An equally dramatic story is recounted by Walter Conn.[2] It is the story of Vic Braden, a successful and famous tennis instructor. Vic grew up in a working-class section of Monroe, Michigan. His father worked in the local paper mill and Vic expected to do the same. Thoughts of a college education were like thoughts of going to the moon: no one in his family or community even considered it. One day, while hanging around gathering stray balls outside a tennis court, the players called him in. Rather than have

69

him steal their balls, they taught him how to play. A natural athlete, he soon found himself playing in tournaments. Many of his tennis colleagues simply assumed they would go on to college. Vic took up the challenge and attended Kalamazoo College. Even so, it took several years for him to realize that, as a member of the working class, he could actually think. He vividly recalls coming home to his brother Paul, who had dropped out of school, and declaring: "We're not dumb, Paul! I've learned. We're not dumb! We're not dumb!"[3]

Vic had been socialized into believing that rationality and learning were a matter of social class. He had assumed, without realizing it, that he could not think. In spite of his aspirations for a college education, Braden was so conditioned "in his belief that he and his family were ignorant lower class, that it was not until years later when he was at Kalamazoo College that he finally comprehended that intelligence was not necessarily a reflection of economic status."[4]

Helen Keller suffered from perceptual disabilities. Vic Braden suffered from social stigma. Both were considered ignorant, unintelligent, incapable of learning. In both cases the contradiction of this myth proved life-changing. Both discovered the power of discovery, a discovery that radically reoriented their configuration of themselves and their worlds. The power of naming, the emotional and psychic revolution brought about by the discovery of discovery, cannot be understated.

In the previous chapters we have explored "embracing travail." In the first two chapters, we explored the travail of encountering ourselves in Jesus as both crucifiers and the crucified. Second, we posed the question of how embracing suffering could go hand in hand with resisting evil. Now a further element has to be explored. If the solution to the problem of evil involves (in some way) embracing pain, going *through* the cross with Jesus, we need to be clear about just who has the authority to name that pain. Who is it that can and should designate the cross that we are to bear?

For most of its history, there has been within the Christian church a dominant elite, the literate if not propertied class, usually men, most often in theological centers in Europe. These men were in a social tier that provided them with the power of learning, the ability to read, the leisure to think, the influence on students, the authority over believers. The good news of Christianity is that there is no sin that is unforgivable and no wound that is unhealable. Still, this rational elite has been the one to define evil, sin, woundedness, and salvation for the cloud of witnesses who have endured the cross throughout the centuries.

The meaning of salvation today, especially if it is to incorporate the cross, must include the power of naming. Those who are the crucified must have the power to discover for themselves the nature of their victimization and their healing. Those who are crucifiers must discover the myths by which they have been enabled to live deceitfully. In short, no one person or group can define for another the travail they must endure. Each must work out his or her own salvation in fear and trembling. Surely a community can and should guide its members toward forgiveness and healing. But communities can only facilitate discernment, and the discovery of discovery is a potent resource on the road to salvation.

My task in this chapter is to explore the role of "naming" in redemption. It is to show how the discovery of oneself as a knower can have a revolutionary impact on one's understanding of sin and salvation. In recent decades the metaphor of "voice" has been used to illustrate this discovery, especially for women. I will begin by exploring the social roots of our knowing and the ways in which we are socialized as "discoverers" or merely "receivers" of knowledge. I will do this with reference to gender and women's ways of knowing, but most of the points are applicable to anyone on the underside of history, by virtue of race, class, disability, sexual orientation, or other factors. I will move on to show the redemptive power of gaining a voice, as well as to indicate a few ways in which Christians have used their own voices to tell the story of redemption.

Voice and Social Location

"Social location" is a code word for the insight that every person is born into a particular geographical place, financial circumstance, family configuration, ethnic subculture, set of social expectations. What has emerged over the last two centuries, and more directly the last three decades, is the realization that this social location has a profound impact on one's ability to claim a voice. For many persons the tools of learning, access to certain professions, and the route to political influence have been unavailable. What *Brown v the Board of Education* did in the United States was to show that the "separate but equal" interpretation of the Fourteenth Amendment was simply a cover story for the subtle silencing of an entire race. The battle for women's suffrage gained (white) women the vote in Canada in 1918 and in the United States in 1920, but the ideal of domesticated silence perdured. Women have found their way into rabbinic circles and ordained ministry in some religious groups yet remain a silenced majority in others.

One remedy to such subtle silencing was to give women a higher profile in the academy. Women's studies programs flourished in the late 1960s and 1970s. Every discipline has come under scrutiny, including history, literature, anthropology, psychology, philosophy, and theology. Feminists have highlighted the male bias of the educational system, of the scholars who have defined history, of those who have determined psychological health, and of the philosophers who have outlined the nature of scholarship itself.[5]

In 1982 the publication of Carol Gilligan's book *In a Different Voice* gained great popular as well as academic attention.[6] Many nonacademics resonated with her description of the "different voice," while in academic circles her work was influential in disciplines ranging from theology to social work to education and ethical theory. The main point that Gilligan makes is that developmental theory (from Freud, through Piaget, Erikson, and Kohlberg) assumes that male patterns of development define what is normal. She redresses this imbalance by listening to the different voice of women. While previous theorists saw moral development as a matter of learning impersonal *justice,* women described moral dilemmas as matters involving networks of *caring.*[7]

Women's studies, the feminist critique of various disciplines, and work such as that of Carol Gilligan all highlight biases in both the theory and the practice of the academy. What is more telling, however, is the underlying assumptions about knowing and gender (or race or class) that support these biases. In Western culture at large, the social location of women and minorities has rendered them (presumably) less than rational. The issue of voice—speaking versus being silenced—takes on a much more significant symbolic role here. Not only have some persons not been positioned to contribute to the public fund of knowledge; they have been assumed to be not even *capable* of such a contribution.

The Western cultural tradition, for the most part, has attributed reason to men, while denying it to women. As far back as Aristotle, a dualism between male and female, reason and irrationality existed. Elizabeth Morelli puts it as follows: "There were, then, two basic tenets that could be combined: (1) Female is the opposite of Male, or woman is not man; and (2) Man is rational."[8] Lorraine Code cites Aristotle's discussion of intellectual virtue: since virtues belonged only to citizens of the city-state, and since women were, by definition, not citizens, they were—by default—

incapable of intellectual virtue.[9] The history of philosophy is full of thinkers who, even if granting women a degree of intellectual capacity, limit it. Hegel claims: "Women are capable of education, but they are not made for activities which demand a universal faculty such as more advanced sciences, philosophy, and certain forms of artistic production."[10] Likewise, Schopenhauer insists: "For women, only what is intuitive, present and immediately real truly exists; what is knowable only by means of concepts, what is remote, absent, past, or future cannot really be grasped by them."[11] The inability to know, or to know *properly*, is tied to women's status as less than human. Again, listen to Hegel: "The difference between men and women is like that between animals and plants. Men correspond to animals, while women correspond to plants because their development is more placid and the principle that underlies it is the rather vague unity of feeling."[12]

The irrationality of women has often been explained in relation to biological functions. Since, it was presumed, a woman's place in the natural order is to reproduce, her energies are undoubtedly directed toward the bearing and nurturing of children. This reproductive role necessarily detracts from her ability to think. The opposite was assumed as well: as recently as a hundred years ago the belief was widespread that women who engaged in intellectual activities would find their sexual organs atrophying. This was given, quite seriously, as a reason to keep women out of higher education.[13]

Add to this the theological element that interprets Eve as the source of evil in the world. Eve, the primordial woman, tempts her husband to disobey God, thus bringing down God's wrath and destroying paradise. Women, in this pervasive worldview, are not only less than human, tied to reproduction and therefore incapable of rational thought; they are also temptresses who seduce *men* away from rational living. Thus, the University of Bologna, one of the two "ivy league" universities of the Middle Ages, not only denied women admission but insisted that the very presence of women was a danger to the male students. In A.D. 1377, they passed the following edict:

> And whereas woman is the fountain of sin, the weapon of the Devil, the cause of man's banishment from Paradise and the ruin of the old laws, and whereas for these reasons all intercourse with her is to be diligently avoided; therefore we do interdict and expressly forbid that any one presume to introduce into the said college any woman, whatsoever, however honorable she be. If this not withstanding anyone should perpetrate such an act, he shall be severely punished by the Rector.[14]

Thomas Aquinas, representing the height of medieval scholarship, had this to say about women: "Woman was created to be man's helpmeet, but her unique role is in conception . . . since for other purposes men would be better assisted by other men."[15]

These cursory glimpses of Western culture do not do justice to the wide range of views and practices in Christian history.[16] Nor do they indicate that women were never great thinkers or leaders. Still, the wisdom of women has most often been relegated to the margins, dismissed as "old wives tales," or disparaged as "midwifery." Women's knowledge has been discredited as mere gossip, and women's expertise has routinely been questioned.[17]

In fact, the well-documented persecution of women for witchcraft was linked to women speaking out independently. Midwives and women herbalists were the healthcare industry of the Middle Ages, before the rise of the medical profession. It did not take much for this community of knowledge to fall prey to accusations that their medical expertise relied on magic, gained through consorting with the devil. Marginal women (the "old nag" or the "loose" young woman), "women who did not fall under 'proper' male authority, women who talked back and led their lives independently, were most likely to be regarded as the town witches."[18] Some scholars see the witchcraft persecutions as an attempt of the growing male medical profession to contain its rivals.[19] The classic manual of witch-hunting connects witchcraft to the lesser intellect of women, which is, in turn, linked to women's bodily dispositions:

> It is not surprising that they [women] should come more under the spell of witchcraft. As regards intellect or understanding of spiritual things, they seem to be of a different nature than men. . . . Women are intellectually like children. . . . And since through the first defect in their intelligence, they are always more prone to abjure the faith, so through their second defect of inordinate passions, they search for, brood over and inflict various vengeances, either by witchcraft or some other means. Wherefore it is no wonder that so great a number of witches exist in this sex.[20]

Independent of accusations of witchcraft, women in the Christian West have been exhorted to silence. Paul's original warrant—"As in all the churches of the holy ones, women should keep silent"—is followed by the exhortation to learn from their husbands: "But if they want to learn anything, they should ask their husbands at home" (1 Cor. 14:33–36). Such exhortations have led to the exclusion of women not only from theology and church leadership but from the voice of independent inquiry altogether.[21] To speak up, to question authority, is to be a nag, a gossip, or a bitch. Thomas More tells of a husband who chopped off his wife's head because she persisted in "scolding" him. The local prince agreed that this was justified since the wife had "asked for it" with her scolding.[22] In Puritan New England in the seventeenth century, women accused of scolding by their husbands would be gagged with special cages designed to keep their mouths shut.[23] Even today, strong leadership is denigrated when exercised by a woman. A female pastor ousted from her church received the following comment: "This church needs a strong leader. A woman pastor is too pushy."[24]

Another important thread here is the relegation of women to the private sphere. Already we have seen that in Aristotle's world women could not be citizens of the city-state. More recently, American history reflects a shift from the family-based economy of the colonial household to the public/private split created by the industrial revolution. In the middle classes, beginning in the early 1800s, men went "out" to work while women tended the home, raised children and conformed to the "cult of domesticity."[25] Women's knowledge thus became relegated to the private sphere, as Lorraine Code points out:

> For the fact that woman is restricted to dealing with things individual and private restricts those things she is in a position to *know* to things discoverable within the confines of this realm. Hence there is a constant, enclosed circle in female life where her morality, traditionally, is based in an excessively narrow cognitive sphere: where the boundaries of her world are close about her, constraining both knowledge and action.[26]

This restriction to the domestic world earned women a certain idealization. In their world, that of the home, they are *above* men intellectually and morally. For this reason, they should avoid public speaking in order to keep themselves pure. In 1911, in response to questions about women's suffrage, Roman Catholic Cardinal Gibbons explained his unhesitating opposition:

> "Why should a woman lower herself to sordid politics? Why should a woman leave her home and go into the streets to play the game of politics? . . . Why should she long to rub elbows with men who are her inferiors intellectually and morally? . . . When a woman enters the political arena, she goes outside the sphere for which she was intended. She gains nothing by that journey. On the other hand, she loses the exclusiveness, respect and dignity to which she is entitled in her home. . . . Woman is queen," said the Cardinal, in bringing the interview to a close, "but her kingdom is the domestic kingdom."[27]

These examples are but a few of the many that could illustrate the restriction, if not complete denigration, of women's capacity to know and speak the truth. Though the examples refer to women and knowing, parallel narratives could be told of other nondominant groups: native Canadians forced into residential schools to learn properly, since their native cultures were considered barbaric; African Americans considered ignorant or, at best, restricted in their educational opportunities to the "truths" of white culture;[28] the welfare mom stereotyped, as Vic Braden was, as dumb and lazy. Certain elements converge: the assumption that particular groups are less human and therefore incapable of rational thought; the connection of this irrationality with undisciplined bodily passions or biological destiny; the restriction of voice and knowledge to certain private spheres, where minorities will not threaten the status quo with unwelcome questions. Most importantly, these converge not only in the structures of the economy and polity but in the cultural narratives by which we understand who we are. Some people inherit a presumption of voice and the confidence to know they are knowers. Others are socialized into silence and are carefully "protected" from discovering that they can make discoveries.[29]

FROM "RECEIVERS" TO "DISCOVERERS"

What does any of this have to do with redemption and the cross? It has to do with the narratives, the stories by which we understand ourselves in relation to the gospel. If a certain dominant elite has presumed others to be irrational and has taken on the role of interpreting and teaching truth to those less enlightened, then the storytelling has been in the hands of the few. This is not to say that the gospel does not speak for itself, that it does not have power to transform, but that those on the underside often have had to discover that power through their own means. Negro spirituals, the diaries of medieval women mystics, the wisdom passed from mother to daughter, the "Bible mothers" of south India who catechized female converts because they couldn't meet in public with men, all attest to ways in which the transforming power of gospel knowing from the underside has perdured.

In the modern era, the issue of knowledge and power has become explicit. It underlies the women's suffrage movement of a century ago, the

American civil rights movement, the claims of native Canadians to sovereignty over their lands, the movement for women's ordination. In these cases, the issue of the *ability* to discover meaning for oneself has had to be defended. The right to claim one's voice, to claim that one can be a *discoverer* of truth and not just a *receiver* of others' wisdom, has been at the heart of these battles. It lies at the heart of renewing redemption as well.

Before drawing out this connection, let us examine in more detail this process of discovering discovery. A study of women's understandings of their own understanding conducted by Mary Belenky, Blythe Clinchy, Nancy Goldberger, and Jill Tarule in the 1980s, illustrates the connection between self, voice, and mind.[30] *Women's Ways of Knowing* reports on in-depth interviews of 135 women from a variety of socioeconomic situations. The subjects were drawn from academic institutions and social agency training programs. Of the 135, 90 were enrolled in educational institutions ranging from a prestigious ivy league college to an urban community college with a mixed ethnic and less advantaged clientele. In addition, 45 women interviewed were from family agencies dealing with clients seeking help with parenting. Having gathered interview data, these researchers coded the interview material into five classifications representing the distinct ways of knowing that they discerned.[31] We will briefly review each of these perspectives.[32]

Silence

Though the researchers found only two or three subjects that they could designate as "silent," other women describe a period of silence in retrospect. What stands out about these women is not their perspective on knowing but that they have none. The silent women live in a world cut off from others, with little or no real communication. Words are seen as weapons of might, used to diminish rather than connect people. Women are expected to be seen but not heard (p. 32). These women describe the barest experience of dialogue with others and indicate no experience of interior dialogue. "When asked to finish the sentence, 'My conscience bothers me if . . . ,' Cindy, a pregnant fifteen-year-old, wrote, 'someone picks on me'" (p. 25).[33]

What is most salient in these women's stories is their social location, the role of authorities, the sex stereotypes involved, and the presence of violence. The silent women came from the youngest and the most socially, economically, and educationally deprived segment of the research sample.

They were found in the social agencies, not the ivy league colleges, and came from families who themselves were isolated from community. The women see themselves as passive, while authorities are all-powerful. Authorities are loud but never explain anything (pp. 27–29). Males are active while women are passive and powerless:

> I didn't think I had the right to think. That probably goes back to my folks. When my father yelled, everybody automatically jumped. Every woman I ever saw, then, the man barked and the woman jumped. I just thought that women were no good and had to be told everything to do. (p. 30)

In the families of silent women "at least one parent routinely used violence rather than words for influencing others' behavior" (p. 32). While violence was apparent in the lives of women of other perspectives, these women seemed particularly impotent: they had no sense of themselves as intelligent initiators of change (p. 29).

Received Knowledge

Unlike the silent women, women of this perspective see words as central tools in the knowing process (p. 36). Listening becomes all-important and is the vehicle of learning. Listening is a very active and demanding process, and receiving knowledge from others can be quite liberating. Ann's experience of childbirth catapulted her into a need to learn. She discovered that the workers at the social agency knew everything she needed to know regarding babies. Their provision of knowledge, combined with a confidence in Ann's own intellectual abilities, served to change Ann's life (pp. 35–36).

Ordinarily, received knowers have little confidence in their own ability to think or speak. Truth is "out there" and comes from knowledgeable others. Even authorities do not generate their own answers; they too receive knowledge from others. When asked why professors are always more or less right, Angela replied: "They have books to look at. Things you look up in a book, you normally get the right answer" (p. 39). When asked what they would do if two advisors at the children's center gave them opposite advice, both Ann and Rachel were confused. Ann denied that this could ever happen, and Rachel finally said she would gather the facts from the "right studies." But if the studies conflict? Rachel found this incomprehensible, but ultimately said she would opt for the one that "most people believe in" (p. 41).

Because women of this perspective rely so heavily on others for knowledge, their conceptions of themselves are largely tied to what others think. Self-reflection is rare. "Who I am" is merely a reflection of "what others think of me." A college freshmen reports: "'Everything I say about myself is what other people tell me I am. You get a pretty good idea of yourself from the comments that other people are saying about you" (p. 48).

Here the power of social definitions of "knowers" is revealed. Since women of this perspective are so vulnerable to others' opinions, if authorities define women as stupid or intellectually inferior, women internalize and believe it. On the other hand, if authorities encourage women to use their intellects and treat them as equal and capable thinkers, women will begin to believe in themselves and discover their own processes of knowing (p. 49; cf. chap. 9). Some women spoke of science professors who communicated their conviction that women couldn't do science. Others indicated experiences in which authorities wielded power to extract sexual favors. The need for female mentors who can communicate a positive sense of intellectual authority becomes apparent (pp. 43–45).

These women typically conceive of themselves as caretakers, accepting the world as hierarchically arranged and dualistic (pp. 45–48). Add to this the expectation that women are not meant to be intellectually independent, and the "fear of success" emerges:

> Women worry that if they were to develop their own powers it would be at the expense of others. Not only are they concerned to live up to the cultural standards that hold that women should be the listeners, subordinate, and unassertive; but they also worry that if they excel, those they love will automatically be penalized. (p. 46)[34]

Exposure to diverse intellectual or cultural milieus can challenge received knowers to shift their perspective. Alternately, being thrust into roles of responsibility (parenthood, earning one's own living) can erode a simple trust in the truth of "them." This shift often comes at a great cost, however. It is because their social worlds break down, and authorities are seen to be unreliable, that women are forced to look to themselves as generators of their own truths. Thus emerges "subjective knowledge."[35]

Subjective Knowledge

Belenky and her colleagues classify as "subjective knowers" those who insist that there is an inner resource that contributes to their knowing. In most cases this involves a rejection of a simple dualism of right and wrong,

as well as a nuanced assessment of authority. In contrast to received knowers, who see truth as external to themselves, subjectivists conceive of truth
as "personal, private, and subjectively known or intuited" (p. 54). One
woman refers to a portion of herself that "I didn't even know I had—intuition, instinct, what I call my gut" (p. 57).[36]

What is most striking is that this shift in understanding knowing seems
inevitably tied to a revolutionary change in personal life situation. It
involves a shift to greater autonomy, yet it is not tied to any age, class, or
ethnic group. What seems to link these women is that they identify this discovery of subjective truth as a profoundly liberating event in their lives
(pp. 54, 56). A Columbian-American women named Inez had been subject
to incest as a child and to an abusive marriage as an adult. She did not
believe that a woman could "think and be smart." The turning point came
when she returned home to California to discover that her father was
known and accepted by the entire local community as a child molester.
Her anger propelled her to leave her past behind entirely, and she now
claims that "I can only know with my gut. I've got it tuned to a point where
I think and feel all at the same time and I know what is right" (p. 53; cf.
pp. 52–53, 56–57).

Indeed, what seems to come through most clearly in these stories is not
only the current reliance on self for knowledge, but the past failure of male
authority (p. 57). Many of these women had had husbands or fathers who
belittled them. Others angrily gave accounts of how their men had been
disenfranchised through economic injustice or racism. Middle-class women
recounted the emotional defections of fathers and husbands who were preoccupied with their own destinies. Most pervasive among these women
was the loss of trust in male authority because of sexual abuse or harassment. The discovery that male resources are not to be trusted was accompanied by a discovery of maternal authority, women mentors who could be
trusted and who encouraged these women to trust their own abilities to
know (pp. 60–62).

For these women, affirming themselves as experts, relying on their own
inner voice, is crucial. They lean toward an antirationalism that is suspicious of scientific expertise, and they trust instead their feelings, intu-
itions, their "gut" (pp. 71–75). However, while their position initially gives
them courage and autonomy, it at times results in stubborn isolation. As
women begin to discover that the inner voice can lie and is not as reliable
as first indicated, their subjectivist position breaks down. Some of them
move on to procedural knowing.[37]

Procedural Knowing

A much smaller group of women than those exhibiting subjective know-ing fall into the category of procedural knowers. Most of these women are privileged, bright, white, and young, and all were involved in some formal educational institution (pp. 87, 93). The shift that occurred in their think-ing came about as a result of further encounters with authorities, benign authorities who challenged them to substantiate their opinions (p. 88). Professors insisted on papers that *argued* a position rather than just *assert-ing* an opinion.

Naomi struggled with the demands of an art history course. Initially she objected to required work on the basis that art history was a merely sub-jective topic in which there is no right or wrong. Though she could have a profound response to a Van Gogh painting, "Wow!" did not constitute a paper that could be graded. The professor eventually provided a five-page guide and Naomi came to see the usefulness of clear criteria: "They give us a way to analyze paintings. Then we analyze the painting and come to a conclusion. There are certain criteria that you judge your evaluation on—the composition, texture, color, lighting, how the artist expresses his feel-ings, what the medium is" (p. 89). No matter what Naomi's personal reaction to a painting, she had to justify her response in relation to the *object,* the painting itself.

Procedural knowers recognize that one's gut is not infallible, that some truths are truer than others. The criteria for justifying an argument demand critical judgment rather than simple assertion of the subject's point of view (pp. 89, 98–99). Attending to and understanding an other, be it a parent, a text, or a painting, are central (p. 91). Learning is not a matter of memorizing right answers; in fact, teachers rarely provide the answers. Rather, access to knowledge involves learning a method, grasp-ing the procedures that lie behind an assertion of truth.[38]

This shift is usually accompanied by a diminishment of voice. Lacking both the derived authority of received knowers and the inner assurance of subjectivists, these women speak softly. "The inner voice turns critical; . . . because their ideas must measure up to certain objective standards, they speak in measured tones" (p. 94). In a few cases, this emphasis on objec-tivity and the demands of procedure lead to personal alienation. In these cases some reclamation of the self is required and constructed knowledge emerges.

Constructed Knowledge

A handful of women in this study moved beyond procedural knowledge. These women seem caught between their own creative forces and the procedures of judgment they have learned. They are seeking to reclaim the self as part of the process of knowing. Through periods of intensive self-reflection they try to grasp just "how I want to think" (p. 136). They discover a need to sort out what they have learned via others from what they themselves know to be true (p. 137). There is a need to weave together reason and emotion, objective and subjective knowing (p. 134). But most central to this position is this discovery: *"All knowledge is constructed, and the knower is an intimate part of the known"* (p. 137). Knowing is not a matter of merely attending to the object; it also involves constructing meaningful explanations.

Several corollaries are attached to this basic perspective. First, for these women passion and intellect are not opposed. The move into constructed knowing is accompanied by the unleashing of a passion for learning: knowing is no longer a cold, distant journey but a lively exciting quest (pp. 140–44). Within this quest there is a tolerance for ambiguity; the rigid dualisms are long gone (p. 137). Further, "real talk" is possible, in which people use words in a collaborative search for truth rather than as weapons or tools to impress others (pp. 144–46). In addition, the knowledge of experts is not ruled out of court, but is taken with careful qualifications (pp. 139–41). Nevertheless, conflicts over voice and silence remain, as constructivist women experience resistance to their abilities to think and articulate truth (pp. 146–48). Though these women have moved to a very sophisticated and nuanced acceptance of themselves as knowers, they often find few who are interested in listening.

VIOLENCE, VOICE, AND DISCOVERY

Let me develop two threads that appear in this *Women's Ways of Knowing*. The first is the connection between violence and voice. Though these researchers did not initially set out to chart experiences of sexual harassment, they found it to be such a pervasive theme that they began to survey women on this issue. Based on a sample of seventy-five subjects, 38 percent of women in schools and colleges and 65 percent of women contacted through social agencies said that they had been subject to incest, rape, or sexual seduction by males in authority over them. Among the college women, one in five had a history of childhood incest. Among women from the social agencies, which drew on a population in which drug and alcohol abuse was prevalent, one out of every two women had been subject to incest (pp. 58–60).[39]

Incidence of physical abuse was not limited to any one group of knowers. However, comments such as the following were made by women labeled as silent: "I deserved to be hit, because I was always mouthing off." "I don't like talking to my husband. If I were to say no, he might hit me." "I had to get drunk so I could tell people off" (pp. 24–25). Among subjectivists the sense of outrage was most prominent, accompanied by a recognition of previous naivete and docile submission. A young mother who had begun to take charge of her own life reflects on why she stayed with a husband who battered her for ten years:

> You know, I used to only hear his words, and his words kept coming out of my mouth. He had me thinking that I didn't know anything. But now, you know, I realize I'm not so dumb. . . . And my own words are coming out of my mouth now. (p. 30)

Though higher education does play a role in developing voice, the power differential between male professors and female students often results in confusion. One woman said: "My whole response to praise, my sense of what I can achieve and how I should achieve is all wrapped up in my past [experience of incest]. I know it has affected my relationships with men and male professors. Maybe there are things in the professional relationship that ought not be there" (p. 59).

From the other side, those who work with women suffering from abuse note the secrecy and shame, the reticence to speak, and the lack of credibility given to women who do speak:

> To add further to their lack of identity, poor self-esteem, and sense of dissociation, victims of abuse often feel that they are isolated and alone. In fact, many such women are kept isolated by their owners, who seem to know that connections with other women might undermine their power. Thus, acts of violence need to be kept secret. *If victims try to break out of their isolation by speaking, they are often discredited and shamed.*[40]

In reference to the history of Western culture, Polly Young-Eisendrath and Demaris Wehr comment:

> Since the female person has not been part of the Western worldview, and since her subjectivity is unrecorded, many women are reticent to speak their

experiences. Women's accounts, especially of suffering and abuse, are fre-
quently perceived as "incredible" and unbelievable, even to themselves.[41]

A second thread I would like to develop is the relation between
"received knowledge" and "discovery." All of us inherit a fund of knowledge from others, knowledge that we simply accept and believe by virtue
of trusting others. In fact, the bulk of what we know is constituted by this
knowledge born of belief. But each of us also has the capacity to determine some things for ourselves. We can examine evidence, even of the
most commonsense variety, and decide for ourselves whether "X" is in fact
the case. It could range from why the car won't start, to why the cake did-
n't rise, to whether or not it is raining. For all of us, our knowledge consists of both what we have "received" and what we have "discovered."

What our review of Western history and recent studies reveals is that
those who are not in the cognitive elite of a culture are restricted in *how*
they are expected to learn. Rather than being given opportunities to discover knowledge for themselves, women and other restricted groups have
traditionally been *taught*, been expected to receive knowledge from others.
This restriction to learning by way of receiving leads over the course of
time to inherited assumptions that one cannot learn in any other way.

What becomes evident in examining the trends in women's ways of
knowing is that the distorted beliefs that have and still do oppress women
are *precisely beliefs about believing and discovery themselves.* Historically, to the
degree that women were considered cognitive agents at all, they were relegated to believing what others told them. Lorraine Code puts it thus:

> Excluded from public intellectual debate, woman is more restricted than
> "real" members of the epistemic community to reliance upon testimony *cho-
> sen for her:* to the tutelage of her patrons, friends, and lovers. Her possibili-
> ties for circumspection are fewer than those available to men. Hence the
> distance she can acquire from her own cognitive endeavors to cast a critical
> eye upon them . . . and the scope of her possible epistemic responsibility is,
> accordingly, narrowed. She is *more than* naturally reliant upon acquiring
> knowledge from others, . . . more at the mercy of those she is *permitted* to
> trust, than is man, who at least is *in a position* to choose more widely, how-
> ever well or badly he may do this.[42]

Many contemporary women, if they are not totally silent, can only conceive of themselves as receivers of knowledge. Even those who move
beyond this to some confidence in their own inner voice find assertion of
their role as discoverers of knowledge to be radical, revolutionary, and
requiring courageous changes in their communities of meaning. Thus, for

many women, exercising what Lorraine Code calls "epistemic responsibility" involves a heroic courage that not only pursues the knowledge sought but affirms the capabilities of the knower as well. This is, Code says, "a form of courage that is difficult to sustain in the face of pervasive and *infectious* feeling on every side that one is bound not to succeed in one's enterprise, be it intellectual, moral, or other."[43]

Belenky's study and others make it clear that there is a profound connection between the socialization of women as *receivers* of knowledge and the social acceptance of *violence* against women.[44] While teaching women to be receivers of knowledge has value in itself, restricting them to this role, while appearing benign, may in fact have tragic social implications. The flip side of this connection is that asserting one's ability to discover truth presents a direct challenge to the (often violent) status quo. Thus, Code's allusion to the courage required to assert oneself as a knower is no mere conjecture but has its concrete reality: the existential commitment arising from the discovery of discovery can put some women at the risk of losing their lives.

NAMING CROSS AND RESURRECTION

The Gospel accounts of the resurrection have at least one thing in common. They are all dramas about "telling." In all but one Gospel account of this unprecedented event, without which the Jesus movement would have withered into oblivion, a single woman or a group of women are commanded directly: "Go tell his disciples what you have seen." And the truth that they are to reveal is not a received interpretation but a discovery. These women witness concrete evidence and draw their own conclusions: Jesus is alive! There is an empty tomb. There are discarded burial cloths. There is an angel or angels. There is Jesus himself. The apparitions speak. In some cases the women actually touch Jesus. In others, they remember his words. Whatever the version, whoever the players, this story is about making a direct, profound, joyful, yet frightening discovery. A discovery that begs to be told.

In Mark, the earliest version, a young man dressed in white sits in the empty tomb: "Do not be amazed! You seek Jesus of Nazareth, the crucified. He has been raised; he is not here. Behold the place where they laid him. But go and tell his disciples and Peter, 'He is going before you to

Galilee; there you will see him, as he told you'" (Mark 16:6–7). Exactly what the women eventually did is not told, only that this challenge to be conveyers of truth terrified them. The earliest manuscript breaks off abruptly: "Then they went out and fled from the tomb, seized with trembling and bewilderment. They said nothing to anyone, for they were afraid" (v. 8). Alternately, "They said nothing to anyone. They were afraid for . . . ."

In Matthew, Mary Magdalene and the "other" Mary are granted a voice twice. First, an angel explains—Don't be afraid; Jesus isn't here; come check the evidence for yourself, and then GO quickly and TELL his disciples he has been raised from the dead. As they run away "fearful yet overjoyed," they meet Jesus, embrace him, worship him, and then hear him: "Do not be afraid. Go tell my brothers to go to Galilee, and there they will see me" (Matt. 28:10).

The effect of the resurrection, the redemption that makes the horror of the cross a moment in a much bigger story, is to create agents of interpretation. Women who could not, with any clout, protest Jesus' arrest, trial, and execution become powerful witnesses. They discover an alternate truth, encounter new evidence that makes the narrative of the cross an entirely different story than they had been led to believe. Moreover, they are the ones called upon to communicate this discovery to Jesus' wider community.

The power of the resurrection is intimately tied to gaining and claiming the right to tell the story. What these women discovered was not just a fact—Jesus was raised—but simultaneously a recognition of something about themselves: Jesus was raised, and they knew that *they* knew it. Their discovery of the resurrection involved a discovery of discovery itself. They had no need to "check with the authorities": their integrity as knowers, their ability to have a voice, was clear to themselves and recognized without apology by Jesus.

This power to tell, this new voice, came with a price. It involved nothing less than a *conversion*, for it demanded a complete reversal of everything they had thought was true—about Jesus, but also about themselves. To go and tell the story, *as they knew it*, was nothing less than an act of resistance. They were up against the other disciples—men and women—who could easily dismiss them as crazy. Their story would challenge their roles as receivers of religious and factual truths. It would undermine their personal structures of self-esteem. Their lack of power, and its comfort, would be forever disrupted: the call to be a (w)holy Self had to be rejected or taken in its entirety. The earliest Markan manuscript leaves us hanging in the grip of this existential dilemma. Other accounts indicate that the women did tell their story, with more or less success.

Indeed, the Gospel accounts reveal how tenuous the witness of these women was. Just after Jesus affirms the women's "power to tell" in Matthew's Gospel, we discover that political "spin" immediately went into effect. The guards reported their failure to secure the tomb to the powers that be, who quickly took counsel. Bribing the guards with large sums of money, they told them: "You are to say, 'His disciples came by night and stole him away while we were asleep.' And if this gets to the ears of the governor we will satisfy [him] and keep you out of trouble" (Matt. 28:13–14). Barely had the women left Jesus than their version of events was doomed to be discredited. Luke's version is even more painful. The women's own community of Jesus-followers dismisses them: "Then they returned from the tomb and announced all these things to the eleven and to all the others . . . but their story seemed like nonsense and they did not believe them" (Luke 24:9, 11).[45]

The role of voice in claiming redemptive meaning expands the points made earlier about embracing travail. First, discovering ourselves in the crucified involves discovering both how we have allowed our deepest and truest Selves to be destroyed and how we have been victimized. Given the tremendous connection between voice and violence, and between victimization and silence, to discover ourselves in Jesus as either victims or perpetrators (or both) will necessarily involve fresh discoveries about our roles as knowers and creators of meaning and value. To identify with Jesus as the crucified, and to discover the power of resurrection healing, will necessarily mean naming our victimization anew. To discover ourselves as crucifiers of Jesus, of our Selves, to grasp that we are nevertheless still (w)holy, is to name complicity with silence and/or pro-active violence, yet claim its new significance.

Second, people enter the narrative of death and resurrection from different points, different social locations. Some inherit confidence in their cognitive agency by virtue of socioeconomic, educational, racial, or gender status. To "repent" may involve eschewing pride of place, letting go of presumed powers to tell the story. Embracing travail may mean embracing silence so that one can hear another, a different story. Like Peter, some may need to follow the lead of those whose story sounds like "nonsense." Others—those that have mostly occupied this chapter—inherit presumptions that they are irrational, stupid, or unable to ascribe meaning accurately. For these, redemption comes about not through "repenting" to a position of listening, but through learning instead to speak. And, importantly, though we may enter the drama from different presumptions about voice, redemption will always involve recognizing in ourselves illicit acceptance of silence as well as false voices of knowledge.[46]

Third, telling the story of cross and resurrection is not an addendum to redemption. Naming the cross, proclaiming its resurrection meaning, is *constitutive* of the redemptive process. This is not to say that persons and communities don't have profound religious experiences that defy immediate description. After all, it took the earliest Christians several decades to make sense of their experience, to discover the Suffering Servant motif in the Law and the Prophets, and to produce Gospel accounts. The "naming" may take generations in a community or decades in an individual's life. But the point is that the process of "making sense" and the cognitive agency and moral autonomy that come with it are themselves vehicles for healing and forgiveness. [47]

Fourth, one of the "crosses" from which we suffer may be precisely the silencing we have examined in this chapter. We may be victims not as a direct result of one agent's action but in the more subtle messages we receive about our capacity to discover truth. For those raised as part of a cognitive elite, the burden of authority, of having to make truth pronouncements when still unsure of one's judgments, can distort the eros of the human spirit. For those on the underside, the sometimes imperceptible ascription of "nonsense" to one's clearest judgments can cut to the bone of self-integrity. To redefine voice, in action if not in words, whether through "penitential" silence or resistant "telling," is at the heart of suffering and its redemption.[48]

Fifth, the discovery of discovery, the power of naming that comes with resurrection, catapults one into an ethic of risk. As the Gospel narratives reveal, discovering a Risen Lord, and the "GO, TELL" that comes with it, challenges one to risk all. One must cross boundaries set by the domination system, and one crosses them without any assurance of success. So far from an ethic of control, the point of this "telling" is not to solve problems, not even to eradicate evil. Rather, through strategic risk taking one hopes only to create conditions of possibility whereby transformation may take place in others. The risk is that one will be misunderstood, dismissed as a conveyor of nonsense, circumvented with status quo "spin." The point is to proclaim transformation, to name one's self as the friend of a Risen Lord, the child of a benevolent Creator, the agent of a Divine Spirit, regardless of who "gets it." The point is to tell a story that must be told, for to not tell it would mean spiritual death.

Sixth, the naming of cross and resurrection is itself an act of resistance. Conversely, claiming voice and integrity, insisting performatively that all are children of God, is a means of proclaiming resurrection. The sass of Linda Brent in the face of her master's abuse, the singing of "Lift Every Voice and Sing" by Maya Angelou's graduating class, the poignant picture of a man on death row in *Dead Man Walking;* all serve as acts of resistance to a system that insists that some persons are less rationally human than others. To tell one's story, to insist that there is meaning in it in spite of horrendous suffering, is an act of surrender and resistance. One surrenders in embracing the pain and in accepting the negligible success of one's actions. One resists by telling the story *in one's own voice* regardless of who is willing to listen.

Seven, one of the main points of the earlier chapters was to insist that pain, suffering, and surrender must be *embraced* rather than avoided. To embrace the travail of discovering oneself as victim as well as perpetrator is perhaps humanly impossible but *can* occur within the embrace of a loving God, one who raises people from death. But this embracing of pain must be accompanied by the power of naming. One cannot insist that people endure pain while imposing the meaning of that pain upon them. For centuries this odd paradox of suffering becoming redemptive has been recognized and proclaimed, but proclaimed by a dominant, learned elite that imbued the good news, however unwittingly, with meanings that perpetuated the status quo. If the core of the gospel message is that somehow, miraculously, suffering can be transformed into new life, the discovery and the naming of that transformation *must* lie in the hands of those who suffer.

Remembering, Retelling, and Reversing Expectations

In earlier chapters I insisted that suffering is always interpreted. The resurrection stories reveal that the meaning of the cross depends on the story that you tell. The experiences of the earliest Christians led them to a profound shift in their understanding of what Jesus' story—and their own—was all about. They thought the story was about painful betrayal, grief-stricken helplessness, and the victory of dominant powers over God's presence in the world. It turned out that the story was about something quite different—the victory of God over evil, the forgiveness of sins, and the healing of wounds.

But it also turns out that this truth is not obvious to all, is not some "already out there now real" that one simply looks at. Rather, we, like the early players, grasp this new story by contributing to it, by participating in the story itself. We must enter the story by going to the tomb, carrying our bags of embalming spices, unsure who will roll away the stone. If we are Peter, we have to listen to the "nonsense" of the women, swallow our guilt and pride, and rush to see the empty tomb. Either way, resurrection—finding meaning in what seems to be a helpless and meaningless situation—engages us in redefining our voice. We must take up the challenge of "epistemic agency," of taking responsibility for what we discover, of recognizing the power of our own ability to know and name truth.

St. Paul represents this reversal of voice, both in his own story and in his teaching. He had been playing a very clearly defined role in the drama surrounding Jesus: that of learned and devout Jew, protector of orthodoxy, and, therefore, persecutor of the marginal cult who called themselves Christians. But then he, not unlike the women at the tomb, was thrust into an entirely different story. Blinded on the road to Damascus, he is left helpless and dependent, waiting for healing, shipwrecked in his ethic of control. Finding himself in this new story, yet now voice-less, he becomes the catechized. When we encounter him in his first letter to the Corinthians he is a "receiver" of knowledge, passing on the narrative he had learned from others:

> For I handed on to you as of first importance what I also received; that Christ died for our sins in accordance with the scriptures; that he was buried; that he was raised on the third day in accordance with the scriptures; that he appeared to Kephas, then to the Twelve. After that, he appeared to more than five hundred brothers at once, most of whom are still living, though some have fallen asleep. After that he appeared to James, then to all the apostles. Last of all, as to one born abnormally, he appeared to me. For I am the least of the apostles, not fit to be called an apostle, because I persecuted the church of God. (1 Cor. 15:3–9).[49]

Paul directly acknowledges his earlier hubris and his current dependence on God's grace. Moreover, earlier in this same letter, he explicitly insists that the cross means a reversal of expectations over who is a knower and who is not. He responds to rumors that the Corinthians are setting up learned elites among the apostles and aligning themselves with Paul, or Apollos, or Peter:

> For Christ did not send me to baptize but to preach the gospel, and not with the wisdom of human eloquence, so that the cross of Christ might not be emptied of its meaning.

> The message of the cross is foolishness to those who are perishing, but to us who are being saved it is the power of God. For it is written: "I will destroy the wisdom of the wise, and the learning of the learned I will set aside."
>
> Where is the wise one? Where is the scribe? Where is the debater of this age? Has not God made the wisdom of the world foolish? . . . For Jews demand signs and Greeks look for wisdom, but we proclaim Christ crucified, a stumbling block to Jews and foolishness to Gentiles, but to those who are called, Jews and Greeks alike, Christ the power of God and the wisdom of God. (1 Cor. 1:17–24)

He goes on to recognize directly that the cross has granted a voice to those who, by any other standards, would be ignored as irrational and ignorant:

> Consider your own calling, brothers. Not many of you were wise by human standards, not many were powerful, not many were of noble birth. Rather, God chose the foolish of the world to shame the wise, and God chose the weak of the world to shame the strong, and God chose the lowly and despised of the world, those who count for nothing, to reduce to nothing those who are something, so that no human being might boast before God. . . . so that, as it is written, "Whoever boasts, should boast in the Lord." (1 Cor. 1:26–29, 31).[50]

Paul's story illustrates the process by which religious experience (of death and resurrection) involves retelling both our own histories and those of our communities. Community plays an indispensable role here, both as a resource for reinterpretation and as the foil against which believers declare new meaning. In the quotation directly above, Paul describes the Corinthian church as a group of voiceless fools who tell their story of transformation over against a contemporary culture that demands signs and expects wisdom. Yet his creedal confession in 1 Corinthians 15 is permeated with the refrain, "according to the scriptures." The new story is told not only over against old meanings but by using them as a resource for reinterpretation. Discovering redemption, naming cross and resurrection, speaking resistance, all involve both challenging current assumptions and reversing them with the help of scripture and tradition. It is what the early Christians did creatively and courageously. It is what we must do today in order to renew the meaning of the cross.

There are many examples of ways in which contemporary Christians are reclaiming the gospel by grasping new voices of proclamation. A recent anthology of articles in feminist theology carries the pertinent title *The Power of Naming*.[51] Its contents illustrate the ways in which women have claimed territory in redefining the theological enterprise. Mary John Mananzan shows how education has been revolutionized by women's studies, citing the particular example of a Benedictine school in the Philippines and the national movement—*Gabriela*—that emerged out of it.[52] Eileen J. Stenzel examines how women have redefined "rape" and "sainthood" by listening to the stories of victims.[53] Diane Neu reviews new liturgies used by women in the Roman Catholic Church, including the "Litany of Naming."[54] Janet Walton examines rites of "blessing"—specifically the blessing of an Abbess or a mother—and suggests new meanings and new ways of engaging in ritual blessings.[55] Most telling, of course, is the effort to revise the language itself.[56] Shifting the *medium* of conversation, which has traditionally overlooked women as well as feminine attributes of God, is a subtle but powerful way of reclaiming the truth of the gospel. All these examples involve engaging in the concrete stories of women, taking existing traditions and reforming them *in light of the tradition* but *over against* the distorted silence embedded in it. This is precisely what Paul and the early Christians did in their retelling of the Jesus story.

In addition to these explicit attempts to redefine theology, Christian history offers grass-roots ways in which those on the underside of society have managed to subvert silence. The sass of African American women served to proclaim dignity in the face of humiliation and abuse by masters, albeit as an ethic of risk since there was little hope that sass would convert the oppressor. Gossip is perhaps the white middle-class woman's version of sass:

> [G]ossip is often an alternative mode of discourse, a rhetoric of inquiry, an invasion and a possible subversion of the domain of the powerful and privileged. It strikes us as morally interesting, for example, that a person can be at the helm of a great nation and still be powerless to make his own children behave. Through gossip, power is defeated.[57]

The author here goes on to insist that gossip can also be a "primary means of building and sustaining communities." Gossip can be used maliciously and manipulatively to wield power. But it can also function as a way of entering into others' narratives of pain and of helping them articulate the resurrection elements within it. Given the severe split between public and private as well as the privatization of religion in our culture, "gossip" may be one way to walk with others in their stories of the cross while protecting their safety with discretion.[58]

James Cone points to the way in which African American slaves used spirituals and theological images to sustain their hope. In reference to heaven he says:

Although African slaves used the term "heaven" to describe their experience of hope, its primary meaning for them must not be reduced to the "pie-in-the-sky," otherworldly affirmation that often characterized white evangelical Protestantism. The idea of heaven was the means by which slaves affirmed their humanity in a world that did not recognize them as human beings. It was their way of saying they were made for freedom, not slavery.

> Oh Freedom! Oh Freedom!
> Oh Freedom, I love thee!
> And before I'll be a slave,
> I'll be buried in my grave,
> And go home to my Lord and be free.[59]

Furthermore, the richness of African American religion lies in the rereading of the Gospel through new eyes:

> To explicate the theological significance of the liberation motif, black theologians began to reread the Bible through the eyes of their slave grandparents and started to speak of God's solidarity with the wretched of the earth. As the political liberation of the poor emerged as the dominant motif, justice, suffering, love, and hope were reinterpreted in its light.[60]

Likewise, in the African context, Jean-Marc Ela insists that the gospel must be re-thought in light of the (albeit ambiguous) history of colonialism.

> The story of the gospel is the place from where there springs up a basic personality who has marked the foundational event of the faith. But our retelling of this event is always done in a particular context. We never speak out of nowhere. We need to come back to the traditions that Africa invents about its own self and avoid the many approaches that were distorted because they applied concepts of Western knowledge to the realities specific to Africa. . . . Reconstructed each time, "the tradition" becomes a resource to update the materials used in art and music, languages belonging to the popular culture, the written and oral stories, the religious and political life. . . . African theologians cannot therefore spare the memory if they want to hear the narrative of the Passion of Jesus Christ in the specific places where the concrete and historical dimensions of the African imagination are rooted.[61]

In a similar vein, Korean Christians are developing *minjung* theology. *Minjung* means "people" and refers to "those who resist in a situation where they are oppressed, those who do not lie down under their fate."[62] A key component of this resistance is reflecting on one's own history:

> [T]he *minjung* are those who reflect upon their history in which they are not in control of their destiny. History is normally written from the perspective

of those who have power and reflects that power and those who govern with it. *Minjung* theology encourages a change in that situation. The writing of history must begin with the *minjung,* with the result that the *minjung* themselves become aware of their own destiny as a vital part of that history.[63]

In the Latin American context, Gustavo Gutiérrez emphasizes the retelling of history, but insists that this is not a matter of reassuring nostalgia or pleasant reveries. "It is a subversive memory, and it lends force and sustenance to our positions, refuses to compromise or equivocate, learns from failures, and knows (by experience) that it has the capability of overcoming every obstacle, even repression itself."[64] Ada Maria Isasi-Diaz includes as a key component of *mujerista* theology the concept "*permitanme hablar.*" "Allow us to speak" is the English equivalent, and it indicates the importance of voice in retrieving the gospel.

> When Latinas use the phrase *permitanme hablar,* we are not merely asking to be taken into consideration. When we use this phrase we are asking for a respectful silence from all those who have the power to set up definitions of what it is to be human, a respectful silence so others can indeed hear our cries denouncing oppression and injustice, so others can understand our vision of just society. . . . For many Hispanic Women who have seldom found anyone to listen to them—to hear them—their permitanme hablar is a way of insisting on recognition of our right to think, to defend our rights, to participate in setting what is normative of and for humanity.[65]

These are just a few examples of ways in which people have or are striving to gain a voice in order to reclaim the gospel for themselves. Just as the earliest Christians had to work to make sense of their devastating experience of Jesus' execution in light of his resurrection, so many today are attempting to put themselves in a Gospel story from which they have been excluded. Dorothy Soelle sums up this necessary process as follows:

> The first step towards overcoming suffering is, then, to find a language that leads out of the uncomprehended suffering that makes one mute, a language of lament, of crying, of pain, a language that at least says what the situation is.[66]
>
> The sufferer himself must find a way to express and identify his suffering; it is not sufficient to have someone speak on his behalf. If people cannot speak about their affliction they will be destroyed by it, or swallowed up by apathy.[67]

The point of all this is to insist that *naming pain* is integral to *embracing travail.* In the Christian context this does not mean "making it up." Rather, we *already* have a story, whose heart is freedom and liberation, healing and forgiveness. We have a *history* at whose center is a real human person who has *been there*. We can enter the story, participate in it and thereby discover both Jesus' divine presence and our own transcendent Self. But entering the story means discovering, however implicitly, the power of discovery. Entering the story means claiming the right to tell the story. Given the distortion of the tradition at times, entering the story means re-telling it, re-claiming the gospel as it was originally experienced and as it is currently manifested. In sum, *gaining a voice* is at the heart of *redeeming redemption*.

5

Redeeming Redemption

Transforming the Tradition

WHILE OUR CHILDREN WERE STILL SMALL and I was being battered, I went to our pastor for counseling. I realized that he meant well, but he laid a heavier burden of guilt on me. His advice was to "pray harder, have more faith, and be grateful for your six fine children."[1]

My pastor's reaction [to news about sexual abuse] was to call and confront me. I hoped for some help, or at least some consolation and advice, but I received only a lecture on having deceived him and the community into thinking we had a Christian marriage. So in my shock and aloneness, I was given no help. In fact, my pastor contributed to my isolation and shame.[2]

He started abusing me when I was five years old. This was when I was beginning my religious training which taught me that women were vessels of sin. It was my sin of incest that made him [i.e., Jesus] hang on the cross.[3]

A Maryland woman who was severely abused over many years told me that when she complained after some attacks that she had sustained injuries, her husband would retort that "your bones are my bones—just like it says in the Bible" [Gen. 2:23].[4]

I have experienced both sexual and physical abuse at the hands of men who believed their gender somehow "entitled" them to be pleased and served by women. Somehow "helpmeet" has been twisted and misinterpreted to serve the interests of the dominant group.[5]

I was very active in a church with male/female co-pastors, women in leadership positions, active in peace and justice issues. It was a myth. The male pastor was sexually abusive to many women, including myself. He always had his way in decisions. He claimed to be a prophet, to have special knowledge of God's will. God's will and "spirit-led" were used to condone my own rape.[6]

96

Ten years ago I was very active in church. I have suffered losses. A twenty-four year marriage came to an end, and then my sixteen-year-old daughter was abducted. Her damaged bike was found, but police have not been able to find her body. We believe she is in heaven, alive, and healed. With both my divorce—"Christians, and especially conservative, evangelical pastors and their wives, don't get divorced"—and the loss of my daughter—for over one year, the church pastor and others were sure she was naughty and ran away—I have come to realize that the (my) organized church did not support me as I had ignorantly assumed they would. Many Christians seem to be judgmental and so intent on being 'right' that they often show little or none of the compassion and love that my God has and is showing me.[7]

One of the great sins of the church is the continuing co-dependency role which is really fostered in women. There is little or no recognition that sinfulness in women is more often related to being too submissive—humility that is self-abasement, pride disguised as martyrdom. . . . How I wish I had been taught as a little girl to take a few risks, to be more assertive. One gets so self-righteous being a "good little girl." At sixty-plus, I'm working very hard to just be human.[8]

I am a survivor of ritual abuse at the hands of the Catholic Church. I have experienced first-hand the effects of abuse of power in a male-dominated system. I was exorcised for sexual abuse—"woman is the temptress"—when I was about four years old.[9]

I often think that the RC church had to convince me of how bad I was (original sin, self-denial) so that I would feel compelled to "buy" what they were selling (sacraments, grace, redemption).[10]

I am not real keen on theology that focusses on humanity's need for forgiveness of sins rather than on the need for helping people find wholeness and healing. Treating me as though I am "sinful" and blaming me for my "sins" fails to recognize that adults are often grown children who were victims.[11]

In the preceding chapter we explored the power of gaining a voice. I insisted that the power of naming is constitutive of the process of redemption itself. If believers are to embrace the travail of confronting their sins and their wounds, if these are to be transformed by God's resurrection love, then believers—especially those who have been silenced—need to enter into the Jesus story and retell the narrative of suffering, death, and resurrection for themselves. The chapter ended with the optimistic claim that, in this retelling, Christians do not have to start from scratch. We already have a story, a history, and a person who has been there before us. Entering the story means appropriating a story that has already been lived and recounted.

What the above quotations indicate, however, is that the story that often has been told is a very debilitating and dehumanizing one. However liberating the core of the gospel message is, it has over time been co-opted into structures of power, into social and cultural systems, in which the burden of sin and suffering—even the burden of redemption itself—has been laid on the shoulders of an underclass. In some cases the tradition, as it has been taught, has been so destructive that either the Christian message needs to be rejected altogether, or needs itself to be redeemed.

The purpose of this chapter is to add some nuance to the "embracing travail" advocated in the first three chapters and the "voice" encouraged in the last chapter. Unfortunately, too often the pain and travail of the cross have come at the hands of Christians themselves. The Christian tradition, though a resource of hope, has also been an instrument of oppression. This chapter faces squarely the fact that Christian praxis, based on Christian theology, can be and has been distorted. It raises the dilemma of how a community, a church, a tradition, can be transformed when these are precisely the vehicles of socialization by which messages about self-worth, sin, and redemption are handed down. How can redemption itself be redeemed?

The first step will be to examine the ways in which such distortions have manifested themselves. That there is a problem that needs resolving must be established. We will do this in two contexts: first, by illustrating the "salvation" messages that have denigrated women, even to the point of justifying physical and sexual abuse and, second, by examining the cultural hegemony of Christian missions and observing the destructive effects that many of these missions had on indigenous peoples.

The second step will be to review briefly a history of interpretations of redemption in Christian theology. Third, we will look at the process of history, outlining the way in which traditions are transformed. We will conclude with a few examples of retrieving the cross anew.

THE STORY OF WOMEN, SIN,
AND THE NEED FOR REDEMPTION

The quotations listed above illustrate the difficulty some women have had in gaining sympathy, advice, concern, and support from the church and its ministers. Carole Bohn summarizes the kind of advice that many women have received when seeking counsel from their pastors—they often hear some variation of the following:

Marriage is sacred and you must do whatever you can to hold it together.

Your husband is the head of your household; do what he tells you and he won't need to resort to violence.

You must have done something to provoke him; go home and mend your ways so he will not need to behave in this manner.

All of us must suffer; it makes us more Christ-like. Offer up your suffering to Jesus and he will give you strength to endure.[12]

Though these mandates have taken many different forms in a variety of contexts through the years, let us take a brief look at the theological traditions that stand behind this sort of pastoral advice.

The roots of blaming the victim go back to several key biblical passages and the way they have influenced Christian practice. The first is the creation story from Genesis 2 and its sequel, the story of the origin of sin, in Genesis 3. This is where Eve is created after Adam, out of his rib, and recognized by him as "bone of my bone." Then Eve is enticed by the serpent to ignore God's command regarding the tree of the knowledge of good and evil. She eats the forbidden fruit and gives some to her husband. Their eyes are opened and they are left exposed to a new world of good and evil.

This story has had the effect of supporting two intertwined beliefs throughout Christian history. There is the assumption that God established an order in creation in which man is closer to God and has authority over woman. Man is created in the image of God (*imago Dei*) while woman is derivative of man, and therefore subordinate to him. Further, a woman was responsible for the entrance of sin into the world, having seduced her husband and caused him to sin. The upshot of these two beliefs is the presumption that women are, by nature, temptresses and need to be controlled and ruled over by men. A hierarchy is established in which women are derivative and less human, or at least further from God, than men are. The hierarchy and women's "natural" vulnerability to sin justify the authority that men wield in women's lives.[13]

These themes were picked up in the early church by the Pauline tradition. The best known passage is from the fifth chapter of Ephesians, with its parallel in Colossians 3. In the aftermath of the cross and resurrection, the hierarchy of marriage is interpreted as an analogy of Christ's redemption of the church:

> Be subordinate to one another out of reverence for Christ. Wives should be subordinate to their husbands as to the Lord. For the husband is head of his wife just as Christ is head of the church, he himself the savior of the body. As the church is subordinate to Christ, so wives should be subordinate to their husbands in everything. Husbands, love your wives, even as Christ loved the church and handed himself over for her to sanctify her, cleansing her by the bath of water with the word, that he might present to himself the church in splendor, without spot or wrinkle or any such thing, that she might be holy and without blemish. So [also] husbands should love their wives as their own bodies. He who loves his wife loves himself. For no one hates his own flesh but rather nourishes and cherishes it, even as Christ does the church, because we are members of his body. "For this reason a man shall leave [his] father and [his] mother and be joined to his wife, and the two shall become one flesh." (Eph. 5:21–32)[14]

Again, now in the Christian context, the hierarchical ordering of male and female is intertwined with the issue of sin. Though the passage does not explicitly say, "women are redeemed by men," the analogy set up between husbands and wives, and Christ and the church, reinforces the idea that men represent Christ and that women need special redemption. Moreover, the passage makes clear that when husband and wife become one body the wife becomes the body (property) of the husband, just as the church is the body of Christ. The author quotes the Genesis story to this effect. While one can read this passage as putting the onus on the husband to love and to make sacrifices for his wife, what seems to have been influential in the ongoing tradition is the emphasis on hierarchy and authority.

These themes are further reinforced in other New Testament passages, such as the discussion in 1 Corinthians about proper attire for worship:

> But I want you to know that Christ is the head of every man and a husband the head of his wife, and God the head of Christ. Any man who prays or prophesies with his head covered brings shame upon his head. But any woman who prays or prophesies with her head unveiled brings shame upon her head. . . . A man, on the other hand, should not cover his head, because he is the image and glory of God, but woman is the glory of man. For man did not come from woman, but woman from man; nor was man created for woman but woman for man; for this reason a woman should have a sign of authority on her head, because of the angels. (1 Cor. 11:3–5a, 7–10)[15]

The hierarchy of authority is clear here and is once again based on the story of creation. The same is true when Paul gives advice to Timothy on the proper conduct of worship:

> It is my wish, then, that in every place the men should pray, lifting up holy hands, without anger or argument. Similarly, [too,] women should adorn themselves with proper conduct, with modesty and self-control, not with braided hairstyles and gold ornaments, or pearls, or expensive clothes, but, rather, as befits women who profess reverence for God, with good deeds. A woman must receive instruction silently and under complete control. I do not permit a woman to teach or to have authority over a man. She must be quiet. For Adam was formed first, then Eve. Further, Adam was not deceived, but the woman was deceived and transgressed. But she will be saved through motherhood, provided women persevere in faith and love and holiness, with self-control. (1 Tim. 2:8–15)

Once again, the creation story is recounted, this time in order to explain liturgical practices. Women are expected to be quiet, modest, and self-controlled because they were created second after men and because they are more prone to deception.

What is at stake here is not the correct exegesis of these passages in the historical context in which they were written.[16] The point is the way in which these passages have influenced centuries of Christian practice. Though Jesus may have promoted an egalitarian, person-centered, holistic approach to both men and women, the Christian church often reverted to its patriarchal cultural context. It clung to passages such as these to justify the hierarchical ordering of family and society and to endorse the extra burden of suffering required for women's salvation. A hierarchy of authority, the lesser status of women as human persons, and the special need of women to be redeemed are themes still evident in the quotes at the beginning of this chapter.[17]

Though it is impossible here to prove exhaustively that these themes had a perduring effect throughout Christian history, one or two examples will illustrate the point.[18] Tertullian, writing two hundred years after Christ, said of women:

> You are the Devil's gateway. You are the unsealer of that forbidden tree. You are the first deserter of the Divine Law. You are she who persuaded him whom the Devil was not valiant enough to attack. You destroyed so easily God's image, man. On account of your dessert, that is death, even the Son of God had to die.[19]

Here, not only is woman guilty of original sin and man's demise; she is the reason that Jesus had to die on the cross. It is the woman who deserves death, in whose place Jesus died instead.

More than a thousand years later, in 1528, the Spanish humanist Luis Vives wrote his *Instrucción de la mujer cristiana,* a guidebook for Christian

women. He assumes not only that men have the authority to beat their
wives but that such suffering is a penance that will lead to a woman's
redemption:

> If he lays hands on you for some fault of yours or in a fit of madness, imag-
> ine that it is God who is punishing you, and that this is happening because
> of your sins, and that in this way you are doing penance for them. You are
> fortunate if, with a little suffering in this life, you gain remission of the tor-
> ments of the next.

This penance is intimately tied to silence. In fact, the onus is on the woman
to exert restraint on herself in order to restrain her husband:

> Swallow your pain at home and do not prattle outside or to others about
> your complaints against your husband, lest you should seem to be asking for
> judgment between him and yourself. . . . In this way your restraint will make
> your husband more restrained, whereas your complaints and offensive chat-
> ter would merely make him more and more incensed.[20]

In general, the bulk of the Christian tradition has socialized women
into silence and self-blame. Christian practice has incorporated certain
notions of sin as well as expectations of virtue that have played a central
role in making women vulnerable to abuse and suffering. With regard to
sin, a few of the culprits include sin as (1) anger, (2) disobedience, (3)
pride, and (4) concupiscence.[21] The exhortation to silence above is implicitly an exhortation against *anger*. Similar spiritual counsels throughout the
centuries have advocated the stoical ideal of equanimity. In this view, any
expression of dissatisfaction, any resistance toward injustice, can be dismissed as sinful. While those in dominant positions of authority have the
right to protest, those in more vulnerable positions of social power are
exhorted to contain their anger.

Likewise, the sin of *disobedience* presumes the hierarchy of authority
that is so embedded in patriarchal culture. A woman's "natural" role is to
be obedient to her husband. This obedience is all the more necessary since
she was the one who originally sinned by disobeying God in the first place.
It doesn't take much, then, to expand a husband's duty to save his wife to
that of making her obey. As one victim of spousal abuse said, "He told me
he would beat me every day, if that's what it took to make me obey."[22]

In a similar vein, sin has been described as *pride*, as the aspiration to be
like God that proved so tempting in the Garden of Eden. The antidote to
such sin is being put in one's place: repentance and humility. Unfortunately, for those on the underside of power, who already have been socialized into self-blame, ruminations against pride only reinforce previously

existing guilt. As one victim explained to her abuser years after the fact, "You're damn lucky I didn't commit suicide. . . . But you really didn't worry about that—you knew I'd been brought up a good Christian, that I would take a good share of the guilt on myself, that I would feel that I was supposed to suffer because I was so sinful."[23]

Finally, there is sin as *concupiscence:* arduous, sensuous longing, sexual desire, or lust. While men are certainly as guilty of this as women, the characterization of women as temptresses, those who seduce men into sin just as Eve seduced Adam, puts the burden of sexual sin on women's shoulders. Men are often exonerated as subject to "natural" desires, and women are responsible for fending off sexual advances. The preservation of a woman's virginity is of utmost importance, and the loss of sexual purity is a woman's or girl's responsibility, even at the hands of a rapist. Thus, the retrospective account of a victim of child sexual abuse, quoted at the beginning of the chapter: "He started abusing me when I was five years old. This was when I was beginning my religious training which taught me that women were vessels of sin. It was my sin of incest that made him [i.e., Jesus] hang on the cross."[24]

The counterpart to such notions of sin is the socialization of children, especially female children, into certain Christian virtues.[25] These include (1) suffering as desirable, (2) the virtue of forgiveness, (3) the value of sexual purity, (4) the need for redemption, and (5) the virtue of obedience to authority. *Suffering* is seen as either a punishment or test sent from God, something to be endured on the road to salvation. *Forgiveness* of perpetrators is demanded as a way of imitating Jesus, and as the antidote to anger. *Sexual purity* is understood entirely in terms of genital sexuality, and the loss of virginity the worst of all sins, even if not provoked or desired.[26] The *need for redemption* often comes in the form of being told one is bad or guilty simply by existing. The natural development of autonomy and a sense of competence is circumvented by the religious message of "redemptive" love. The virtue of *obedience* to authority has already been evident in our review so far, and is especially salient for children, who, de facto, have less power in an adult world. All these "virtues" can prove detrimental in the socialization of women and children. They are especially damaging to those suffering from physical or sexual abuse, for whom questions of boundaries, of power, of forgiveness, of purity, redemption, and punishment are profoundly expanded.

In sum, at times the Christian tradition has itself contributed to the victimization of women and children. We have yet to address whether it has been so damaging as to be irretrievable, and how a positive recovery of the tradition might take place. Suffice it to say, at this point, that much of the Christian tradition surrounding women and redemption has, in practice, led to the blaming and silencing of victims.

THE STORY OF THE CROSS AND THE SWORD: THE REDEMPTION OF BARBARIANS

The misuse of theologies of redemption has also played itself out in the last five hundred years of missions to the "heathen." Marco Polo opened up a route to Asia in the thirteenth century, but it was the great advances in sea navigation in the fifteenth and sixteenth centuries that prompted European colonization, imperialism, and evangelization. Columbus "discovered" America in 1492; the Portuguese and Spanish competed for ownership of the new lands in the sixteenth century; and the British, Dutch, and French began staking claims soon after. An economic impetus drove explorers and investors to Africa and around the tip of South America to the Pacific Islands and Asia. Along with economic and political goals, Christian missionaries, endowed with genuine even if culturally naive motives, felt the imperative to preach the gospel to the "barbarians" so that they might be saved from eternal damnation.

Such a concept of salvation carried with it many of the presumptions implicit in the views of women discussed above: the world, as created by God, had a hierarchical structure to it, whereby some persons (in this case aboriginal peoples) were less human, more prone to the temptations of evil, and therefore in greater need of redemption than others (Europeans). The hierarchy in this case was primarily a cultural one: European culture was normative, and others, regardless of climate, temperament, or native traditions, had to be brought up to standard. This standard incorporated a religious and racial hegemony. While non-whites could hardly be expected to change their color, they could at least—due to the expansive mercy of God—be baptized and saved from eternal hell.[27] The good news was that Jesus had died, even for them. The bad news was that, in order to comprehend grace, aboriginals had to be convinced of sin, a concept foreign to many indigenous cultures.

> The upshot of this was that the sword and the cross were introduced simultaneously: The cross was not only an instrument and a sign of salvation and the well-being of the people to whom it was brought. It had a somber and violent aspect as well. One is reminded that the cross as a means of salva-

tion or damnation triumphed in many instances because it went hand in hand with the sword. It was used not only to proclaim salvation to the people but it was also used in the process of crushing and subjugating others. As one writer put it, "the redeeming Cross was stained with blood. Not that of missionaries. Only that of indigenous peoples."[28]

This combination of cross and sword, of European religion and military conquest, led to the violent deaths in America of over ninety million Indians. Brazil, which at the time of European discovery had two to five million natives, today has only 220,000 Indians out of a total population of 150 million.[29] Only seventy years after 1492 the indigenous population of Latin America had been reduced to 15 percent.[30] Add to this the legacy of the slave trade. When Brazil gained its independence from Portugal in 1822 two-thirds of the population of four million inhabitants were Africans. However pure the intentions of the missionaries, the cross nevertheless served as an agent of domination: "Many times they were baptized by force before embarking on the slave ships so that if they died during the crossing they would not die as pagans. History has even registered cases where they were branded like cattle with the sign of the cross!"[31]

Not only did the cross and the sword go hand in hand, two images of Christ dominated the conquest of Latin America: a dead Jesus and Jesus as a ruling monarch. The Spanish brought the image of Jesus dying on a cross, arising from their own experience of exploitation, suffering, and conquest at the hands of Arabs and Muslims. They themselves knew what it was to suffer, and they identified with Jesus in this way. But they combined it with images of Jesus looking very much like a Spanish or Portuguese king—seated on a throne, extravagantly dressed, ornamented with a golden crown. Again, whatever the intentions of the missionaries, the message to native inhabitants amounted to the following: the triumph of Jesus, and the power he wields, lies squarely in the hands of terrestrial agents, the Spanish or Portuguese king. The conjunction of these two images—cross and crown—have played a tragic role in Latin America: "When, on the one side, the power of Christ is transferred to heaven in the image of the effective terrestrial power of the king and, on the other side, a defeated Jesus is left for identification with and devotion of the people, systems of domination are obviously being supported."[32] The poor and exploited natives were expected to cling to the cross for their salvation, while distant rulers made judgments with the authority of God.

The marriage between throne and altar appeared in similar guise in South Africa. The apartheid system and its racist philosophy had their roots in British imperialism and were solidified under Dutch rule. In the seventeenth century the British imperialists undergirded their conquest with the belief that they were the new Israel, elected to dominate the world and thereby save the heathen. Cecil Rhodes insisted that only one race— his own—was destined to fulfill God's purpose on earth and bring nearer the reign of truth and justice.[33] When the Dutch later defeated the British, they too brought a sense of calling. The Afrikaners argued that they had been commanded by God,

> to act as the guardian, master and spiritual leader to the Black man. To do that the white man has to have at his command the authority needed to uplift, Christianize and evangelize the black man; the purpose is that the Black man who is still a child from the point of view of civilization, shall grow and develop in due course in his own area, with his own language according to his nature and traditions.[34]

One outcome of this attitude was that black people were expected to bear the brunt of suffering under the shadow of the cross. The cross and suffering were assumed to be their natural lot in life. Simon Maimela observes:

> What is particularly painful in all this is not so much that black people have been experiencing this seemingly unending Good Friday but rather that racist white Christians attempted to abuse the theology of the cross by encouraging their black victims to carry their cross of suffering with dignity and without complaint as Jesus Christ carried his.[35]

Maimela goes on to agree with Jürgen Moltmann, who says:

> The church has much abused the theology of the cross and the mysticism of the passion in the interest of those who cause the suffering. Too often, peasants, Indians and black slaves have been called upon by the representatives of the dominant religion to accept their sufferings as "their cross" and not to rebel against them.[36]

The cross, in these cases, has been an instrument of justified torture, with a population considered less than human bearing the brunt of suffering, once again, in silence.

The story in Asia and the Pacific tells a similar tale. Andreas Yewangoe acknowledges that, "in most countries of Asia, the cross is certainly not seen as the symbol of suffering but as the symbol of the Church's pride and arrogance."[37] Jill Raitt, a white Roman Catholic, tells of her discovery of the abuse of Polynesian peoples when she attended a series of conferences on

Polynesian spirituality in Hawaii. Speaker after speaker talked of the trauma visited upon their people through the Christian missionaries. The most telling revelation came from reading a historian, Edward Joesting:

> The great damage the missionaries did was an unintentional one, a harm they would have been hard pressed to understand. Christianity was a Western religion, and to be a Christian one had to have the conscience of a Western man. The Hawaiians were Polynesians, and the concept of Christian sin missed the Polynesian mind. So missionaries attempted to destroy the old Hawaiian standard and substitute Western ideals of right and wrong. Only when this had been done would the concept of sin be realized and the need for Christ be apparent.[38]

Converts had to be indoctrinated into the guilt of their depraved ways in order to discover the wonderful love and mercy of God!

In the case of Hawaii, most of the missionaries were Americans, Congregationalist ministers sent from New England, having been trained at Yale College or Amherst College. Their job was not only to convert the heathen but to train them in the ways of New England propriety. The moral superiority of Euro-American culture is evident in the journals of the missionaries. Rev. A. W. Murray wrote, "Never have I enjoyed a season of deeper, purer interest than in meeting these tamed savages, these happy Christian converts from amid darkness the most deep, depravity the most profound, and pollutions the most loathsome."[39] Hiram Bingham saw his task as "civilizing" the "savages": "From what has been exhibited of native character previous to the commencement of intercourse with whites, it will readily be admitted that it was degraded in the extreme. Consequently the contact of a better race must necessarily cause some moral improvement."[40]

In all of these cases, several themes emerge, themes also apparent in women's socialization. First and foremost is the assumption of a hierarchy, a hierarchy of cultures as well as of genders. This hierarchy presumes a natural order of both racial superiority and moral superiority. It is the duty and responsibility of the dominant class (male Europeans) to train the savages (or the weaker sex) through obedience and even harsh punishment. Though Christian women were generally socialized into these assumptions, indigenous peoples around the world—at least in the first generations—had to be taught how depraved they were, indoctrinated into a sense of sin, so that they could thereby be saved. In all cases the cross and resurrection became symbols not of the liberation of the powerless but of the triumph of the powerful. Though this occurred more often as a result of missionary ignorance rather than malevolence, "in an ironic twist, the Jesus who himself fell into the hands of the powerful and was crucified by them ended up as an accomplice in the crucifixion of others."[41]

THE HISTORY OF "REDEMPTION": HOW DID WE GET HERE FROM THERE?

A theologian from Haiti declares: "This is perhaps the most serious question today: the Jesus who had been assassinated by a coalition of the powerful, tortured like a slave—how did he manage to become . . . (as for example in Haiti) the God of the strong, the God of the powerful?"[42] Though a full-blown examination of the history of ideas regarding redemption is impossible here, a few historical tidbits are necessary. We will examine some of the metaphors used to explain the meaning of the cross and its role in salvation. We will also look at the political and social changes that affected Christianity's rise to power and the transferral of the cross from a symbol of liberation to a symbol of power and domination.[43]

The first step is to recognize the experience of the earliest disciples and the radical shock they had in having to deal with the cross at all. Jesus' message was not first and foremost about "redemption" as we now know it. Jesus preached the kingdom of God—that a new power of God was breaking into the world. His followers were preoccupied with messianic questions: When would the Messiah come? What changes would he make? How would he be recognized? Jesus was executed on political grounds because his message of a new kingdom and his power to touch the hearts and minds of the people threatened both the religious and political establishment. As the Gospel narratives make clear, Jesus' followers themselves had a variety of messianic expectations for Jesus: political revolutionary, religious reformer, mystical guru, miracle worker, and healer.

One further thing becomes clear in reading the New Testament: no one, whatever their messianic hopes, expected the man to whom they had pledged their lives to die on a Roman cross. The New Testament writings reveal this first generation of Christians struggling to make sense of their shock over the crucifixion. They were convinced that it *did* make sense because of their experience of the resurrection and of the ongoing presence of the Risen Lord. A new reign of God was indeed upon them, but this "kingdom" did not fit any of the narratives or categories they had previously known. They had to regroup and devise new images that would shed light on a Messiah who had died at the hands of the hated Roman Empire.

In the context of their lived experience and their socialization, either into Jewish tradition or Greek culture, these early Christians used their imaginations and the metaphors at hand to tell their story. As Elizabeth Johnson says,

> An event becomes a meaningful force in history by being narrated. The early communities of disciples began "telling the story" of Jesus the Living One in the context of their new life praxis. In the context of these narratives, they employed a dazzling variety of imaginative metaphors to interpret their experience of salvation in Jesus.[44]

The images used to convey this experience were diverse. In fact, "redemption" was one of these original metaphors: it was a financial category, a fee paid to release someone from slavery. Jesus paid this price just as a citizen would pay to purchase a slave's freedom. Likewise, the term salvation came from a common reference in both Hebrew and Greek, denoting being rescued from peril as well as being healed of a malady. Other images used in the New Testament include justification before the law (as in Paul's letter to the Romans) and cultic practices such as sacrifice, sin-offering, and expiation. The Letter to the Hebrews refers to Jesus as both the high priest offering the sacrifice and the sacrificial offering itself. Jesus' work is also described in political terms, as a liberation or victory over an oppressor (death, Satan, evil powers). Reconciliation after a personal rift—atonement—is another way disciples expressed their new relationship to God.[45] Medical images of healing or being made whole also appear. John speaks of Jesus as a light that brings new knowledge of God to believers. John uses also the figure of new birth into the family of God. Paul uses family imagery as well, but speaks in terms of adoption.

In the postbiblical world the fertility of images continued in a variety of contexts. As the gospel moved beyond the confines of Palestine and Jewish communities, and as theologians began defending their faith over against local cultures, new explanations of Jesus' work abounded. In the Greek east "divinization" took hold: through rebirth in the Spirit humanity is drawn up into the divine nature so that we are ultimately freed from corruption and death.[46] The Roman west had a more legal bent and thus emphasized metaphors of forgiveness, focusing on the debt paid by Jesus on the cross in order to reconcile us to God.[47]

When scholars summarize developments in soteriology (the issue of how we are saved), they generally discuss three approaches.[48] The earliest interpretation (second to sixth centuries) is called the classic, or dramatic, view and features Christ as Victor. This rendition of the Jesus story tells about the conflict between God and his enemies. Jesus' life and his struggle on the cross are the stage on which God fights the evil powers, even Satan himself. There is biblical precedent here in Paul's reference to a cosmic struggle against "principalities and powers." The victory of God over Satan is evidenced by the resurrection of Jesus from the dead. There is present in these interpretations the notion of a contract or transaction: God allowed Satan to take Jesus' life in order to free sinners who are Satan's slaves. Jesus' life was the ransom God had to pay (or in some versions, even owed) to Satan in order to save humankind. God, of course, had the last laugh, outwitting Satan with the resurrection.[49]

The second and third approaches came in the early Middle Ages, as theologians attempted to systematize their understanding of salvation, to develop coherent theories rather than metaphorical stories. Abelard (1079–1142) was the greatest defender of what is often called the Moral Influence Theory, featuring Christ as Exemplar. Abelard rejects the notion that a debt had to be paid because of sin. He abandons the drama of a cosmic struggle between God and evil powers. The essence of sin, for Abelard, lies less in actions than in intentions; it is our deepest affections that need to be freed. The problem to be solved is the estrangement between humans and God. The incarnation and death of Christ bring about this reconciliation through example: Christ's life, death, and resurrection communicate to us God's wonderful love. This demonstration of love, in turn, draws us out of ourselves, into a loving union with God.

Abelard strongly opposed the leading rival of his day, the third approach, which was advocated just before his time by Anselm (1033–1109). Anselm is responsible for what is called the Satisfaction Theory of atonement. Though Anselm first proposed this in a systematic way, the seeds of such an approach had existed for centuries. The context of Anselm's approach was that of feudal lordship, in which vassals owed allegiance to their lords, and lords, in turn, vowed to protect the countryside. Anselm thus saw the problem of sin as one of justice. Humanity had sinned against God by not rendering to him what was his due, namely, honor and subjection to his will. God, because he is just, cannot simply remit sins out of free mercy but needs "satisfaction" for this dishonor. By his nature God must preserve the honor of his own dignity and cannot forgive sins without some payment.

Further, the satisfaction must be adequate to the crime; in this case the only satisfaction would be the punishment of death. This is a satisfaction no sinner can make. Yet God cannot forgive without payment. The satisfaction needs to be paid by a human, yet the satisfaction required is so great that only God can pay it. The only solution lies in a sinless person dying, to pay not for his own sins but for the sins of others. If this sinless person were human but more than human, his satisfaction would be great enough to apply to all humankind. Thus, God became human in Christ, a blameless man who willingly submitted to death and thereby provided the satisfaction by which the whole human race is saved.[50]

This theory of satisfaction, with its many variants, became the most influential explanation of salvation in the Christian West. Elizabeth Johnson says:

> I sometimes think that Anselm should be considered the most successful theologian of all time. Imagine having almost a one-thousand-year run for your theological construct! It was never declared as a dogma but might just as well have been, so dominant has been its influence in theology, preaching, devotion, and the penitential system of the Church, up to our own day.[51]

John Driver assesses its influence on Protestantism:

> Protestantism has not only tended to reaffirm the satisfaction view but has made it more dominant and more nearly a test of faith than had been the case in the Middle Ages. This has been true for both established and free church Protestants, for Lutherans, Calvinists, and Arminians alike. The Thirty-nine Articles of Anglicanism, for example, contain one of the most forthright statements of Anselmian penal satisfaction theory: . . . "The offering of Christ once made is that perfect redemption, propitiation, and satisfaction for all the sins of the whole world, both original and actual, and there is none other satisfaction for sin, but that alone (Art. XXXI)."[52]

Notice several things about the story of the stories of redemption that I have been telling. First, Christians' experience of being saved, of the power of God's resurrection, was expressed in the first millennium in a wide variety of images, metaphors, analogies, and narratives. Not all of them focused on the cross or even on sin and judgment. After Anselm the variety dissipated and narrowed down to variations on the theme of penal substitution—we, because we had offended God, deserved to die, but God sent Jesus to die in our place, freeing us from damnation.

Second, most of the early attempts to explain salvation were put forward in narrative and symbolic forms. These forms were assumed to have an analogous meaning: "My experience of the Risen Lord, of new life, is *as if.* . . ." This "as if" dimension was implicit and presumed by audiences everywhere, allowing them to make up better analogies if they could find them. Anselm tried to systematize a theory of salvation, yet his explanation was, in fact, just as metaphorical as the others. Whether Anselm himself confused the metaphorical with the literal, Anselm's approach became codified as reality. It was not "as if" God were a feudal lord and had been offended. God *is* an omnipotent Lord, has been offended, and needs satisfaction. We humans are the guilty parties who deserve death, and without Christ's satisfaction we would, indeed, be justly doomed to eternal death.

Third, this literal reading of an analogous situation led much of Anselm's cultural baggage to be handed down as if it were the core of the gospel message. The early medieval world of feudal hierarchy, the offense against a lord's honor, and the need for payment of the offense made sense in Anselm's world. They functioned as a way of touching the hearts and minds of believers. But even though the world changed drastically after Anselm, even after the rise of cities and universities, of craftsmen, and guilds; the printing press, modern capitalism, modern science, and democracy, the feudal structure of God's saving plan continued to be hailed as a timeless reality. Long after feudalism no longer held sway, Christians were taught that God is a distant lord who by his very nature demands punishment for sin. Even Anselm's original intent, to show that "God's mercy is incomparably greater than anything that can be conceived," was lost as his metaphor perdured as literal truth.[53]

Finally, even though Anselm's explanation began with a personal question, "How am I saved?" and is written as a dialogue over personal issues with Anselm's friend Boso, it answers the question in theoretical and metaphysical categories. As the discussion unfolds, it becomes apparent that the real issue for Anselm is to reconcile God's mercy with God's character. How could God, an infinitely wise lord and judge, have granted humankind forgiveness without violating his own nature? The point is that, unlike the earliest Christians who attempted to explain their experience of God's love, Anselm begins the shift toward theory, which prescinds from concrete human experience. For this reason, Anselm's theory has at times been called the "objective" approach—dealing with a barrier between God and humanity that exists either in God or in the moral order.[54]

In sum, from the early Middle Ages and beyond in the Christian West, the narrative and multivalent power of symbols and stories of new life were reduced to variations on a single theme. This approach took literally what had been just another analogy for the relation between God and humankind. Theological concerns then revolved around explaining God's point of view and socializing believers into a structured reality in which God is an all-powerful judge and humans are innately sinful creatures deserving death.[55]

To make this story complete, we need to add a few more elements. First, there is the story of Christianity moving from being a marginal cult to being a dominant, white, European power. Second, there is the influence of Greek asceticism and the inversion of pleasure and pain.

First, Christianity began as a marginal cult, a subsection of Judaism. As it spread and grew in its geographical and cultural reach, it eventually became a threat to both Judaism and the Roman way of life. For several centuries periodic persecutions of Christians by Roman powers emerged, with fatal consequences for believers. But in the fourth century all of this changed when the emperor Constantine became a Christian. This led to a major transformation in the status and power of the church, "when it changed from a scarcely tolerated and often persecuted minority missionary movement into an established, official institution with the power to determine life for its members as well as for society."[56] The church, which had already begun to take on hierarchical and centralized structures of authority, adopted its new status with barely a second thought. The hierarchy between genders and among social classes became entrenched, justified theologically by the biblical passages we have already discussed. The other side of the gospel, the hints of a new covenant in which men and women, slaves and free persons would be equal, fell into utter oblivion.[57]

Another influential development was the rise of Islam (ca. A.D. 520–629). Islam, like Christianity, was a missionary religion—a very successful one—and soon captured the hearts and minds of people in Asia Minor and North Africa. Whereas Christianity had begun as a circle of influence surrounding the Mediterranean, manifested in a variety of races and cultures, the fall of the Roman Empire in the fifth century and the success of Islam in the sixth century forced Christian powers to entrench within the confines of Western Europe. By the early Middle Ages Christianity had become a white European religion that, despite the inroads of Islam, nevertheless asserted its political, cultural, and religious superiority under the ideal of "Christendom." This ideal—that Christ would reign both politically and religiously throughout the world—justified the violent persecutions incited in the Crusades and established the principle that infidels (non-whites, non-Europeans, non-Christians) should be converted at all costs. A religion that had started with a small group of Semites following a marginal Jew now manifested itself as the domination system, with a philosophy of military conquest in the name of salvation.[58]

Second, besides the shift in the political and geographical power of Christianity, the development of Christian faith took another important turn in its adaptation to Greco-Roman culture. Finding themselves in a Greek world influenced by Platonic thinking, Christians (from Paul onwards) tried to make sense of their faith in relation to Hellenistic categories. One of the most influential aspects of this worldview was its dualistic point of view. Though Aristotle, who was not a dualist, would later influence medieval Christianity, the Platonic view, which divided the world between matter and spirit, left a lasting impact on early Christianity. Though there were many variations on this theme, matter and spirit were generally considered to be in conflict, and spiritual freedom came through successfully mastering the flesh. In other words, a hierarchy existed in which things of the mind, things spiritual, were considered good, and in conflict with things material, including human embodiment.

Among the Christians of the early centuries debates arose as to how and whether such a cosmic dualism was compatible with Christian faith. By the early Middle Ages orthodox Christianity had incorporated a modified dualism, not assuming an ultimate conflict between mind and body, spirit and matter, but endorsing a complementarity between the two. Nevertheless, this complementarity presumed a hierarchy of higher (spiritual) and lower (material embodiment) realities. Since mind and spirit were assumed to be male attributes, while women were considered naturally closer to bodily functioning (childbirth), the complementary view of a hierarchical world incorporated moral designations of gender. Beverly Harrison and Carter Heyward explain it this way:

> On the basis of Neoplatonic cosmology, early church fathers explained their religious experience as essentially that of breaking tension between such oppositional realities as spirit and flesh, male and female, light and dark, good and evil. . . . Such opposites as spirit and flesh, male and female, could be cooperative only insofar as the higher was in control of the lower—and as the lower accepted its place as a weaker reality, both naturally and morally subordinate in relation to the higher. . . . Patristic theological discourse bears written testimony to social relations of domination and subjugation in which "the fathers" of the family (both civil and ecclesial households) believed that they should be in charge of women, children, slaves, and all other creatures—and in control, moreover, of their own "lower" selves: flesh, body, passions, and eroticism.[59]

It is this latter control over the lower passions that led eventually to the inversion of pleasure and pain. Put very crudely, one needed to control, or even deprive, oneself with regard to bodily appetites (hunger, sleep, sex) in order to ascend to the spiritual heights. Pain, as the deprivation of sensual pleasure, came to be seen as an important element in attaining the joy of salvation. The early centuries of martyrdom under Roman rule had elevated this pain and sacrifice to the level of hero worship: the greater the evidence of suffering in the martyrs' stories, the holier they obviously were. Still, "it is one thing to accept suffering for the sake of a moral or religious good when confronting unjust power, and another to perceive suffering as itself an intrinsic moral or religious value, the point to which much institutional Christianity came after the collapse of the Roman Imperium."[60]

We can see the elements beginning to fall together. Suffering, a legitimate ideal under martyrdom, gets taken up as a spiritual discipline to foster holiness. Redemption comes to be understood (under Anselm's influence) as the requirement of a distant, omnipotent God for the satisfaction of his honor. God's mercy gets lost in the idealization of punishment and suffering, and God is seen as sadistic and bloodthirsty. Such a God and the acceptance of our deserved punishment become necessary in order for the message of salvation to mean anything. The flaw here is that suffering and pain become not the *by-product* of a life of prophetic union with God but a *necessary means* to union with God. This applies both in interpreting Jesus' life and in understanding believers' lives. Pain becomes, at worst, an end in itself or—not much better—a means to an end, cultivated in an effort to imitate and sustain intimacy with Jesus.[61]

Put this symbiotic and distorted spirituality—believers undertaking (deserved) suffering in order to please a sadistic God—in the context of the power differentials permeating Christian culture and society. The lower realities (embodiment, passion, appetite) need to be controlled, denigrated, and even punished so that the higher realities (spirit, mind, eternal salvation) can flourish. When the lower realities are intimately associated with female, slaves, non-whites, non-Christians, then the justification of their control, denigration, and even punishment, *for their own good*, becomes evident.[62]

Our review of "redemption" has no doubt been cursory and one-sided. I have made no attempt to defend the tradition nor to explain the positive elements behind some of the metaphors and meanings that have emerged. The point has not been to retrieve exhaustively or accurately what certain persons said, but to indicate how, in spite of original intentions, certain meanings and categories have taken on a life of their own, have served to support the powers that be. The fact is, as illustrated in earlier sections of this chapter, that theologies of the cross and notions of suffering and redemption have left a legacy of oppression, pain, and suffering. The church itself is guilty of preaching salvation as a domination system. The tradition itself, and many Christians socialized into it, need to be redeemed from false teachings about redemption.

TRANSFORMING THE TRADITION: HOW DO WE GET THERE FROM HERE?

The idea that the Christian tradition, or the Christian church, might have elements of corruption within them may strike many as disturbing. However, this is not the entire story. While structures of power or certain metaphors taken literally have dominated some aspects of Christian living, there is, throughout history, evidence of renewal, of ongoing transformation in believers' lives. We turn now to examining the process of transformation in history. If corruption, power, and domination are to be turned around, if resurrection is to make new what is dead or corrupt, how does this happen? By what process can we renew meanings and liberate redemption?

This dilemma can be posed in another way. We learn our faith through community. Our access to the good news comes from a long historical tradition into which we are trained, either as children or as adult converts. But if, as I have been suggesting, a particular tradition has developed certain skewed beliefs and practices, if the tradition we are socialized into has some blind spots and corrupt expectations, we too will be prejudiced in our appropriation of the good news. How can those who have been influenced by a distorted framework of meaning see clearly the possibility of liberation? How can they step outside their communities to grasp and claim the resurrection elements? Won't their ability to grasp and proclaim any good news from the tradition be forever handicapped?

To explore these issues we must first establish that history itself, and the Christian tradition in particular, involves two dynamic processes. We can call them the "conservative" and the "revolutionary," or the "institutional" and the "prophetic." Whatever the labels, in every era and social context there are structures and institutions that carry coherent meaning for a culture. These structures include family, educational systems, religious traditions, economic practices, political arrangements, means of communication. At the same time, every social group has within it elements of change. Some persons recognize the flaws in their social worlds and seek to reverse corruption, whether explicitly and with the blessings of the whole, or in clandestine and condemned forms. The point is that these two forces are what drive historical developments. These two elements are always in tension in society and culture, regardless of whether it is a healthy, creative tension or a destructive and damaging conflict.[63]

Rosemary Haughton speaks of these dynamic elements in reference to the Christian tradition. In *The Transformation of Man* she develops the categories of *formation* and *transformation* as two ways in which persons enter into the Christian story.[64] The idea of formation is to use all the influences of culture—all the structures and institutions mentioned above—to help people understand themselves and their world, to adjust to both without excessive stress, and to come to the point where they can contribute their own talents, insights, and gifts to the community. Transformation, on the other hand, involves the complete and utter reversal of all that is considered good and perfect. Transformation leads to the dissolution of all that one ordinarily values. The death of the old and ordinary self leads to the birth of the whole self—healed, renewed, and restored, both in its communal and personal dimensions.

Notice the relationship between these two. "Without the long process of formation there could be no transformation, yet no amount of careful formation can transform. Transformation is a timeless point of decision, yet it can only operate in the personality formed through time-conditioned stages of development, and its effects can only be worked out in terms of that formation."[65] There is a perduring paradox here: one needs to be socialized into faith in order to open up the possibility of renewal and rebirth, but such socialization, by itself, simply perpetuates the status quo and curtails transformation. At the same time, transformation cannot be programmed but remains an elusive and serendipitous occurrence.[66] The two elements are de facto a part of personal and communal life and can never be separated. Still, there is no simple causal relationship between the two, only an ongoing tension or "dialectic," what Bernard Lonergan describes as "linked but opposed principles of change."[67]

The dynamic tension between formation and transformation is an example of a deeper dialectic that is intrinsic to human development. This has to do with how we learn and grow. Frederick E. Crowe addresses the question as follows: "[O]n what basis can we unite tradition and innovation, gift and achievement, heritage and development, docility and personal creativity?"[68] He insists that the answer involves the interaction of two ways of learning: the way of "heritage" and the way of "achievement." Lonergan speaks of the knowledge "born of belief" in contrast to "immanently generated insights.[69] I made the contrast in the last chapter between "received" knowledge and "discovery." The point behind all of these labels is that human development (affective as well as cognitive) is always a matter of both socialization and discovery. Some things we know, feel strongly about, or believe, simply because we have been told. Other things we know, feel strongly about, and endorse because we have discovered them for ourselves.[70]

This process has its communal as well as personal dimensions. In fact, all traditions—the stories, the wisdom, the teachings, the principles, and the proverbs—begin originally as sets of insights and consequent practices. Someone discovers a profound truth and shares it with others. As similar insights are elicited in a group, shared wisdom and customs develop. These original discoveries and actions are then handed on to the next generation, and the tradition takes on a life of its own. Oral tradition evolves, and new angles on the original wisdom emerge. Oral tradition becomes a written record: Plato writes of Socrates, an anonymous author gathers the proclamations of Jeremiah into a narrative whole, an early generation of Christians sets down the stories of Jesus as the first disciples begin dying off. Written narratives are superseded by codified laws, creeds, and declarations of councils. People devise methods of teaching these truths, so catechisms are written, disciplines are established, rules of life hold sway. Before long, traditions become Tradition, understood as a single *deposit* of faith.

The danger that always arises is that the dynamic interaction between natively creative discoveries and tradition will stalemate. A tradition only continues as a living and vibrant way of life if succeeding generations continue to experience what the original generation found transforming. Each generation, indeed, each person, must have the insights for him- or herself or religious life simply becomes a set of strictures preventing real flourishing. Ultimately, all the artifacts of a religious tradition—rituals, songs, narratives, artwork, icons—are meant to be vehicles of transformation. They serve to move us out of ourselves to a grasp of that which is ultimately beyond us. To the degree that such vehicles become merely religious trappings they neither elicit the needed insights nor point beyond themselves. The tradition itself becomes the object of worship, and the dynamism between creative discovery and socialization into a community is curtailed.

In fact, Christian history reveals that such dynamism cannot ultimately be shut down. Whenever a tradition begins to stagnate, a new person or generation comes forward with transformative experiences that renew and challenge the received expectations. In A.D. 540 Benedict realized that the disciplines of asceticism needed to be ordered within a community dedicated to balancing mind, body, and spirit. Benedict touched a chord in the hearts and minds of his generation, and his *Rule* spread throughout Europe. Several generations later, the *Rule* had become a dead letter of the law. The monks living in the Abbey of Cluny discovered again the power of this way of living and reformed Benedictine life (A.D. 909). A century later even this revision had fallen stale, and the Cistercians revived the best of the original vision for their day (A.D. 1098). Not long afterward, Francis of Assisi had his own powerful experience of transformation and insisted that owning property was the bane of all religious life; the poverty of Jesus had to be rediscovered (ca. A.D. 1209). In their own day, the Protestant Reformers saw the oppression of conscience that certain religious practices perpetuated. They discovered anew the power of God's free gift of love, and in so doing revived the conversion element of faith. In his turn, Ignatius of Loyola saw the same corruptions and developed a set of spiritual exercises with the express intent of promoting transformative encounters with God. As years passed, Protestant traditions solidified into, for example, Puritan strictures, while some arms of the Jesuits developed into cadres of papal henchmen, reducing conversion to a matter of allegiance.

Having established this tension in a number of ways, let me point out that the opposition at work here, both in individual and communal development, is not an opposition of ultimate conflict or contradiction. It is, rather, a complementary opposition, in which the two poles are *linked* as well as opposed. This means that the resolution of the tension is not a matter of one trajectory overtaking or defeating the other trajectory. Rather, the tension is resolved through balance, through accepting the inevitable ambiguity of paradox, where two seemingly contradictory principles are simultaneously true.

Further, this kind of complementary tension is also at the heart of the Judeo-Christian notion of God. Early on, in its revolutionary adoption of monotheism, Israel rejected the notion of a god or gods who represented forces that were battling against each other. Creation is not the result of skirmishes between rival powers, nor is it the fruit of lust or jealousy between gendered gods. God is singular and transcends all such polarities. At the same time, God is intimately involved in God's creation. The advent of Jesus, Christians proclaim, signifies this intimate involvement in a historically unprecedented way. So we have a God who is both ultimately transcendent and incomprehensible at the same time we have a God who is utterly incarnate and involved, to the point of suffering our pain. To take one side of this paradoxical truth as the only or more salient truth is to mistake a complementary and dynamic tension as an oppositional conflict.

This dynamic tension—in experiences and conceptions of God—has also played itself out in history. One generation experiences the intimate concreteness of God in the world: through taste, touch, sight, and smell they become aware of God's presence. They set up shrines to mark the spot, design icons to depict the newfound insight, write hymns to celebrate the epiphany, devise new rituals to rehearse the revelation. After a while, the icons, the shrines, the rituals are assumed to be the very locus of God's presence. People cling to the artifacts they have devised for certain assurance of God's good will. Soon enough, the concrete, earthy, sensuous reminders of God become idols of God. Rather than effect transformation and transcendence in believers, they encourage believers to contain God in designated rubrics.

When this happens, a new generation arises to name and condemn the idolatry that has become entrenched. This generation experiences the ultimate mystery and transcendence of God and declares the good news of God's incomprehensibility. The spiritual morbidity of clinging to sensuous reminders of God is overcome with powerful and inexpressible mystical experiences. Out of these powerful experiences this new generation of believers perceives that idolatry is the obstacle to union with God. They smash icons, denounce artwork of any kind, reduce the extravagance of liturgy, empty their places of worship of all depictions of God.

It doesn't take long, however, for this reform to become its own idol. The incomprehensibility of God becomes a dogma that gets codified, leads to rules that must be obeyed, produces an austerity that is rigid and kills creativity. The fact that human persons are embodied, that we need to taste, touch, see, smell, and hear God is forgotten. The fact that God became incarnate himself is forgotten. Forgotten, that is, until a new prophet discovers what his generation has missed: a St. Francis, for example, discovers God in the simple joys of the created world. So the cycle repeats itself, the mystics and iconoclasts (destroyers of images) rising up against the aesthetes and sacramentalists (who see God in all things created) and vice versa.

Now, note how this dynamic tension interfaces with the tension between socialization and transformation. One can be socialized into *either* an iconoclastic tradition (e.g., Anabaptism) *or* into an strongly sacramental tradition (e.g., pre–Vatican II Roman Catholicism). Both embody and pass on a rich heritage that reflects and facilitates authentic experiences of God. Both suffer from the danger of clinging too closely to the medium in which they find God. Both suffer from the danger of making God in their own image, of mistaking their grasp of God with God herself. In both cases, the socialization is only "successful" to the degree that it promotes its own transformation. It is the reversal inherent in transformation that restores the *dynamism* of the tension. Every tradition needs to be transformed, not only because new generations need to experience God anew, but because our conception of God itself is in jeopardy without such continual renewal.[71]

The significant point in all of this is that authentic religious faith cannot be contained or prescribed. To be authentic is to live in the in-between of the dynamic tension, both the tension between our formation and our unpredictable transformation, and that between an omnipotent, transcendent God and an immanent, incarnational God. Because of the tendency for our notions and experiences of God to become rigid and prescribed, we—both individuals and communities—need to stand ever ready to have our religious experience and ideas about God broken wide open.

The true enemy here is, in fact, "certitude." A personal faith or a tradition that seeks to cling with certainty to its ideas about God, or to its prescriptions about how to know God, risks idolatry of the worst sort. Idolatry is, at root, not worship of images, but taking what is tangible and finite and giving it ultimacy and transcendence. Even iconoclasm, which intends to root out idols, can become idolatrous by clinging with certitude to its path to God. The temptation to contain God in this way is ever present in Christian life. The only antidote for such a danger is to embrace the ambiguity and unpredictability of waiting for the insights that open the door to transformative decisions while trusting God's grace to bring them about.[72]

We have arrived at the point of stating explicitly the question we have been intimating all along. If history reveals corruption and continual reform in the unfolding of Christian lives, how can we trust the tradition to be authentic? If we can't trust the tradition, how will we know what authentic faith is? What *are* the grounds of religious authenticity?

On the basis of the dialectical tensions we have been examining, we can, at the very least, say what the grounds of authenticity are *not*. Religious authenticity is not a matter of opting for one side of the polarity over against another. It is not the case that the tradition has the answers and any innovators are heretics. Nor is it the case that the tradition is all wrong, totally corrupt, so that rejecting it is a sign of transformation. The tradition is *both* corrupt *and* holds the seeds of renewal. Likewise, authentic faith does not opt for a mysterious, omnipotent God over against an incarnate, embodied God. God is both, so authentic faith will involve both tangible, sensuous vehicles for God's communication and mystical, silent, empty spaces. Authentic faith means embracing the ambiguity of living in the middle, unable to control God or our own revelatory moments. It means embracing the insecurity of travail. Inauthentic faith succumbs to the temptations of certitude and control, packages God and prescribes salvation.

Is there, then, any absolute truth about redemption? Are our interpretations of redemption ever subject to fluctuation? The answer to both questions is yes. There is at the core of the Christian tradition good news that has, does, and will continue to transform lives. Our formulation of that message of salvation can be delineated in general principles pertaining to human lives, principles that we hold apply to all people, in every time and place. Nevertheless, both the formulation of these principles ("doctrines," if you will) and the application of them to concrete lives take place *in* specific times and places. So each new generation, each new culture and historical situation cannot avoid that task of discernment and application. This task may involve rejecting formulations that are no longer adequate to the truth at hand. Or revising practices that no longer promote healing and forgiveness. But to revise and rediscover only testifies to the perduring truth of the redemptive process and its work in peoples' lives. The need to remember and retell reveals the deep longing for truth inherent in the human heart.[73]

Those who cling to formulations as unrevisable sacrifice truth for certainty. Those who reject the tradition outright and refuse to explore the evidence of redemptive truth within it are equally curtailing questions relevant to unveiling salvation. In both cases bias operates to squelch the search for truth in favor of ideological security.[74]

So redeeming redemption involves both the ambiguity of the search and the conviction that we hold the truth. The ambiguity, like the travail of embracing ourselves as both sinners and victims, means abiding in the struggle of discernment, patiently working yet waiting for the relevant insights to emerge. The conviction of truth, like faith in resurrection healing and forgiveness, means asserting what we do know to be authentic even while we are open to further revisions of our grasp of these affairs. Redeeming redemption is part of the redemptive process itself and involves faith that God is present no matter how corrupt we or the tradition have become.[75]

EVIDENCE OF RENEWAL

My own project in this book has been to suggest a new version of the meaning of the cross, one that embodies rather than contradicts what the earliest Christians experienced and what Jesus was all about. The key revision here is to name an aspect of redemption that has been overshadowed by the emphasis on sin as pride that offends God's honor and must be accounted for. The other side of the story involves the experience of victims, of the powerless and silent, for whom messages of repentance and forgiveness are misplaced. The cross and resurrection mean not only forgiveness but also healing, and in Jesus we can discover our woundedness as well as our culpability. The "as well as" is central here, since these two poles are not oppositional but linked: to discover one is to understand the other.

I am not alone in retrieving this other side of the cross. The need to reconsider theories of atonement has been widely stated.[76] Counter-traditions within Christian history are being retrieved.[77] The importance of Jesus as a vulnerable victim with whom we can identify is being recognized from a variety of perspectives. The experience of child abuse has revealed the importance of Jesus as God-made-vulnerable.[78] In Latin America the reality of the "crucified peoples" has brought the cross new meaning.[79] African American theologians are recovering the power that the broken and unjustly murdered Jesus had in sustaining hope among North American slaves.[80] African Christians are working to renew their understanding of Christ in a postcolonial world.[81] Mujerista theology is the work of Hispanic American women who are working to replace the ideology of suffering with the positive power of "la lucha" (the struggle).[82] White Eurocentric feminists are putting forward new angles on pain, suffering, and the cross.[83] Theologians in various parts of Asia are attempting to relate the meaning of Jesus to their non-Christian contexts.[84] At the same time, persons with a heritage of dominance are engaging in rituals seeking forgiveness for the blindness and oppression of their forefathers.[85]

In all of this work three themes are most salient regarding the meaning of Jesus' death and resurrection. First and foremost is the emphasis on identifying with the crucified Jesus as unjustly accused, tortured, and executed. This stands in contrast to the tradition that sees Jesus' crucifixion as a just payment of a debt owed to God. Second, the meaning of Jesus' death cannot be understood apart from Jesus' life and message. The good news of the kingdom and Jesus' loving treatment of outcasts and sinners are part and parcel of the meaning of Jesus' death and resurrection. To focus only on Jesus' suffering makes the meaning of the good news too narrow. Finally, it is important to understand suffering as a *consequence* of union with God, not the *means* to it. Jesus' suffering and death were a by-product of his prophetic life and his intimacy with his Abba-Father-God. Our suffering is to be interpreted in this light. In neither case is suffering either an end in itself or a means to union with God.

6

A Theological Model

Grace, Conversion, and the
Law of the Cross

BETWEEN THE AGES OF ELEVEN and fourteen I suffered from a series of relational injuries, feeling hurt and excluded by others close to me. My response was to "go underground," lying awake each night in my bed, nursing wounds, trying to resolve my difficulties. I literally talked to the darkness, to some unknown imagined someone who would understand my cause and vindicate me. I could not go to sleep without meditating on my situation and presenting its latest developments to this unknown listener.

In tenth grade I gradually got involved in a Christian outreach program to high school students. Though innately shy, I attended rowdy Young Life meetings every week. In December I was talked into going on a weekend retreat at Camp Laurelville, in the Laurel Mountains of Pennsylvania. I listened intently to the talks about Jesus, which concluded with the Saturday night call to conversion. As that talk ended, we were asked to leave the assembly without speaking to anyone, to spend twenty minutes in silence. I wandered through the rainy, cold woods without clear direction or purpose. No flashes of lightning, no voices from heaven. After twenty minutes I went back to my cabin, soaking wet, where other girls and our counselor were sitting on their beds and talking. As I listened to these people speak of their very personal faith, it simply but clearly dawned on me: "That darkness I have been talking to really is a Someone. This is what all these people mean by accepting Jesus into your heart."

This discovery fascinated and haunted me. I took it home with me, a changed person. My "darkness" became God, known as my friend Jesus, and my ruminations became prayer. Though few of my problems were solved and my wounds weren't immediately healed, I was not alone, and that made all the difference. My energy, attention, and habits shifted: I wanted to know everything I could about this Someone in the darkness who was now my friend, who had a name, Jesus.

Many many years later I had learned a lot about Jesus. I had spent hours in theological discussions with every Christian leader, minister, teacher, and friend I had ever known. I had taken religious studies courses in university, I had learned Greek in graduate school, I was doing rudimentary biblical exegesis on my own. I had begun theological studies at an evangelical Anglican seminary that I was assured by friends was "safe" (meaning theologically orthodox). But my deep desire to understand the Bible with critical tools was met with disdain by those who felt the high road of criticism was the low road to heresy. I was sure that if I just kept moving deeper into the text I would one day get to the heart of truth, have the certitude I needed to clinch my faith once and for all.

Uneasy with such a "safe" environment, I moved to a Roman Catholic institute (no doubt quite "unsafe" in the opinion of my evangelical friends), where my first M.A. course was "Foundations of Theology." When we came to the section on "The Mediation of Revelation through Scripture" my anxiety surfaced. I went to the professor full of questions and doubts, determined once and for all to straighten out my confusion over the authority of scripture.[1] After I kept pressing her with the question, "How do I know the Bible is true?" she finally observed, quietly but profoundly, "I think what you are asking is 'How do I know *anything* is true?'"![2]

This set me on a long course of "self-appropriation" by which I discovered that certitude (meaning having no further doubts or questions) was not the criterion of authentic faith at all. Instead, I took a course called "Conversion," where I discovered a dynamic but intelligible framework for understanding my befriending of the darkness years earlier.

Eventually I came to see not only that certitude has its limits but also that critical thought can only resolve so much. Talking to Jesus in the darkness returned as a viable medium of faith, though in an entirely new way. The devotional and liturgical life I had spurned in my critical quest for the true source of Christian faith began to become acceptable as a legitimate way of life. I discovered spirituality as a valid arena of thought and inquiry, and discernment became just as important as intellectual acumen. As the hard knocks of life jostled me, logical answers, biblical propositions, and doctrinal theology seemed less and less salient, while liturgical and sacramental life became more and more important. My evangelical roots and my low

Anglicanism began moving "up," as the Eucharist gained a central place in my life. Both conversion and the cross became central to my theology.

This book is an extension of this journey. I have been exploring a new way of approaching the cross and the significance of suffering in believers' lives. I have been weaving meanings together, working in and out of concrete examples, suggesting new categories, presenting theological hints and guesses. In this chapter I stand back and reflect on some of the qualities, properties, and characteristics of the process of salvation as I have re-presented it. My aim is not some abstract or universal account of redemption that will settle once and for all the meaning of Christ's work on the cross, but a gathering together of some of the elements common throughout my previous chapters. My objective is to articulate constituent categories in a new theological model: interrelated terms that it is good to have around when one is interpreting concrete situations.[3] I begin with a discussion of the human condition, move on to explicate the intervention of grace into cycles of alienation, explore different aspects of conversion, and, finally, explain further the "law of the cross" as the solution to the problem of evil.[4]

THE HUMAN CONDITION:
ALIENATION AND MORAL IMPOTENCE

The human person is dynamic, developing, and imbued with an eros and energy oriented toward understanding reality, discovering truth and value, choosing authentic living and abiding in love relationships. To the degree that one has attained the age of reason one can choose either to live according to this orientation or to ignore her spontaneous quest. Still, no one attains the age of reason without being indelibly marked by his community of meaning, and such communities are all mixtures of intertwined value and disvalue, truth and error, love and disdain. So the transcendent spontaneity that marks us as human, the positive orientation of our native intelligence and intersubjectivity, is often tainted by prejudice, curtailed by limited horizons. We may reach the age of reason but have been taught to be "reasonable," meaning we ought not to ask unsolicited questions. We may reach the point at which we are considered responsible for our actions yet have a distorted sense of whom we are responsible for and why. In short, our essential freedom (our propensity to seek intelligibility, truth, value, love), which can never be taken from us, has been severely limited to the much shallower domain of our effective freedom (what we can, in fact, choose and hope to achieve).[5]

The alienation of the human condition is precisely this disjunction between the inherent orientation of the human spirit—toward discovering intelligibility, knowing truth, knowing and choosing value, and falling in love—and the inability to actualize this potential. The roots of this alienation can be found in both human finitude and human sin.

We are creatures and have creaturely limits. The reach of our imaginations, our questions, our aspirations, is unlimited, but the attainment of this reach is hampered by time and space. We do not have time to ask all the questions that we need or want to ask. We do not have the resources to undertake all the possible relationships, works of art, and worthy tasks that could be pursued. In addition, to ask questions, to create imaginative lives, our minds need to be working accurately, which means healthy bodies that are well fed. So there is immanent within the human condition a certain "alienation," namely, the tension between the unlimited eros of the human spirit and the very limited conditions of embodied existence.[6]

This tension inherent in being intelligent creatures has been exacerbated and immensely complicated by sin. Sin is the limitation of human endeavor, not through embodiment and finitude but through the willful choice to deny the human spirit and its eros. Sin is the "flight from understanding," the choice not to ask questions that arise spontaneously, not to act on insights that may occur, not to pursue the questions for action consequent on discoveries that we make.[7] Sin is not a codified list of indiscreet behaviors but the basic attitude that underlies such behaviors. It is the refusal to be just what one is: an embodied and limited creature whose orientation is toward what lies beyond himself. It is to err either on the side of pride—the presumption of power that overlooks our finitude—or on the side of denigration—the refusal to recognize and claim the full Self as oriented to beauty, truth, love, self-agency.

This basic sin has consequences, infecting many lives. Human alienation, *my* alienation, is not just of my own making but is also the fruit of other peoples' refusal to be self-transcendent. Perhaps my grandmother refused to ask what went on between her husband and her daughter while she worked the late shift, even though there were clear indications that something was amiss. My mother may have learned to hide shameful things and thus have taught me to be ashamed of asking certain kinds of questions. This will have left me with an entire set of emotive and intellectual habits oriented toward asking some questions but refusing others, not even aware of the elements needed for my health and flourishing. Thus, while an individual may overtly choose at times to deny her own call to self-transcendence, to ask, to grow, to pursue truth and value, it is also the case that her entire self-concept, her habits and skills, fears and aspirations, may have been socialized into an alienated pattern.

The human condition is, thus, one of unlimited aspiration and limited creaturely existence. This tension, contrary to some types of theology and piety down through the ages, is not in itself evil. Creaturely existence is not the ultimate source of alienation but its precondition. Self-transcendence —full human flourishing—involves accepting our innate spiritual orientation and actualizing it *within* the limits constraining us.

The root of sin lies in misunderstanding and denying this healthy tension. We live within the taut balance of both "limitation" and "transcendence."[8] Basic sin is the refusal to accept this tension, either by moving in the direction of too much transcendence (through presumption of unlimited human powers) or by too much limitation (by denying the aspirations of the human spirit). Moral evils are the cumulative consequences of such distortions, so that a clear perspective on this duality is clouded, and choosing authentic balance becomes more and more difficult.[9]

Here the categories of "victim" and "perpetrator" enter in. For most of Christian history, sin has been understood as one-half of the equation, that of pride, of taking our ability to go beyond ourselves in knowing, creating, and loving to the extreme. Sin has been understood as usurping the role of God, forgetting our creaturely finitude, foolishly thinking that the unlimited *reach* of our desire to know truth and value is a guarantee of its *attainment*. The solution to such sin has been the humility of faith, modeled after the *kenōsis* of Jesus himself. What feminists have unveiled, and I have been developing, is the idea that sin indeed has another face, that of "too much limitation." Some persons fail to be (w)holy human by denying their spiritual orientation to learn, grow, understand, create, love themselves and others. These persons need to overcome sin by discovering discovery, claiming the transcendent dimension of themselves, the eros of their spirits, and acting on it. Humility and *kenōsis*, in this case, only further promote the illness that needs curing.

As illustrated in previous chapters, this distortion between limitation and transcendence can become embedded in social arrangements and cultural values. One culture, because of its technological advancement, claims a monopoly on the higher powers of human potential and presumes that other cultures are made up of barbarians or savages. One gender takes the operations of the human mind as native only to its own kind, designating the other gender as non-rational, irrational, or a-rational.[10] One race, taken with its ability to order the world around it, presumes that other races are less advanced, innately more limited, and therefore available to serve the "higher" aspirations of "human culture."[11] Individuals are then socialized into such distorted self-identities (on both ends of the spectrum) that the potential actualization of authenticity becomes skewed from the start.[12]

It is precisely this "skewing" that the Christian tradition has designated with the term "original sin." I have used the term "alienation" but the point is the same: we are so stuck within cycles of distortion that we cannot even see clearly what the issues are and how to address them. We are socialized into an entire nexus of distorted assumptions about what it means to be human (the privileged as well as the oppressed). These distortions are not only sets of ideas but are embodied in neural transmitters that codify our hopes, fears, aspirations, and self-concepts. To break out of these distortions one needs clear insights into and intentional decisions to change the errors of these assumptions. But the communal context is so imbued with distortion that it will not naturally yield the needed revelations and incentives. Even our psychic conditioning is such that it will block whatever transformative discoveries and imaginative choices may be ready to burst forth. In short, the human condition is not only one of alienation but also one of moral impotence: we cannot cure ourselves because the very means by which the cure might come are themselves tainted.[13]

The fact that we are historical beings contributes to this dilemma. What is needed to correct these false cycles are insights, judgments, and decisions regarding the erroneous elements in them. But the requisite insights depend on prior correct judgments or decisions, and until we have grown to the point where these occur, our efforts to heal may further infect the situation. As the Pennsylvania Dutch say, "Too soon old, too late smart." The addict cannot learn about the nature of addiction until he stops drinking, but unless he understands the nature of addiction, he will not be able to stop drinking. The slave cannot use his capacity for learning unless he claims his right to an education. But he does not know how to claim his civil rights unless he has the skills developed through an education.

Who will save us, then, from this cycle of dehumanization?[14] The Christian tradition, while maintaining the dead-end nature of these cycles of alienation, also claims that such moral impotence is not the complete story. There is some other element that operates in history, some other process by which new and unforeseen discoveries emerge, some healing element that manages not to correct the situation in its entirety but to shift the probabilities so that authenticity is more likely to occur. This is what Christians have called "grace" and what is imaged in myriad ways in the New Testament, as a tiny mustard seed, as leaven, as the inbreaking of the reign of God. Let us examine this work of grace more closely.

GRACE

Grace operates as an intervention into the distorted cycles of alienation. This intervention is at the same time extraordinary and quite ordinary. It is *ordinary* in that it involves insights and choices that are just like any and all other insights and choices that we have each day. The intervention of grace does not circumvent our natural ways of knowing, deciding, and being in the world. Grace is *extraordinary* in that we are given the required insights and the requisite willingness before we have taken the steps needed to generate them. The cycle of alienation stops or shifts because we unexpectedly see something in a new light and/or respond to values in a new way. C. S. Lewis got on a bus at the bottom of a hill and when he got off at the top he knew that God existed. Roberta Bondi, walking down the hall between her kitchen and her dining room, realized that she no longer believed in the crucifixion. Charles Colson wept uncontrollably in his darkened car one night and found himself praying in spite of his doubts. As mere insights or simple feelings these are only nascent hints, ones that need to be further understood, examined, confirmed, acted on. But they come, sometimes unsolicited, and certainly not as direct acts of will on our part.

Grace, then, is an intervention into cycles of alienation that manifests itself concretely in our lives through shifting our understanding and our willingness, our knowing and deciding. First, grace intervenes through our *understanding*. It occurs when we grasp new meanings, have insights that open up new interpretations of the world, ourselves, our relationships, our actions. Transformative religious encounters (as borne out through centuries of religious conversions) involve some "Aha!," some new grasp of meaning, some previously evasive truth that opens up new horizons of comprehension and possibility.

Second, grace intervenes in our *deciding*. Even when we grasp accurately what needs to be changed in our lives, we don't necessarily have the will to do it. This is often the case in the course of ordinary life but is even more so when it comes to the surrender and resistance needed for dysfunctional or oppressive situations. So grace intervenes not only through insights but by shifting our appetites. St. Paul spoke of the Holy Spirit flooding our hearts with love (Rom. 5:5). Thomas Aquinas spoke of infused virtues, the theological virtues (i.e., habits) of faith, hope, and love.[15] Earlier I discussed the touching of our deepest Desire, a Desire and a touch that can carry us beyond ourselves, to horizons we would never have otherwise imagined. This grace can occur with regard to specific choices in concrete circumstances. It can also involve the general stirring up of Desire that grants us *antecedent willingness*. In this case we are moved in a deep and perduring way to long for, seek, and abide in communion with God, which, in turn, leaves us open to whatever actions God might call us to.

So grace comes as the new ordering of our desires toward authentic love, even though our desire for love has been tainted. Grace comes as faith, trust in the knowledge born of love, even though we don't have all the requisite understanding. Grace comes as hope, even though we live in an ethic of risk, without control over the outcomes of our actions. The intervention of new desires, or newly ordered desires, makes the insights of grace effective and heightens the probability of their occurring. When such insights do occur, we have the desire to pursue and confirm them, the courage to act on them. When such insights are not forthcoming, we wait patiently for their emergence, undertaking disciplines that will increase their likelihood.

Note this interaction of understanding and will with regard to grace. A new grasp of reality—such as C. S. Lewis's realization that God exists—can lead to further questions for action and a shift in the ground of our Desire. At the same time, being touched at a deep level by transformative feelings can be the occasion for a renewed understanding. Charles Colson was moved by his friend's account of deep intimacy with God: he longed and prayed for such as he sat outside his friend's house in the dark. Much later he came to understand just who Jesus was, and who he himself was, including the nature of his sins. Dorothy Day was drawn by her experience of pregnancy to feel the presence and beauty of a Creator. Such an encounter led her to seek to know such a God, eventually taking her into catechism classes and baptism.

Not only does one aspect of grace lead to the other, the two must go together if the full fruit of grace is to be manifested. Revelations of truth that stall at the level of intellect can lead to pompous rationalism and doctrinaire creedal orthodoxy. On the other hand, being caught up in the sweep of God's love, no matter how it transforms one's desires, can degenerate into myopic pietism and self-centered, irrational devotion. Transformed Desire is empty unless bolstered by accurate understanding. Clear understanding can be lifeless without the passion of Desire.

Further, while grace may enter our lives as gifts unmerited or unsought, we have an active role in pursuing or ignoring such serendipitous offerings. An insight—the "Aha" that grasps us in a moment of grace—is only potentially transformative. It is the operative grace—God's action on us—that yet requires cooperative grace. We cooperate with God by examining just what this revelation means, checking and rechecking the correctness of the original bright idea, and pursuing whatever further questions need to be asked. Likewise, we may be touched by God at a deep level of our conscious feelings. But we can still choose to reject this glimpse of Desire fulfilled, and even if we choose to follow it there is much work entailed: discerning the value apprehended by this undercurrent, working out the implications for our living, our communities, our world.[16]

In addition, grace operates in us as both *healing* and *elevating*. We began the chapter with an account of human alienation and have spoken of grace as an intervention that can reverse dysfunctional cycles. As such, grace heals the wounded and the perpetrator alike, making reconciliation possible. Such reconciliation generates yet more gifts of forgiveness and healing. Still, God's work in our lives is not *merely* therapeutic. It not only addresses the distortion of sin; it transforms the limitations of finitude. Even if sin were not operative, we would remain creatures restricted in our reach toward truth, value, and love. The touch of God on our understanding elevates our minds to grasp what otherwise we could not reach. God's undergirding presence touching our Desire opens horizons of relationship, encounters with beauty and love, that our ordinary consciousness could not fathom. The gift of God's relationship with us does not end our creatureliness, but it draws us up into communion with the Divine, meeting the eros of the human spirit, fulfilling our deepest Desire, before we have arrived at it of our own accord.

The taut balance between limitation and transcendence is distorted by sin and convoluted into complex dysfunctional cycles in individuals and in social systems. Healing grace is needed to right the balance and shift the cycles. Yet the key to such reorientation is the ultimate self-transcendence that is involved in an other-worldly falling in love. Elevating and healing grace are distinct but not separate: they are two functions of one gift, the gift of God's communion with the world. This is why psychotherapy must ultimately involve a spirituality, why self-help techniques and New Age fads eventually prove empty. As humans we are oriented to the ultimate, the reach of our questions and desires is unfathomable. Grace is the fulfillment of these yearnings in spite of our natural limitations as well as our willful resistance.

A few final points, made earlier in the book, need to be highlighted. First, there is the important role of the community with regard to grace. Persons can be socialized as well as converted into a "graced" worldview. Horizons of ultimate meaning, habits of feelings, wisdom in decision making all come to us initially through the community of meaning in which we are raised. We are socialized into a whole nexus of interpretations of the world, its ways of functioning, and our roles within it. This nexus includes parameters of good behavior, actions that are taboo, virtues that are expected, and images of the Divine that sanction or propel such behavior. We learn prayers that presume relationship with the Divine, are taught that God has created a certain order and meaning to the universe.

Still, such communities of faith are not exempt from the distortions caused by finitude and by sin. Communities, like individuals, suffer the limitations of human endeavor and need to be continually reformed. They need to be ever renewed through the transformation of understanding and willing brought about through elevating grace. Likewise, communities, even religious communities, embody and perpetuate the sin that exacerbates an imbalance between limitation and transcendence. So we find ourselves in the ironic position in which the insights of grace and the liberation of Desire often involve discovering and changing errors within our religious communities themselves. We and our communities must be purged, through healing grace, of distorted desires and misleading "truths." The church, though embodying the communion of saints and serving as the body of Christ in the world, is itself in need of constant renewal and healing.

Furthermore, the effect of grace in our lives, both individual and communal, is not a matter of instant and/or permanent solutions. Grace doesn't "fix" anything, like a magic potion or the instant-win lottery. What the intervention of grace does is shift probabilities. New understandings make it more likely that we will accurately grasp a situation and its healing possibilities. Altered appetites, renewed Desire, heighten the chances that we will be able to make the requisite choices. In a world operating within cycles of alienation, the entrance of grace "solves" nothing: it merely opens up new possibilities and thus makes authentic living more likely.

This means, of course, that we are not masters of grace. An ethic of control presumes that human ideas and actions can fix the ills of the world. So, too, an approach to grace that assumes we can manufacture either healing or elevating experiences degenerates into spiritual pride and manipulation. Just as grace merely increases the probability of authenticity and healing, so our seeking of grace—through disciplines of any sort—does not ensure transformative insights or desires but only heightens the likelihood of their occurrence. A theology of grace must be grounded in an ethic of risk, lest grace be robbed of its very nature as gift.

In sum: Redemption is the restoration of the integral balance between human limitation and the human orientation to transcendence. It reestablishes the integration of ourselves as limited creatures with an unlimited eros to know truth, create value, and abide in love relationships. Grace, as the agent of such restoration, comes as a third element in this tension, comes as an intervention into the distorted cycles of victims and perpetrators as these occur at the individual level, within social configurations, and within sets of cultural meanings. Grace opens us to the fulfillment of Desire which we would never, otherwise, encounter. Such grace is needed by religious communities as much as in the secular world. It is not something over which we have control but occurs and bears fruit according to probabilities. Reordered desires heighten the likelihood of graced insights and undergird their movement into judgments and decisions, which in turn confirm the new ordering of our desires. The conjunction of such insights with the liberation of our desires is what Lonergan has called, and the Christian tradition has always meant by, *conversion.*

CONVERSION: RELIGIOUS, MORAL, INTELLECTUAL, AND PSYCHIC

Grace, as I have been presenting it, is not so much a state (of being in or out of God's favor) as it is a process of growth. This process, while operating within the ordinary structure of our knowing and doing, often involves an about-face, a dramatic reversal of previously known meanings and values. Such reversal is what *conversion* is all about. Though it can be dramatic and sudden, it can also be dramatic and subtle. In the weavings of our lives, we can shift instantly from purple thread to red thread or we can gradually mute the tones of purple, begin using deep blues, unfold the blues into lighter shades, and then gradually introduce red tones. So conversions are woven into our lives, dramatically or subtly, through grace.

Religious conversion, according to Bernard J. F. Lonergan, is an "otherworldly falling in love," a "being grasped by ultimate concern."[17] It

involves the fulfillment of what I have referred to as Desire—our deepest
longing for some Other. The attraction of such completed desire is so powerful that it draws all our resources to itself. It becomes the undertow of
all our questioning, deciding, living:

> Being in love with God, as experienced, is being in love in an unrestricted
> fashion. . . . Just as unrestricted questioning is our capacity for self-tran-
> scendence, so being in love in an unrestricted fashion is the proper fulfill-
> ment of that capacity.
>
> That fulfillment is not the product of our knowledge and choice. On the
> contrary, it dismantles and abolishes the horizon in which our knowing and
> choosing went on and it sets up a new horizon in which the love of God will
> transvalue our values and the eyes of that love will transform our knowing.[18]

Dorothy Day entered into this love very subtly with her experience of
pregnancy and a growing wonder at creation. Thomas Merton discovered
beauty in his childhood in southern France long before his conversion to
Catholicism. C. S. Lewis engaged in intellectual disputes over theism, but
in the end was simply transformed at a level deeper than conceptual
debate.[19] Roberta Bondi glimpsed a beautiful God while studying Hebrew
and reading Genesis and later rediscovered such a God in the early monas-
tics, until this "desirable" God completely transformed her childhood
faith.[20] I befriended "the darkness" only to discover later that it had an
existence and a name.

Though the essence of such conversion has to do with our deepest
Desire, this is not to say that religious conversion is always an emotional
experience. Lonergan refers to the feelings that are "easily aroused and
easily pass away." The "other-worldly falling in love" is not of this sort
(though any particular event may involve such emotional reactions) but
pertains instead to more deeply seated feelings:

> But there are in full consciousness feelings so deep and strong, especially
> when deliberately reinforced, that they channel attention, shape one's hori-
> zon, direct one's life. Here the supreme illustration is loving. A man or
> woman that falls in love is engaged in loving not only when attending to the
> beloved but at all times. Besides particular acts of loving, there is the prior
> state of being in love, and that prior state is, as it were, the fount of all one's
> actions. So mutual love is the intertwining of two lives. It transforms an "I"
> and "thou" into a "we" so intimate, so secure, so permanent, that each
> attends, imagines, thinks, plans, feels, speaks, acts in concern for both.[21]

The simple point here is that it is such love, the "we," not of a man and
woman (though this, too, can have powerful transformative effects) but of

a person with the Transcendent, that elicits redemption. And this is precisely because it is such a love, Desire with a transcendent focus, that energizes us to seek reintegration of our distorted living. Such love does not change everything at once, but it dismantles and abolishes our currently flawed horizons and sets up a new horizon in which the love of God transforms both our understanding and our choosing. This love becomes the ground out of which the insights of grace and the energy of willingness can and do emerge. This love is the embrace of God in which we have the courage to embrace travail. This love is grace as operative because it is a gift yet grace as cooperative because we can choose it or reject it. In choosing it, over and over, in whatever proportions, with myriad inadequacies, we are "saved," we are transformed into the "we" that is one more instance of God incarnate.[22]

Moral and intellectual conversions are further aspects involved in the working out of such salvation. *Moral conversion* is not the choosing of a specific lifestyle or a set of Christian behaviors but is a change in the very criterion by which we make our choices. As children we are trained to be good, and most often the reason for good behavior is the expectation of rewards and the avoidance of punishment. The pleasure/pain principle rules and though, at a certain age, pleasure and pain shift very subtly to be social rather than physical, the criterion remains the same.[23] Moral conversion is a move beyond this and involves both insight and choice. The insight is that not everything that feels good really is good, and that not all that hurts is truly bad for us. The choice "consists in opting for the truly good, even for value against satisfaction when value and satisfaction conflict." "Moral conversion changes the criterion of one's decisions and choices from satisfactions to values."[24]

Such conversion involves setting up new habits of decision making, developing the skills of discerning between urges toward satisfaction and desires oriented to self-transcendent values. It is a conversion because it is a radical shift in one's entire existential horizon. It is ongoing conversion because it never happens just once. One's previous ways of operating need to be scrutinized. The biases of one's community need to be discovered. One's own egoism in pursuing beauty, truth, honesty, health, will be unveiled over and over again, so that one discovers the deceptive subtleties of satisfaction.

These deceptive subtleties weave their way into our lives as victims and sinners. The distortions into which we are socialized, and our own choices to sabotage yearning, destroy value, and even despise its realization in others, have a certain pleasure and satisfaction about them. Even when such relationships or actions are hurtful to ourselves, there is a (false) peace in conforming to designated roles, an odd joy in being true to our victim status or our macho image. Moral conversion is the stark recognition that even such heavily loaded and morally sanctioned pleasures may be, in fact, not coextensive with true value. The deepest desires of our hearts may be reaching for something else, something more (w)holy human.

Such a possibility comes as a graced intervention. Still, however thrilling such a discovery may be, it comes with the choice to engage in a long journey of discernment. More significantly, it comes with the realization, overt or implicit, that to live a morally converted life means taking responsibility for one's own self, one's own moral agency. As Lonergan puts it: "So we move to the existential moment when we discover for ourselves that our choosing affects ourselves no less than the chosen or rejected objects, and that it is up to each of us to decide for himself what he is to make of himself."[25]

In a broken world this recognition and choice cannot be anything other than a choice for the cross. To live according to the truly good, even when value and satisfaction conflict, is necessarily to opt for resistance and surrender: resistance to the distortions of our interpersonal and intrapsychic lives, surrender to the grief of broken hopes and expectations. Such moral conversion, with its sacrificial implications, can hardly be sustainable without the undertow of transcendent love. In Christian terms, the experience of resurrection must precede, undergird, surround, and permeate the sacrificial aspects of moral conversion, lest moral conversion become either self-righteousness, on the one hand, or self-immolation, on the other.

Note that suffering is not itself one of the values one is choosing here. The radical shift in the criterion of our choices that is moral conversion is most essentially a choice for value and for new moral and affective habits. It means choosing truth, honesty, beauty, health, love, communion with God, and being willing to take whatever steps are necessary to pursue and create these values. Though pain, sacrifice, and the cross may be intimately entailed, these are not ends; they are by-products. Though moral conversion (and thus authentic resistance and surrender) involves *accepting* suffering, it does not make of suffering a criterion of true value. To do so simply reduces us again to the level of pleasure and pain as arbiters of the good, and it is precisely this reduction from which moral conversion liberates us.

Just as moral conversion is much more profound than living by a set of prescribed behaviors, so *intellectual conversion* is not merely an assent to a list of propositions. Rather, intellectual conversion is what I discussed earlier as the "discovery of discovery," the realization of one's own role in knowing. It is a shift in the way one understands knowing itself, not knowing as an academic topic, but knowing as a set of operations that I myself engage in everyday.[26]

For Lonergan, the core of intellectual conversion is a specific insight and judgment. He says:

> Intellectual conversion is a radical clarification and, consequently, the elimination of an exceedingly stubborn and misleading myth concerning reality, objectivity, and human knowledge. The myth is that knowing is like looking, that objectivity is seeing what is there to be seen and not seeing what is not there, and that the real is what is out there now to be looked at.[27]

In contrast to this myth, Lonergan insists:

> Knowing, accordingly, is not just seeing; it is experiencing, understanding, judging, and believing. The criteria of objectivity are not just the criteria of ocular vision; they are the compounded criteria of experiencing, of understanding, of judging, of believing. The reality known is not just looked at; it is given in experience, organized and extrapolated by understanding, posited by judgment and belief.[28]

Now the important point here is the existential shift that occurs with such a discovery. It involves recognizing that I, as a subject, participate in my knowing in ways that go beyond just looking, realizing that the criteria of truth and objectivity and authentic action lie within my own consciousness. While part of authentic knowing involves confirming insights with the evidence at hand, the *criteria* for knowing and deciding are implicitly operative in my very awareness. There are inherent in my human striving notions of truth, value, and authenticity. Such notions (not formulated categories or concepts) serve as the barometer of whether or not I am successfully grasping truth, understanding value, consistently acting on my value judgments. If I am trying to solve a puzzle, I am agitated until I "get it." Once I get it, I not only get it but I am aware that I have no further doubts. When I am trying to make a decision, I am restless until I hit upon the course of action that is clearly right. My body relaxes, my sense of conviction firms itself up, my conscience is at peace. I not only know what to choose; I realize that I know it, and the notion of value innate within me has found its mark.[29]

Thus, objectivity in knowing involves much more than merely seeing (or hearing).[30] Integrity in choosing is much more than complicit conformity. Both involve "authentic subjectivity." And authentic subjectivity is quite the opposite of the subjectivism that undergirds relativism. It is not a matter of thinking what one pleases or acting on certain values because they happen to follow *my* opinion. Rather, it involves a good deal of confirming that one's judgments are grounded in the evidence. But this confirmation is not merely a matter of looking, hearing, or—in the case of value—conforming to expectations. It is a matter of developing skill in determining when evidence is sufficient. It involves consistently following the inherent transcendental precepts: Be Attentive, Be Intelligent, Be Reasonable, Be Responsible. One attends to the evidence; one seeks to understand it; one confirms that one's theories and beliefs match the evidence at hand; one chooses to pursue one's questions of value, even if the answers may not be what one had hoped for.[31]

While this epistemological position may seem to be a matter merely for academic debate, in fact, intellectual conversion has powerful existential, communal, and political ramifications. To discover that one brings the criteria for discovery and choice to one's pursuits rather than merely responding to some "already out there now real" is to claim cognitive and moral agency. It is to declare oneself a dynamic, creative, and potentially self-transcendent human person. It is to insist that the eros of the human spirit is a part of one's being, and that authenticity, valor, dignity, and integrity lie not in conformity to some set of standards "out there" but in being true to oneself. This is an existential position to take, and it is so contrary to much of what common sense, philosophical theory, and even our own animal instinct tell us, that to make such a discovery and take such a position is nothing less than a conversion.

At the same time, such an intellectual conversion can involve a kind of *kenōsis* for those who have traditionally taken their speaking and knowing privileges for granted. To discover that the process of knowing is not just a matter of seeing clearly what is obviously the case, nor of constructing value by fiat, but of confirming one's views on reality in the evidence, of confirming and testing one's potential decisions through careful discernment, is to admit the limitations of one's cognitive and moral imperialism. One may speak with confidence from a position of power, but one's truths are not true because one has authority; they are true if the evidence confirms one's claims. One may choose specific actions with certainty, but such actions are not good merely because one declares them so. To admit that truth and value are not a matter of the "already out there now real" nor of arbitrary preference is to recognize that the criteria for objectivity and integrity are innate within human consciousness. If this is the case, then to prejudge others' views because of their social class, race, or gender is to deny them their very humanity.[32]

Intellectual conversion thus overlaps with moral conversion: Will one, upon discovering that the criteria of truth and value lie in one's own exigencies to be attentive, intelligent, reasonable, and responsible, commit oneself to such imperatives? Or will one ask only the questions that suit one's purposes, submit to innate criteria of truth and value up to a point and then abandon the quest in favor of satisfying illusions? To follow up on the implications of intellectual conversion will demand the sacrifice recognized and chosen in moral conversion, and this sacrifice can only be sustained when it is held in love by some ultimate concern. This mutual influence occurs in the opposite direction as well: to fall in love with the Divine transforms one's knowing and choosing, so that one gains the courage to question epistemological assumptions, to challenge privileged cognitive powers, to claim oneself as a discoverer.[33]

All three of these radical shifts in horizon are thus intertwined and mutually dependent. But there is yet another dimension. We are not disembodied intellects nor ephemeral spirits. Our understanding, choosing, and loving are grounded in organic biochemical systems. All of our knowing and doing is permeated by the powerful force of the sensitive psyche. Even intellectual conversion involves the discovering of the pure *desire* to know, and the discovery of discovery conveys a passion to follow its imperatives. Thus, an entire nexus of psychic images and energies comes into play in conversion of any sort.

Robert M. Doran has extended Lonergan's conversion triad to include psychic conversion.[34] *Psychic conversion* has to do with the boundary between what is conscious (but not necessarily known) and what is unconscious. Consciousness involves the entire arena of experience to which we are self-present but to which we have not necessarily attended, unobjectified experience that is *conscious* but not *known*.[35] The sensitive psyche is this complex flow of experiential consciousness, whether drawn up into higher integrations of knowing (through attention, understanding, and judging) or not. It is the "polyphony, or, as the case may be, the cacophony, of our sensations, memories, images, emotions, conations, associations, bodily movements, and spontaneous intersubjective responses" and the symbolic integrations of these that emerge in active imagining or in dreaming.[36] The unconscious involves the manifold of neural transmitters of which we are entirely unaware. It is energy at its physical, chemical, and biological levels. "The unconscious is all energy that is not present to itself, all energy save that which becomes psychic energy in animal and human consciousness"[37] As such, the unconscious needs "the higher integration of at least the sensitive consciousness of the psyche to attain an elemental luminosity."[38]

Even at its most elemental levels, the energy of the unconsciousness is oriented, as is our knowing, toward synthesis and integration. The psyche serves to pattern the unconscious neural manifold into images, symbols, feeling complexes, and the like, which have an "elemental luminosity" that, in turn, is oriented toward the further integration of knowing and acting. In the optimal situation, such sensitive experience provides the energy of willingness as well as the images and symbols that serve as catalysts for insight and action. This optimal process is hampered, like all our living, on two counts. First, there is our finitude, which simply means that not all our unconscious energy can be catalyzed into images or symbols that are then attended to or otherwise used in the integration of knowing and doing. Second, there is the fact of sin, in which damage done to us through interpersonal relations, often the result of generations of power differentials and unjust economic arrangements, reaches even to the level of what is allowed to emerge into consciousness and what remains hidden. In other words, the damage of sin reaches to the very depths of the unconscious, through repressing the very energy that could supply us with the images, insights, desires, and passions we need in order to flourish. Not only are our understanding and choosing distorted; our elemental experience itself is tainted.

The problem of moral impotence rears its ugly head again: in order to reorder our lives we need access to the power of willingness, the attraction of transcendent love fulfilled. In order to grasp the changes that must be made in our lives, we need images that will yield the requisite insights. But unless we have the antecedent willingness to seek such images and insights, unless our passion for the Other is released from fear, unless the requisite questions are free to emerge, the necessary energies will lie dormant beyond our conscious awareness.

Psychic conversion is another instance of the intervention of grace. In this case it is an intervention that changes the relationship between the conscious and the unconscious, the sensitive psyche with its rich resources and the merely biochemical energy of the neural manifold:

> The process of liberation from oppressive patterns of experience is ineffec-
> tual unless feelings are touched and stirred by the movement that brings
> healing insight. For the psyche is the locus of the embodiment of inquiry,
> insight, reflection, judgment, deliberation, and decision, just as it is the

place of the embodiment of the oppressive forces from which we can be
released by such intentional operations. . . . To the extent that our psychic
sensitivity is victimized by oppression, the embodiment of the spirit is con-
fined to an animal habitat, fastened on survival, intent on the satisfaction of
its own deprivation of the *humanum*. To the extent that the psyche is
released from oppressive patterns, the embodiment of the spirit is released
into a human world, and indeed ultimately into the universe of being. A true
healing of the psyche would dissolve the affective wounds that block sustained self-transcendence; it would give the freedom required to engage in
the constitution of the human world.[39]

The shift that takes place in psychic conversion is a change in the way
the gatekeeper between consciousness and the unconscious operates.
"Psychic conversion is a transformation of the psychic component of what
Freud calls 'the censor' from a repressive to a constructive agency in a person's development."[40] Like any other conversion, the transformation of
one's censor comes as an intervention of grace, often as the effect of
falling in love, of religious conversion. Such falling in love not only trans-
values one's values and transforms one's knowing; it reorients the spontaneous patterns of one's psyche. It reorders one's emotive habits toward
faith, hope, and love, and these become concretely embodied in a new pat-
terning of neural energy. Where before one lived by reactive impulse, now
the possibility of living by intentionally chosen values opens up.

In psychic conversion, "the criterion of one's responses is shifting from
impulse to value."[41] Impulses are connected to the satisfactions that currently drive one's decisions. Values move one toward self-transcendence,
and since values are apprehended in feelings, the liberation of one's feelings means the freedom of new discernment. The shift from impulse and
repression means that psychic energy is released in the interests of growth,
healing, development. But just as grace is operative in its intervention
through love, so grace is cooperative through human choice. There is no
magic here that gets one off the hook of responsibility for self. The most
important opportunity that opens up with the liberation of desire is the
opportunity to face and "own" one's own psychic wounds. This will involve
"compassionate but responsible negotiation of one's rigidified energic
psychic complexes that are keeping one from being an incarnation of personal value" and "assuming responsibility for one's own emotional darkness, and for the havoc that it wreaks on oneself and others."[42]

Embracing travail cannot be avoided here. The radical conversion of
one's censor from the status quo to a new and constructive agent, while liberating, also means befriending one's shadow side, "assuming responsi-

bility for one's own emotional darkness." Choosing value over mere satisfaction—moral conversion, cooperative grace—will here mean sacrifice in
the sense of facing one's demons, confronting the old and distorted patterns which need to be reordered. The intellectual conversion that involves
recognizing oneself as a cognitive and moral agent will imply an active
seeking of graced insights, even when such insights are into a network of
great pain—either the pain of victimization or the pain of repentance or,
most likely, both. The comfort of the psychic status quo must be surrendered, the superego must yield to an intentional conscience, and guilt
must give way to Desire. The moral evils embedded in the distorted cycles
of one's affectivity can be overcome but only by courageous resistance,
only through "the experience of withstanding the potential destructive-
ness of precisely the same kind of manifestation of evil that previously, and
perhaps very early in one's life, was the source of one's most crippling victimization."[43]

THE LAW OF THE CROSS

We have been working with a concept of the human person as dynamically
oriented toward movement beyond herself, an orientation manifested in
questioning, in seeking to make sense of experience, in trying to understand it correctly, and in longing to know and create value. This dynamism
incorporates the grounds for determining its own fulfillment: inherent
notions of truth, value, and authentic love serve as measures of when and
if our questions have been adequately answered, our decisions properly
resolved, our Desire fully met.

Still, we noted that this transcendentally oriented dynamism comes
embodied in creaturely existence. Thus, the challenge of human authenticity is to discern and live within the creative tension of limitation and
transcendence. Basic sin is the willful refusal to accept such a tension,
involving a distortion on either the side of too much transcendence
(pride) or too much limitation (self-denigration). The effects of this basic
sin are cumulative, perpetuating alienation at the personal, social, and cultural levels. Further, this intertwined alienation mires us in vicious cycles,
so that our attempts to right unbalanced relations simply skew the dialectic in the opposite direction. We are stuck, and the cycles of victim and
perpetrator, as they operate within us and between us, are destined to
reproduce themselves unless some other force intervenes.

Grace is just such an intervention, and it manifests itself quite concretely in our lives at the level of both understanding and will. Now let me make clear what was implicit in earlier sections of the book. Grace, as manifested in conversion, breaks the cycle of alienation and restores the distorted dialectic of our living, not from within the distortion but by drawing our minds and hearts to a new level ("elevating grace"). One gains a higher viewpoint, from which the previously lived alienation makes sense in a completely new and encompassing way. And though there remain many further questions or elements to be incorporated, the new overarching set of meanings and values provides a framework from which to engage in further inquiry. At the level of will, new habits of love form schemes of recurrence that incorporate earlier affective cycles. Just as the plant is a higher integration of chemical processes, a unity dependent on yet distinct from such processes, so transcendent love draws all our feelings, thoughts, and aspirations into a new synthesis.

The implications of this are manifold. It confirms my earlier point that the solution to the problem of evil involves a "third" element; it is not complete at the level of human aspiration alone. Human aspirations are so distorted that the only way out of alienation is a higher synthesis, a higher synthesis that integrates rather than destroys the native tension between limitation and transcendence.

Further, this latter tension, between our finitude and the unrestricted reach of our spirits, involves a *complementary* tension. This means that the opposing elements (limitation and transcendence) are not ultimately contradictory. This is a dialectic of "both/and" rather than a relation of "either/or." The tension is resolved through balance and integration, created by the higher synthesis of transcendent love, rather than by one tendency defeating the other.

There is another kind of dialectic in which the two factors *are* ultimately contradictory. This is the "either/or" kind of relationship in which the two elements cannot be reconciled. Either something is true or it is false. Either it is the right thing to do or it is not. There is no integration of true and false, right and wrong here: one must exclude the other. The Christian tradition has viewed good and evil in this light: good contradicts evil, is ultimately opposed to it. The tension between the two is resolved not through balance but by one overcoming the other.[44]

What is important here, even essential, is to recognize that the tension in human living between limitation and transcendence is *not* this latter type of oppositional relationship. In other words, the solution to the problem of human alienation *does not lie* in the victory of the erotic spirit over embodied existence. *Neither* does it lie in the *kenōsis* of human aspiration, in denying one's transcendent orientation. Rather, it lies in integrating limitation and transcendence within the synthesis of Divine relationship.

Certain variations of Christian theory and practice have foundered on precisely this point. The mind/body dualism, the Hellenistic insight incorporated into much of Christian theology long ago, was correct in its grasp of the duality of human existence. It was wrong in taking this duality to be an opposition of contradictories rather than a complementarity to be integrated. Consequently, salvation and spiritual integrity came to be seen as a matter of the spirit *conquering* bodily appetites. To the degree that men were associated with mind and women with reproduction, this erroneous grasp of the nature of this dialectic had disastrous consequences. At the same time, the notion of sin as pride, as too much aspiration, held sway. Women got it on both accounts: too "bodily" to be rational, their defeat was symbolically aligned with the solution to the problem of sin, while any evidence of rationality or transcendent spirit was met with admonitions to silence and humility.[45]

The distinction between a complementary dialectic and a dialectic of ultimate contradiction, and the insistence that the tension between finitude and transcendence is the former, provides tremendous potential for understanding redemption. Redemption involves the higher *integration* of embodied spirit, not the *dissolution* of this reality. To fail to recognize this is to remain within the system of domination that so badly needs to be transcended. To fail to recognize this is to perpetuate the oppressive suffering that so badly needs to be transformed. To propose a solution to the problem of evil that fails to acknowledge the higher synthesis needed, that seeks a solution through compensating one side with the other, through "defeating" the imbalance, will only perpetuate the distortion that must be reordered. Victimizing perpetrators so that they will "know what it feels like" or giving victims power to conquer their oppressors resolves nothing.

Note, further, that though the tension between bodily existence and spiritual orientation is a complementary one, there *is* a purely oppositional dialectic involved in the process of transformation. There is an either/or relationship, but it lies not between limitation and transcendence but *between the integral balancing of these and their distortion*. These two—balance and distortion—should not, indeed cannot, exist together. Health, goodness, (w)holiness, lie in the integrity of a creative, taut balance. Pathology, alienation, brokenness, lie in a skewing of the balance. And the integral living that is a healthy tension is not possible without a higher integration, the transformation of one's knowing and willing through transcendent love. In this view, the either/or choice lies between such a higher synthesis and its rejection. And since the higher integration is a result not of our aspiration and achievement but of God's prevenient love and God's gifts of grace, the contradiction involved in transformation lies between our acceptance and our rejection of such gifts.[46]

Still, there is another element here, and this is where the stumbling block of the cross enters in. As I outlined the various conversions occasioned by grace it became apparent that, though liberating, each conversion has its challenge, the place where healing encounters unavoidable pain or sacrifice. This characteristic of conversion has its source in the very nature of human alienation and its solution. Because the distortion of alienation permeates all levels of human living and because not everyone has embarked on the journey of healing and communion with the Divine, because those who have are still growing, living an integrated life will necessarily seem counterintuitive to many observers. To live an integral life, whether nascent or mature, will be countercultural. It may even be countercultural to the point where others consider this integral living the source of evil itself, as was the case with Jesus, and has been the case repeatedly, from Gandhi to Martin Luther King to Yitzhak Rabin. To live out of the higher integration of love for the transcendent will be heralded by a few but despised by many. In sum, in an alienated world, to receive and cooperate with the grace of God necessarily involves embracing consequent suffering.

To put this another way, there is an *apparent* intelligibility to solving the problem of evil by equalizing one distortion with another. It *seems* obvious that if some group has too much power, the antidote is to wrest power away from them and grant it to another. It *seems* clear that if one's psychic pathology lies in having had to repress anger, then healing will come through expressing such anger. Surely social injustice needs to be countered with the establishment of right relations. One sin needs to be redressed with an equivalent punishment. All of these things are true to the extent that such righting of imbalances *emerges from* or is *the occasion for* the higher viewpoint of love. They are not true to the extent that they are understood to be the *means by which* integral balance is established. In essence, the solution to the problem of evil lies in love, not mere retributive, or even distributive, justice. Retribution and right relations may *flow* from redemptive love or *be its catalyst,* but such kinds of justice *alone* are not redemptive.

This very important point is related to the nature of the intelligibility involved in solving the problem of evil. To counter evil with evil, as in the apparent intelligibility of the above discussion, presumes that evil itself makes sense, that if one only thought long and hard enough one could have the "Aha!" that would clear up all one's confusion. But the fact of the matter is that evil is radically unintelligible. Basic sin, the choices at the root of human evil, simply make no sense:

> What is basic sin? It is the irrational. Why does it occur? If there were a reason, it would not be sin. There may be excuses; there may be extenuating circumstances; but there cannot be a reason, for basic sin consists, not in yielding to reasons and reasonableness, but in failing to yield to them; it consists not in inadvertent failure but in advertence to and in acknowledgement of obligation that nonetheless is not followed by reasonable response.[47]

The consequences of basic sin are the moral evils that result, which heighten the possibility of further basic sins. And while one may be able to trace certain consequences back to their source in a specific act, cycles of retaliation and revenge, which *seem* to be making "sense" out of the "nonsense" of the situation, so complicate it that such moral archaeology yields limited results. In fact, there is no getting back to the root of evil, no making sense of it, since even were one to find the original basic sin it itself would make no sense. Instead, we live always with a "social surd," a portion of lived existence that is simply unintelligible.[48]

Still, to recognize this unintelligibility is a gain, since to force the non-sense of basic sin into an intelligible framework is nothing other than rationalization, that is, making reason where there is none. To grant intelligibility to evil when there is none is a grave error, not only in the intellectual realm but in lived reality. For such "sense" when there is none, so far from solving the problem of evil, only perpetuates its craziness. It is far better to name the non-sense, to acknowledge the surd, to embrace the pain of evil's unintelligibility.[49]

Such acknowledgment is an instance of what Lonergan calls an inverse insight. This is an "Aha!" that opens up new horizons, but does so precisely by discovering that the intelligibility one was seeking is simply not there to be discovered. Lonergan contrasts *direct insight* (the kind we have been referring to all along) with *inverse insight*:

> While direct insight grasps the point, or sees the solution, or comes to know the reason, inverse insight apprehends that in some fashion the point is that there is no point, or that the solution is to deny a solution, or that the reason is that the rationality of the real admits distinctions and qualifications.[50]

Imagine trying to solve a puzzle in a puzzle book, perhaps for weeks and months, only to contact the publishing company and be told that the puzzle was insoluble. Imagine being told a joke, and not being able to get it, until everyone around you admits that there is no punch line, that they were all laughing in order to fool you.[51] We *presume* intelligibility, which is why the inverse insight is so startlingly strange. Yet, with regard to the problem of evil, this startling strangeness, this discovery of unintelligibility, can be the catalyst for a different intelligibility, a "sense" that goes beyond mere logic.[52]

For what the Christian tradition claims and embodies is the conviction that there *is* an intelligibility to evil and its suffering consequences. But such sense lies not in the acts and their consequences themselves but in the higher viewpoint that emerges from conversion. Such a higher viewpoint arises precisely as the insight that comes with an other-worldly falling in love. This higher viewpoint is what Pascal meant when he said that "the heart has reasons which reason knows not." This is the intelligibility of God's solution to the problem of evil, the law of the cross, according to which "the divine wisdom ordained and the divine goodness willed, not to take away the evils of the human race through an exercise of power, but to convert those evils into a certain highest good."[53] The solution to the problem of evil is not to cancel out evil by destroying the human freedom that makes evil possible, but to appeal to that freedom in love, and so offer the possibility that love will make of evil the occasion of goodness.

Thus, what I have called the insights of grace will necessarily involve both the inverse insights into the unintelligibility of the social surd and the higher viewpoints by which love grasps' meaning anyway. And the shift in our willingness will necessarily engage us in (authentic) surrender and resistance. With regard to the solution to the problem of evil, Lonergan comments:

> The dialectical method of intellect consists in grasping that the social surd neither is intelligible nor is to be treated as intelligible. The corresponding dialectical attitude of will is to return good for evil. For it is only inasmuch as men [sic] are willing to meet evil with good, to love their enemies, to pray for those that persecute and calumniate them, that the social surd is a potential good. It follows that love of God above all and in all so embraces the order of the universe as to love all men [sic] with a self-sacrificing love.[54]

Let me highlight once again the provisional nature of this solution. While I have presented a resolution of the human dilemma as a participation in the higher viewpoint of divine love, such a solution only provides new conditions for the possibility of healing. It leaves human freedom intact, and this means that healing and forgiveness occur as a matter of probability, not as a matter of direct causality. An ethic of control, precisely because it seeks intelligibility and resolution *within* the tension between limitation and transcendence instead of *beyond* it, seeks to cancel out evil in a definitive and determinative way. This ethic necessarily ends up in coercion, in the "final solution" that eliminates (some peoples') human freedom. The higher synthesis that I insist is constitutive of the resolution of evil leaves human freedom intact, and, precisely because it does so, it is an ethic of risk.[55] It is a provisional solution in the sense that it merely shifts probabilities, it sets conditions that increase the possibility of authentic living. It is permanent, not in the sense that evil will no longer be operative, but in that the conditions of its transformation are forever available.[56]

Epilogue

Redemption Revisited

O N A BRILLIANT MORNING IN LATE SUMMER I was heading down a highway in northern Ontario. The sky was cloudless, the woods glowed with a multitude of greens, there was already a touch of fall in the air. We passed shimmering lakes, saw wisps of color on far shores, felt bits of breeze hinting at the woolly wildness farther out on the open water. I had just picked up my daughter after her week at camp—a moderately evangelical camp that combined the best of nature, fun, and faith—and we were headed home to face her rite of passage into middle school.

Carolyn had had a wonderful week. I heard in graphic detail about each tent-mate, rated on a scale of "great," "okay," and "a little bit weird." She recounted the high qualities of her counselor, Mozzy, and the odd words she used. (She was from Zimbabwe; "mozzy," apparently, is short for "mosquito.") The food had been great, and I got a blow by blow of the evening adventure games, all involving counselors named Hyena, Pickles, Froggy, and the like. There had been Bible studies each morning and quiet time each afternoon. She had learned to flip a canoe, right it, and empty it. The devotional music involved a five-piece electric band with a sound system any recording studio might envy: a far cry from the "Kum Bah Yah" of my camper days. Then came the bomb: "I just don't get the part about Jesus dying for our sins. What does that mean?"

I was rendered speechless. It had been eleven and a half years since that freezing February night when Carolyn's entrance into the world had revealed to me the coincidence of death and birth, pain and rejoicing. Years of explaining, refining, reexamining the cross for and with students had intervened. I had, after all, just spent two years trying to get it straightened out in book form. Eighty thousand words later, with a publishing contract in hand, I had no idea what to say to this simple, innocent question.

151

As the highway descended from the Haliburton highlands, we caught a glimpse of Lake Ontario on the horizon. I took a stab at sin and alienation from God, others, the earth. I explained that some people in the past had thought of it as a debt we owed to God, or that we deserved death because of our sin, and that Jesus had suffered the punishment in our place. The whole thing sounded absurd as I recounted it to a young girl on the verge of womanhood, at the edge of the third millennium. We managed the complicated traffic patterns around Toronto and then rode along beside the brilliant great lake waters. I began talking about hurt and brokenness and how we could be healed by befriending the Risen Jesus and participating in his story today. This, however, still didn't take care of the "dying for us" part. By the time we crossed the voluminous, fuming water of Lake Erie funneling into the narrow Niagara River, crossing the Peace Bridge into the United States, I had just about expended my repertoire. It *all* sounded pretty much like nonsense, and I couldn't make out whether the silence from the passenger seat was meditative pondering or bored dismissal. I thought of Thomas Aquinas who, at the end of his career, disclaimed his mighty works as nothing but straw.

It will be years, if ever, before I know whether anything I said stuck with my daughter. Unfortunately, it will only make more sense to her when and as pain becomes a companion: suffering will be the better teacher. Still, this effort to explain "Jesus dying for our sins" humbles me as I come to the conclusion of my task here. In the end, I don't have a lot to say, except to finish with a few hints as to how my exploration in this book might affect the way we think about the nature of redemption, albeit in language that my eleven-year-old daughter would undoubtedly not understand.

The divine solution to the problem of evil consists of a series of ironic reversals, and these are imaged in myriad ways in the New Testament, as the antitheses between the old law and the new covenant, the first and second Adam, the old man and the new.[1] But the prime symbol of this ironic solution is not only a symbol but an event: the life, death, and resurrection of the incarnate divine one, Jesus. The coming of Jesus signals God's offering of incarnate love as the catalyst for the liberation of human desire. The death of Jesus—accepted by Jesus in union with God's will—indicates God's unwillingness to solve the problem of evil through a system of domination, circumventing human freedom. The resurrection of Jesus reveals that evil can be transformed, that suffering can have meaning, that the human condition need not be mired in alienation.

Thus, Christians claim that the inner word of God's solution to the problem of evil has been quite concretely manifested in history. The outer word of the resolution of evil is nothing other than Jesus Christ himself, the Word of God made incarnate.[2] Jesus' life, death, and resurrection serve as God's act of communication to human persons about their situation:

> The redemption is the outstanding expression of God to man [sic]. . . . We express ourselves, we communicate, through the flesh, through words and gestures, the unnoticed movements of the countenance, pauses, all the manners in which, as Newman says, "cor ad cor loquitur," the heart speaks unto the heart. And the incarnation and the redemption are the supreme instance of God communicating to us in this life. In heaven we shall know as we are known, but now our chief means of knowing God is through the fact of the incarnation and the act of redemption.[3]

The task of theology is to mediate this communication to the world. The authors of the New Testament interpreted this communication in Jesus with images and ideas available in their contexts: reign of God, body of Christ, sacrifice, ransom, and so on. Later generations expanded these and developed other catalysts, such as the deal made between God and the devil (Origen) or the shift to systematic reflection which introduced the notion of satisfaction (Anselm). Theologians today work in a host of contexts, with an endless variety of cultural worlds, meanings, and values into which the gospel must be translated. Pastors, teachers, academics, lay workers, all have the task of making sense of the core of Christian truth—God's meaning in sending Jesus, permitting his death, and raising him from the dead—to the communities in which they live. Contemporary theologians can aid this work by articulating redemption in a way that will endorse the healing elements already at work in a certain situation as well as critique the elements that distort human flourishing.

The task of Christians is to hear the good news, not only to hear it but to bask in its meaning. And since the means of communication is the incarnation of God himself, to receive this communication is to participate in a relationship, to abide in communion with the triune God, thereby allowing the meaning of God's communication to unfold.

There are two moments in the receiving of this communication. The first is to discover oneself in the narrative. Like any good story, the Christian story is only effective if it draws the hearer in, if one can identify with it. So God's communication is effective when the (potential) believer discovers that this story is not just about a man who lived years ago but is also about herself. The resurrection is central here because the claim of the story is that Jesus is risen, alive, and reigning, very much still present in the midst of his followers. So to discover oneself in this story is not to enjoy and identify with characters of a by-gone age (though it may be that as well) but to enter into an ongoing and current narrative.

Thus, the second moment in understanding God's communication in Jesus is to choose to participate in the narrative itself. Not only does one discover oneself in the story, not only does one discover that the story continues; one opts to help create the ongoing tale. Here one moves from identifying with Jesus to imitating Jesus. And through this imitation one becomes an originator of value, one becomes an agent of God's communication, a co-creator in the redemptive action of God in the world.

My work here has added some nuance to these two moments. First, I have maintained that discovering oneself in Jesus involves grasping very concretely the experience of being crucified and of crucifying. One discovers in the Jesus story one's own wounds and, with exaltation as well as fear, sees that these wounds have been and can be healed. One sees oneself as willing to crucify the Lord of glory—as having in fact sabotaged one's own Self and destroyed others in the process—while joyfully recognizing that such sabotaging can be redressed, overlooked, forgiven.

The corollary to this is that choosing to follow Jesus means embracing pain, choosing to love, forgiving others, letting go of justice as revenge. So one becomes an agent of God's communication, an architect of salvation, through resistance and surrender. Such resistance and surrender require a great deal of discernment and no small measure of resurrection love. Imitation of Jesus is not sweetness and light. Nor is it masochism. It involves choosing to be a Self oriented to God and abiding in God's love in a way that courageously confronts evil as woundedness and evil as sin.

In addition, I have insisted that the two moments are intimately connected. In order to imitate Jesus authentically one needs to have discovered oneself in Jesus. In order to fully understand oneself in the Jesus story, one needs to become an author of the story, to imitate Jesus, to undertake the resistance and surrender that will make one not only a recipient of salvation but an agent of salvation.

Finally, the demand for a new theology of redemption carries with it the irony that the agent of evil, by which many have been wounded, is often none other than the Christian church itself. Though we supposedly live in a Post-Christian era, most who call themselves Christian in the Western world have not *discovered* the Christian narrative but have been *socialized* into it. And this socialization itself has often involved very destructive elements, particularly for the self-understanding of women and those on the underside of socio-cultural power. To enter into the Jesus story means *re*-discovering its meaning, means identifying with the risen Jesus as he grieves with yet forgives his church. It means authentic resistance and surrender with regard to one's own religious tradition, one's own community of faith.

Furthermore, my attempt to make sense of this process of redemption has led me to discover several basic parameters within which Jesus' "dying for us" must be interpreted. First, to the degree that Jesus' death on the cross is understood as a sacrifice, as vicarious satisfaction, as surrender to suffering, this is not to be understood as capitulation to the "limitation" pole of existence. Jesus did not, in accepting his fate, yield his dynamic humanity. To the contrary, he withstood evil by embracing suffering without giving up his Self-in-divine-relation, by claiming his identity as a transcendently oriented human being. Likewise, our imitation of Jesus, to the degree that it involves sacrifice, should not be interpreted as a call to deny the upward thrust of our desire to know, create, and love. Instead, it will involve the power of the discovery of discovery, of claiming our dignity as knowers and co-creators of a meaningful world.

Second, from the higher viewpoint of religious love it is clear that what Jesus chose was love, not suffering. It is essential to grasp that Jesus chose suffering only as the indirect consequence of choosing to be himself, to fulfill his mission, to love the world. Suffering, sacrifice, ransom, were not objects of choice. Jesus *accepted* suffering, he did not *choose* it. Likewise, our entrance into the Jesus narrative may result in suffering, but what we choose is positive, to be in communion with the Risen Lord, the Creator, and the Spirit, to love the world with their love. Grief, sorrow, and suffering are intimately intertwined with this love for a broken world, but we are called to *choose* love and *accept* suffering.

Third, this makes of God something quite other than a divine child abuser. God did not choose Jesus' death as his solution to an evil world. Rather, God lovingly created human freedom. And in creating humans with freedom he permitted evil. God's solution to evil was then consistent with the world God created. The solution leaves human freedom intact; it redresses evil through communicating love rather than by destroying freedom. What God chose in solving the problem of evil was love, communication, relationship. What God accepted was that in a world of human freedom this incarnate communication of love could be rejected.

Fourth, however one interprets Christ's work, one cannot make sense of the cross without the resurrection. Without resurrection love, the suffering of the cross is entirely meaningless. It is only within the higher viewpoint of resurrection that one can grasp the solution to the problem of evil. And just as Jesus' death is only intelligible in light of the resurrection, so our suffering is only meaningful within the purview of religious conversion. The corollary is, of course, that any suffering is *potentially* meaning-full, even though it may be experienced as meaning-less.

Fifth, the intelligibility of redemption, of Christ's work, involves a dramatic reversal rather than a logical deduction. It is a reversal of expectations, and therefore to expect some logical coherence is to be mistaken. To discover the meaning-full-ness of Christ's death and resurrection is to have the inverse insight that evil is radically unintelligible and, therefore, that the meaning of Christ's redemptive work is not to be grasped at the level of logical coherence. To try to interpret redemption without this element of reversal, without the inverse insight, is to make of redemption a transaction of retributive justice and thus strip it of its power, reduce it to an ethic of control.

Sixth, this is why the transaction models of redemption simply don't work. If sacrifice is interpreted as an appeasement of the gods, if redemption is seen as a financial transaction, if vicarious satisfaction means satisfying God's demands for justice, if merit means earning a just reward, then Christian theology has got it all wrong. It is possible that these metaphors have retrievable centers by which they may have been and may continue to be catalysts for conversion. But to frame the issue as that of how God's demand for justice was met is to miss the point altogether. God didn't want retribution; God wanted and wants love and communion with (w)holy human persons. Justice—as in the domination system—is, so far from being the solution, at the root of the problem.

Seventh, what God communicated and continues to communicate in Jesus' death and resurrection is not justice as retribution but love and sorrow:

> The sufferings of Christ, then, are the expression of God's detestation of sin. They are also the expression of Christ's own detestation of sin. . . . His love of us did not in the least, and could not, lessen his detestation of sin. On the contrary, his detestation of sin, combined with his love of us, caused in him the greatest sorrow that we had sinned. He was sorry for our sins because of his love for us in a manner that we can hardly be sorry, because we do not possess his knowledge of God and his love of God. Christ, the Son of God, because of his perfect knowledge and love of his Father, could detest sin as sin is to be detested, and because of his love of us could feel a sorrow such as no sorrow can equal. It is the combination of love and deepest regret involved in a single situation and about the same persons.[4]

Thus, our participation in resistance and surrender, our embracing of travail, will emerge with love and grief. This is good grief, which is utterly distinct from the grief of meaningless suffering, and quite far from the guilt that an ethic of control (and much of Christian practice) would foster.

Finally, understanding redemption must take account of "mystery." This is not mystery as a problem to be solved but mystery as signifying the vast reach of our desire and the limited scope of our understanding and action. We may make sense of Christ's work, we may even grasp that this "sense" must incorporate the dramatic reversal that recognizes the ultimate "non-sense" of evil. But no matter how well theologians mediate such intelligibility to the world, and no matter how deeply Christians embed themselves in the Jesus narrative, the higher viewpoint will always be beyond our grasp. For this reason we abide in hope, we have faith, we live with the unseen in confidence. Theology gives way to liturgy, poetry, symbol, dance, artwork, prayer, meditation, song. As the beloved English hymn reveals, "My Song Is Love Unknown":

> My song is love unknown,
>   My Savior's love for me:
> love to the loveless shown,
>   that they might lovely be.
>   Oh who am I,
>   that for my sake,
>   my Lord should take
>   frail flesh, and die?
>
> Here might I stay and sing,
>   No story so divine:
> never was love, dear King,
>   never was grief like thine.
>   This is my friend,
>   in whose sweet praise
>   I all my days
>   could gladly spend.[5]

Notes

CHAPTER 1
ENTERING THE DRAMA: CRUCIFIED AND CRUCIFIERS

1. Carlos Fuentes, *The Good Conscience*, trans. Sam Hileman (New York: Noonday, 1961). See also Anne E. Patrick, "Christian Ethics and 'The Good Conscience': Building a Course around a Novel," in *The Annual of the Society of Christian Ethics*, ed. Diane Yeager (Washington, D.C.: Georgetown University Press, 1988), 249–53.

2. Sebastian Moore, *The Crucified Is No Stranger* (London: Darton, Longman, & Todd, 1977).

3. Now published under the same title in *Église et Théologie* 28 (1997): 245–63.

4. See M. Shawn Copeland, "'Wading Through Many Sorrows': Toward a Theology of Suffering in Womanist Perspective," in *A Troubling in My Soul: Womanist Perspectives on Evil and Suffering*, ed. Emilie Townes (Maryknoll, N.Y.: Orbis Books, 1993), 109–29.

5. Maya Angelou, *I Know Why the Caged Bird Sings* (New York: Bantam Books, 1969).

6. See further discussion below, in chapter 3.

7. Joanne C. Brown and Carole R. Bohn, eds., *Christianity, Patriarchy, and Abuse: A Feminist Critique* (Cleveland, Oh.: Pilgrim Press, 1989).

8. Roberta C. Bondi, *Memories of God: Theological Reflections on a Life* (Nashville: Abingdon Press, 1995), 113.

9. Valerie Saiving Goldstein first articulated the insight that the understanding of sin as pride arose from a male-dominated tradition in which "separation" is problematic and "connection" (reconciliation) is the solution. She presented the notion that, for women, pride is not the primary sin; rather self-deprecation is. Judith Plaskow picked up this theme and used it to analyze the theologies of Reinhold Niebuhr and Paul Tillich, which she concluded both suffer from this one-sided understanding of sin as pride. This critique is now commonplace in feminist discussions of sin. See Valerie Saiving Goldstein, "The Human Situation: A Femi-

158

nine View," *Journal of Religion* 40 (1960): 100–112; and Judith Plaskow, *Sex, Sin, and Grace* (Lanham, Md.: University Press of America, 1980). Two clear overviews of this position can be found in Sally Alsford, "Sin and Atonement in Feminist Perspective," in *Atonement Today*, ed. John Goldingay (London: SPCK, 1995), 148–65; and William J. Cahoy, "One Species or Two? Kierkegaard's Anthropology and The Feminist Critique of the Concept of Sin," *Modern Theology* 11 (1995): 429–54.

The term "the underside of history" comes from Gustavo Gutiérrez. See *The Power of the Poor in History*, trans. Robert Barr (Maryknoll, N.Y.: Orbis Books, 1983), esp. 192, 169–234. Gutiérrez uses the term to refer to the poor in Latin America. I use it in this book to refer to all who have been left out of the telling of history, those whose voice has not been allowed a public forum. See chapter 4 below.

10. Moore, *Crucified*, x. Here, and in other direct quotations from the book, I retain his exclusive language. In addition, Moore relies heavily on a Jungian analysis of the human person, speaking in terms of *persona, ego*, and *self*. While I continue to employ some of this terminology, I do so without any claim to Jungian orthodoxy. Rather, I understand the concept of Self to mean that we live within a tension between who we are and who we could become, between the many roles we play in life and the larger mystery of our whole person. This "whole," this "other who is ourself," finds both its origins and its orientation in God. It is what previous generations have called the *imago Dei*, a Latin label for the insight that even as finite creatures we have a divine dimension, one which, ironically, we tend to destroy. This spiritual mystery of who we are is a mystery of communion: we are created by community and called into union with the divine Selves as well as with a communion of saints. In sum, the Self as I understand it is not a psychological construct nor a "thing" somewhere inside of us. It is, rather, the recognition that "what you see is not what you get," that whoever we think we are, there is more: an infinite "more" that finds its full flourishing only in the embrace of God's community of love.

On the notion of persons being created in the image of God, and for a feminist critique and retrieval of this notion, see Mary C. Hilkert, "Cry Beloved Image: Rethinking the Image of God," in *In the Embrace of God: Feminist Approaches to Theological Anthropology*, ed. Ann O'Hara Graff (Maryknoll, N.Y.: Orbis Books, 1995), 190–205.

11. Moore, *Crucified*, x.

12. Ibid., 2.

13. See ibid., 13.

14. Ibid., 11.

15. Ibid., 13.

16. Delores Williams makes a similar point in her retrieval of a womanist notion of sin. She says, "Feelings of personal 'unworthiness' expressed in the Black women's narratives used in this study indicate problems in women's self-esteem. . . . [T]he womanist notion of sin in this essay takes seriously Black women's

depleted self-esteem. Thus elevating and healing Black women's self-esteem figures into womanist notions of what constitutes salvation for the oppressed African-American community." See "A Womanist Perspective on Sin," in *Troubling*, ed. Townes, 147.

17. My use of these accounts involves a free reading of their meanings, in the vein of midrash or homiletics. For a more precise reading of the texts as texts, in a more exegetical framework, see Gerard S. Sloyan, *The Crucifixion of Jesus: History, Myth, Faith* (Minneapolis: Fortress, 1995), chap. 1, esp. pp. 28–29.

18. Unless otherwise noted, all biblical quotations in this book are taken from the *New American Bible*.

19. See Max Scheler, *Ressentiment*, ed. Lewis A. Coser, trans. William W. Holdheim (New York: Free Press of Glencoe, 1961).

20. Desmond Tutu, "Apartheid and Christianity," in *Apartheid Is a Heresy*, ed. John de Gruchy and Charles Villa-Vicencio (Grand Rapids: Eerdmans, 1983), 46–47, as quoted in Simon S. Maimela, "The Suffering of Human Divisions and the Cross," in *The Scandal of a Crucified World: Perspectives on the Cross and Suffering*, ed. Yacob Tesfai (Maryknoll, N.Y.: Orbis Books, 1994), 46.

21. Mark 1:15 records Jesus entering Galilee, proclaiming the good news of God: "This is the time of fulfillment. The kingdom of God is at hand. Repent, and believe in the gospel." The Greek root word *metanoia* is here translated as "repent." It means to turn around, to reverse direction, and, thus, can also be translated "convert." While "repentance" connotes a confession of sin, which indeed may be involved in turning one's life around, "conversion" carries the more general yet more radical notion of shifting one's entire horizon of life.

22. Since a flow of blood, in Jewish law and ritual practice, was a sign of defilement, this woman's medical problems also left her religiously and socially isolated. Not only would she not be able to participate in ritual and worship; others would be prohibited from touching or even speaking with her, lest they, too, become ritually unclean.

23. Christine Gudorf, in her book *Victimization: Examining Christian Complicity* (Philadelphia: Trinity Press International, 1992), analyzes in greater detail the way in which Christianity has contributed to the perpetual victimization of "the poor." She discusses the intricate relations between poor and non-poor in the process of transformation. While her purpose and her approach are different from mine, she does insist on the great costs, *to the poor themselves*, of trying to change oppressive systems (see especially pp. 43–53).

CHAPTER 2
EMBRACING TRAVAIL: VICTIMS AND PERPETRATORS

1. Both of these terms are loaded with connotations, mostly ones unhelpful to my purpose here. "Perpetrators" conjures up images of scruffy men accosting

innocent children in lonely places. "Victims" has had its own critique recently from AIDS patients and cancer patients, who prefer to be considered active *survivors* rather than passive and helpless *victims* of a disease. I use the terms here mostly because they are the best that I could come up with, given the alternatives. It will be clear from what follows that I see victims as anything but passive objects. Indeed, their ability to choose and act is central to my presentation. I understand perpetrators to include the most subtle of manipulators and nice guys, and would not restrict it to the monsters created by the media.

2. Let me say from the beginning of this analysis that these two processes are not exactly parallel. For those on the underside of power, taking responsibility for their actions is much more complex and difficult, since the arena of their choices is greatly curtailed by a lack of opportunities and resources. In many of these cases, mere survival is the best that can be hoped for, so that "recognizing complicity and co-dependence" might, at best, yield better skills at manipulating the system. Thus, for the oppressed, taking responsibility will involve "strategic risk-taking" as discussed below in chapter 3.

3. One of the best illustrations of misbegotten efforts at healing that simply perpetuate dysfunction and sin can be found in the novel *The Good Conscience,* by Carlos Fuentes, as discussed in chapter 1 (see chap. 1 n. 1 above).

4. The discovery of these truths and the practice of them in healing addiction have been manifested for years by Alcoholics Anonymous (AA). This group has recognized and preached the key elements of (1) embracing pain (whatever pain the addiction has sought to numb), (2) taking responsibility (confessing and apologizing to those one has harmed), and (3) admitting a need for a higher power to assist in this transformation. See *Twelve Steps and Twelve Traditions* (New York: Alcoholics Anonymous World Services, 1952). For a discussion of how the philosophy and practice of AA intersects with Christian theologies of sin, see Linda A. Mercadante, *Victims and Sinners: Spiritual Roots of Addiction and Recovery* (Louisville, Ky.: Westminster John Knox Press, 1996).

5. Monty Roberts, *The Man Who Listens to Horses* (New York: Random House, 1996).

6. Ibid., 95–96.

7. The story reveals how important claiming "voice" is for victims. When his father finally sat—reluctantly—to listen, Monty did not beg permission or understanding but simply stated his convictions. The issue was not whether his father would accept them, but that Monty took ownership in spite of his father's disapproval: "Something clicked; I recognized my opportunity. This was not a conversation now. I was telling him what was going to happen" (*Man Who Listens,* 96).

This story also reveals the connection between inter-human violence and the domination and degradation of nature. Interestingly, the healing of human–horse relationships came through listening to the "voice" of the horses. Roberts insists that the key to his success is his learning "Equus"—the body language that horses use to communicate. In many instances, listening to horses becomes the occasion for healing humans. See below in this chapter, under the section on grace.

8. "The Narrative of Bethany Veney" opens with "Aunt Betty" recalling a childhood incident in which she and other children were batting apples out of a tree. Their mistress came along and questioned what they were doing. When the children did not answer her queries directly, Miss Nasenath took them aside and explained how one day the whole world would burn up, and that every little child that had told a lie would be cast into a lake of fire and brimstone. Frightened to death, Bethany ran home and asked her mother if this were true: "To my great sorrow, she confirmed it all, but added what Miss Nasenath had failed to do; namely, that those who told the truth and were good would always have everything they should want." This illustrates the profound power of socialization: the issue is not that Bethany was told be honest, but the loaded way in which she was taught never to consider "truths" anything that her mistress or master might consider "lies." See "The Narrative of Bethaney Veney, A Slave Woman," in *Collected Black Women's Narratives*, ed. Henry L. Gates, Jr. (New York: Oxford University Press, [1889] 1988), 7–8.

9. For an early critique of modern therapy and culture along these lines, see Karl A. Menninger, *What Ever Became of Sin?* (New York: Hawthorne Books, 1973). For a more recent discussion of this perspective, see William J. Doherty, *Soul Searching: Why Psychotherapy Must Promote Moral Responsibility* (New York: Basic Books, 1995).

10. The Million Man March in Washington, D.C. (1996) illustrates the popular shift on the part of African American men toward taking responsibility. On a similar theme, see Glenn C. Loury, "Black Dignity and the Common Good," in *Moral Issues and Christian Response*, ed. Paul T. Jersild and Dale A. Johnson, 5th ed. (New York: Harcourt, Brace, Jovanovich, 1993).

11. See Barbara Dent, *My Only Friend Is Darkness: Living the Night of Faith with St. John of the Cross* (Washington, D.C.: ICS Publications, 1992); and Constance Fitzgerald, "Impasse and Dark Night," in *Women's Spirituality: Resources for Christian Development*, ed. Joann Wolski Conn, 2nd ed. (New York: Paulist Press, 1996).

12. Bernard J. F. Lonergan defines "dialectic" as a "concrete unfolding of linked but opposed principles of change" in *Insight: A Study of Human Understanding*, ed. Frederick E. Crowe and Robert M. Doran (Toronto: University of Toronto Press, 1992), 242. We will pick up the topic of dialectical tensions again in chapter 6.

13. These two phrases come from, respectively, Paul Tillich and Bernard J. F. Lonergan.

14. On the difference between *expectation* and *hope*, see Gerald May, *The Awakened Heart: Living Beyond Addiction* (New York: Harper Collins, 1991), 80–83. See also the section on this topic in chapter 3 below.

15. This latter phrase reflects the title of a recent and excellent anthology: *In the Embrace of God: Feminist Approaches to Theological Anthropology*, ed. Ann O'Hara Graff (Maryknoll, N.Y.: Orbis Books, 1996).

16. See Viktor Frankl, *Man's Search for Meaning: An Introduction to Logotherapy* (Boston: Beacon Press, 1962), 39. See also the recounting of this incident in Mar-

jorie H. Suchocki, *The Fall to Violence: Original Sin in Relational Theology* (New York: Continuum, 1995), 131–32.

17. On the notion of God as a community in relation, see Elizabeth A. Johnson, *She Who Is: The Mystery of God in Feminist Theological Discourse* (New York: Crossroad, 1992); and Catherine M. LaCugna, *God For Us: The Trinity and Christian Life* (San Francisco: Harper & Row, 1991).

18. This is not to minimize the important work of retrieving the meaning that the fathers attributed to Jesus through this language. My task here is not to do such historical retrieval, but to try to make sense of Jesus' person and work in light of the modern worldview.

19. For interpretations of the "Son of Man" as the incarnation of the (Jungian) Self, see Walter Wink, *The Bible in Human Transformation: Toward a New Paradigm for Biblical Study* (Philadelphia: Fortress, 1973), esp. 60; and Elizabeth B. Howes, "Son of Man—Expression of the Self," in *Intersection and Beyond* (San Francisco: Guild for the Psychological Studies, 1971), 171–97. Both are cited and discussed in Carter Heyward, *The Redemption of God: A Theology of Mutual Relation* (Lanham, Md.: University Press of America, 1982), 69.

20. I have constructed the terms "(w)holy" and "(w)holiness" to indicate the relation between psychic wholeness and religious holiness. Still, to be precise, wholeness and holiness are not the same thing. Holiness (understood as much more than moral righteousness) involves being drawn up into communion with a transcendent God and living life out of this relationship. Wholeness on a psycho-social level does not necessarily create such transcendent engagement. Still, as I have already indicated, full human flourishing, full human wholeness does not entirely meet its goal unless oriented toward and embraced by such transcendent relationship. Wholeness is not the same as holiness but is oriented toward it. Jesus was unique in embodying both psychic *wholeness* and spiritual *holiness* as complete and utter commitment/involvement with God. Indeed, it was the latter that made the former possible for Jesus.

21. See Sebastian Moore, *The Crucified Is No Stranger* (London: Darton, Longman, & Todd, 1977), 23.

22. Ibid., 19. Moore has a more recent book entitled *Jesus, the Liberator of Desire* (New York: Crossroad, 1989). See also the review symposium on this latter book in *Horizons* 18 (1991): 92–129. Moore's other books include *The Fire and the Rose Are One* (New York: Seabury Press, 1980) and *Let This Mind Be in You: The Quest for Identity Through Oedipus to Christ* (Minneapolis: Winston Press, 1985).

23. Moore says the following on this subject (*Crucified*, 29–30):

It might appear that "communion with an archetypal suffering Christ" and "historical recalling of a man who once suffered" are two perfectly distinct operations, neither one requiring the other. But these alternatives so understood do not fit the Christian contemplative experience. . . . At every stage of my personal entry into the mystery, the Christ that I have *not* yet become is a man who somehow *is*, and not a platonic anthropos-image. This tension seems to be essential to the encounter. Resolve it by dissolving the thought of the Jesus who actually was on that cross, and the encounter itself, with all its power to evoke in me the self, falls to pieces. . . . Make of *him* simply the as yet unappropriated self, and the tension and realism of the encounter collapses. The suffering-of-sin that I have not yet found in myself and found myself in, is in a real body nailed to a cross.

24. See Michael Winter, *The Atonement* (Collegeville, Minn.: Liturgical Press, 1995), 46.

25. Moore, *Crucified,* 8–9. I take the liberty, here and in the following quotation, of adding "healing" as the complementary piece that I think is necessary if the two poles of victim and crucifier are to be taken into account.

26. Ibid., 16.

27. Emilie M. Townes, ed., *A Troubling in My Soul: Womanist Perspectives on Evil and Suffering* (Maryknoll, N.Y.: Orbis Books, 1993).

28. Sharon D. Welch makes a similar point in *A Feminist Ethic of Risk* (Minneapolis: Fortress, 1990), 14–15.

29. This is not to say that questions over God's integrity and the fact of evil have never plagued the oppressed. See, e.g., William R. Jones, *Is God a White Racist: A Preamble to Black Theology* (Garden City, N.Y.: Doubleday, Anchor, 1973). See also M. Shawn Copeland, "'Wading Through Many Sorrows': Toward a Theology of Suffering in Womanist Perspective," in *Troubling,* ed. Townes, 109–29, esp. n. 5; as well as Cheryl Kirk-Duggan, "Theodicy in White and Black," chap. 3 of her *Exorcizing Evil: A Womanist Perspective on the Spirituals* (Maryknoll, N.Y.: Orbis Books, 1997).

30. See Simon S. Maimela, "The Suffering of Human Divisions and the Cross," in *The Scandal of a Crucified World: Perspectives on the Cross and Suffering,* ed. Yacob Tesfai (Maryknoll, N.Y.: Orbis Books, 1994), 36–43, at 38.

31. A more extended explanation of theories of redemption as they developed through Christian history is given below in chapter 5.

32. This is what is often called "the turn to the subject." See Michael Himes, "The Human Person in Contemporary Theology: From Human Nature to Authentic Subjectivity," in *Introduction to Christian Ethics: A Reader,* ed. Ron Hamel and Kenneth Himes (New York: Paulist Press, 1989).

33. I am using the term "Desire" here to emphasize the deep and perduring yearning of all persons for wholeness and communion with the transcendent. This is not to say that such Desire is somehow distinct from everyday longings or desires. It is of a piece with them, as my discussion of "appetites" indicates. I merely want to highlight that there is such a deep, fundamental, and existential core to our affective lives and the decisions that emerge from them.

34. Roberts, *Man Who Listens,* 245–46.

35. In "The Dry Salvages" T. S. Eliot speaks of the "unattended moment" when we catch the "hints and guesses" of incarnation. Aside from these moments, "the rest

is prayer, observance, discipline, thought, and action." See *T.S. Eliot: The Complete Poems and Plays, 1909-1950* (New York: Harcourt, Brace, & World, 1971), 136.

36. On operative and cooperative grace, see Bernard J. F. Lonergan, *Method in Theology* (New York: Seabury Press, 1979), 107, 241, 288-89.

37. These groups, of course, can in turn prescribe certain allowable insights and feelings, so that the transformative efforts themselves become ideological. See Cynthia S. W. Crysdale, "Feminist Theology: Ideology, Authenticity, and the Cross," in *Église et Théologie* 28 (1997): 245-63.

38. See Cynthia S. W. Crysdale, "The Social Construction of Self-Appropriation," in *Lonergan and Feminism,* ed. Cynthia S. W. Crysdale (Toronto: University of Toronto Press, 1994), 88-113. See also chapter 4 below.

39. In the Middle Ages, the issue of God's response to a person doing *quod in se est* ("that which is in us," or "that which one is able to do") was the subject of theological debate. See Alister McGrath, *Iustitia Dei: A History of the Christian Doctrine of Justification,* vol. 1 (Cambridge: Cambridge University Press, 1986), 83-91.

CHAPTER 3
EMBRACING TRAVAIL: SURRENDER AND RESISTANCE

1. Sharon D. Welch, *A Feminist Ethic of Risk* (Minneapolis: Fortress, 1990).

2. Ibid., 19.

3. Ibid., 20.

4. Ibid., 25.

5. Welch uses the United States quest for national security via the arms race as her primary example of an ethic of control. See *Ethic of Risk,* chap. 2.

6. Ibid., 21.

7. Welch borrows this term from Johann Baptist Metz, *Faith in History and Society: Toward a Practical Fundamental Society* (New York: Seabury Press, 1980); see Welch's discussion of this in *Ethic of Risk,* 154-56.

8. Welch, *Ethic of Risk,* 22. Welch uses the Logan family, from the novels by Mildred Taylor, to illustrate such strategic risk taking (see ibid., 71-81). See also Mildred Taylor, *Let the Circle Be Unbroken* (New York: Bantam Books, 1983); and eadem, *Roll of Thunder, Hear My Cry* (New York: Bantam Books, 1984).

9. Welch, *Ethic of Risk,* 22.

10. Walter Wink, *Engaging the Powers: Discernment and Resistance in a World of Domination* (Minneapolis: Fortress, 1992). Welch and Wink approach their subject matter from different angles. Welch's background is that of feminist theory and postmodern literary interpretation, using the work of thinkers such as Michel Foucault. Wink comes from years of work as a biblical scholar, entering into these issues through biblical interpretation. Nevertheless, their key insights do converge and are useful catalysts for my work here.

11. *Engaging the Powers* is, in fact, the third in a series that Walter Wink has written over the course of a decade. The previous two books are *Naming the Powers: The Language of Power in the New Testament* (Philadelphia: Fortress, 1984) and *Unmasking the Powers: The Invisible Forces that Determine Human Existence* (Philadelphia: Fortress, 1986). He has recently published a further book, *The Powers That Be: Theology for a New Millennium* (New York: Doubleday, 1998).

12. See Wink, *Engaging*, chap. 1.

13. Ibid., 18. This is only one of the many cartoons or media stories that Wink reviews. See his discussion (pp. 21–22) of *Get Smart*, in which Smart and Agent 99 try to overcome the enemy, KAOS, and work for an agency called CONTROL.

I think that, in reading the Babylonian myth into current popular media, Wink misses a step. He himself acknowledges that the Jewish tradition introduced a very different notion of creation, particularly the notion that creation is good and that evil is an aberration. The Christian tradition incorporated this worldview, delineating a notion of evil as the deprivation of the good. Thus, whereas the ancient myth understood good and evil to be constitutive of being, and in constant conflict, Western civilization bases its "myth of redemptive violence" on the conviction that being is good and that evil can be ultimately eradicated, conquered. Though I do not necessarily disagree with this position, it cannot be denied that such a worldview heightens the propensity to an "ethic of control" as Welch has defined it. The modern myth of redemptive violence presumes that the hero can, through decisive action, conquer evil once and for all, whereas the ancient myth considers it obvious that the cycles of conflict will continue forever, that such cycles are what grants existence its very being.

14. Ibid., 19.

15. Ibid., 22.

16. Both Welch and Wink use their categories to critique U.S. public policy regarding national security (Welch, *Ethic of Risk*, chap. 2; Wink, *Engaging*, 25–31). Welch finds the ethic of control alive and well in both the American public and foreign policy analysts. Surprisingly, she also finds that peace activists operate implicitly with this same ethic. When gains have been incremental, such as the 1987 Intermediate Nuclear Forces Treaty between the United States and the Soviet Union, many activists have failed to rejoice. Lacking "success"—complete bilateral nuclear disarmament—the peace workers sensed failure rather than reward. Wink engages in a similar critique of nationalism and its reliance on force. He adds to this a scathing analysis of Christianity's role in fostering the myth of redemptive violence.

17. Welch uses this novel as the basis of chapter 3 in *A Feminist Ethic of Risk*. See Paule Marshall, *The Chosen Place, The Timeless People* (New York: Random House, 1984).

18. Welch cites, as an example of the implicit arrogance of Harriet's charity, Harriet's encounter with two hungry children in their meager hut. Their parents are off cutting cane, and Harriet cannot bear the suffering of these hungry chil-

dren. Finding half a dozen eggs in the hut, and over the loud protests of the children, she breaks and scrambles the eggs over the fire. She is shocked later to discover that the eggs were meant for sale at the local market, that the children had been beaten for allowing her to cook them, and that, in fact, the children had left the cooked eggs untouched. Harriet simply had not taken the time to understand the system of economic meaning in which she was (supposedly) acting as an agent of change. See Marshall, *Chosen Place*, 175–81, and Welch's discussion of this, *Ethic of Risk*, 57–58.

19. Wink, *Engaging*, 29.

20. Ibid., 44. He relies here on the work of Raine Eisler, *The Chalice and the Blade* (San Francisco: Harper & Row, 1987).

21. Wink, *Engaging*, 45, citing Abraham Heschel, *The Prophets* (New York: Harper & Row, 1969), 1:166. After citing Heschel, Wink lists the many passages in which prophets denounced the characteristics of domination (*Engaging*, chap. 2 n. 59).

22. On the "Beloved Community," see Welch, *Ethic of Risk*, 158–67. For Wink's contrast of the domination system with God's reign, see his chart in *Engaging*, 46–47.

23. See Wink, *Engaging*, chap 6.

24. Ibid., 46. For a more thorough examination of these shifts in Christian history, see chapter 5 below.

25. Wink clearly understands this point and has a nuanced grasp of the dynamics here. He simply doesn't provide categories for this "underside" of the domination system. He alludes to the paradox in passages such as the following (*Engaging*, 98):

> This is the paradox of moral maturity: we are responsible for what we do with what has been done to us. We are answerable for what we make of what has been made of us. Our capitulation to the delusional system may have been involuntary, but in some deep recess of the self we knew it was wrong. We are so fashioned that no Power on earth can finally drum out of us the capacity to recognize the truth.

26. Helen Prejean, *Dead Man Walking: An Eye Witness Account of the Death Penalty in the United States* (New York: Random House, 1993). See also *Dead Man Walking*, directed by Timothy Robbins, Grammercy Pictures, 1995.

27. Prejean, *Dead Man Walking*, xiii.

28. M. Shawn Copeland, "'Wading Through Many Sorrows': Toward a Theology of Suffering in Womanist Perspective," in *A Troubling in My Soul: Womanist Perspectives on Evil and Suffering*, ed. Emilie Townes (Maryknoll, N.Y.: Orbis Books, 1993), 109–29.

29. Ibid., 121.

30. Ibid., 122. Copeland is citing Harriet Jacobs [Linda Brent], *Incidents in the Life of a Slave Girl* (1861; New York: Harcourt Brace Jovanovich, 1983), 38–39.

31. Wink, *Engaging*, 191. Wink gives several other amusing examples here of ways in which people have engaged in nonviolent protest.

32. Maya Angelou, *I Know Why the Caged Bird Sings* (New York: Bantam Books, 1969), 154–56.

33. In his chapter on Jesus and the cross, Wink has an extended discussion of René Girard and his scapegoat hypothesis. See Wink, *Engaging,* 144–55. See also René Girard, *Violence and the Sacred* (Baltimore: Johns Hopkins University Press, 1977); idem, *Things Hidden Since the Foundation of the World,* with Jean-Michel Oghourlian and Guy Lefort (Stanford: Stanford University Press, 1987); idem, *The Scapegoat* (Baltimore: Johns Hopkins University Press, 1986). Another extended interpretation of the scapegoat theory can be found in Raymond Schwager, *Must There Be Scapegoats?* (San Francisco: Harper & Row, 1987). See also the review article, Leo D. Lefebure, "Victims, Violence, and the Sacred: The Thought of René Girard," *The Christian Century* 113 (1996): 1226–29; and idem, "Beyond Scapegoating: A Conversation with René Girard and Ewart Cousins," *The Christian Century* 115 (1998): 372–75.

34. For an effort to constructively retrieve some of this theology, see Charles C. Hefling, "A Perhaps Permanently Valid Achievement: Lonergan on Christ's Satisfaction," *Method: Journal of Lonergan Studies* 10 (1992): 51–76.

35. See Carter Heyward's "re-imaging" of Jesus in *The Redemption of God: A Theology of Mutual Relation* (Lanham, Md.: University Press of America, 1982), chap. 2. See especially her discussion of power, pp. 41–44.

36. See Wink, *Engaging,* chap. 6.

37. See Sebastian Moore, *The Crucified Is No Stranger* (London: Darton, Longman, & Todd, 1977), 50.

38. Wink, *Engaging,* 141.

39. Ibid., 143.

40. See John of the Cross, *The Collected Works of St. John of the Cross,* trans. Kieran Kavanaugh and Otilio Rodriguez (Washington, D.C.: Institute of Carmelite Studies, 1973). See also Barbara Dent, *My Only Friend Is Darkness: Living the Night of Faith with St. John of the Cross* (Washington, D.C.: ICS Publications, 1992). See also two articles by Constance Fitzgerald, "Impasse and Dark Night," and "The Transformative Influence of Wisdom in John of the Cross," in *Women's Spirituality: Resources for Christian Development,* ed. Joanne Wolski Conn, 2nd ed. (New York: Paulist, 1996).

41. See Welch, *Ethic of Risk,* 20: "Responsible action does not mean the certain achievement of desired ends but the creation of a matrix in which further actions are possible, the creation of the conditions of possibility for desired changes."

42. Though the resistance that I am discussing here has to do with moral evil, there are significant parallels in dealing with physical pain. See the excellent and extensive treatment of these issues in Pamela Smith, "Chronic Pain and Creative Possibility: A Psychological Phenomenon Confronts Theologies of Suffering," in *Broken and Whole: Essays on Religion and the Body,* ed. Maureen A. Tilley and Susan A. Ross (Lanham, Md.: University Press of America, 1993), 159–88.

43. I have borrowed this latter phrase from Bernard J. F. Lonergan. See *Insight:*

A Study of Human Understanding, ed. Frederick E. Crowe and Robert M. Doran (Toronto: University of Toronto Press, 1992), 197–98, 311–12, 314–16, 328–29. A fuller discussion of authenticity and community as they unfold through history is taken up below in chapter 5.

44. I believe that this is what Sharon Welch is up to in *A Feminist Ethic of Risk.* See also Kathleen M. Sands, *Escape from Paradise: Evil and Tragedy in Feminist Theology* (Minneapolis: Fortress, 1994); and Wendy Farley, *Tragic Vision and Divine Compassion: A Contemporary Theodicy* (Louisville, Ky.: Westminster/John Knox, 1990).

45. One of the best illustrations of the higher integration that I am referring to here comes in C. S. Lewis's *The Last Battle,* the last in his series of children's books, all of which carry Christian theological overtones. The conclusion of these stories is, indeed, a colossal battle. But the victory comes not in that the forces of good overcome the forces of evil. Rather, at the strategic moment in which all seems lost, the hero gathers up his courage to barge into a small hut in the middle of the battle, where all the horrid forces of evil have taken up residence. No one who has entered has emerged; instead, blood-curdling screams have issued forth. However, when the hero does finally jump into the darkness inhabited by evil he finds himself in a wood surrounded by dazzling light and unspeakable beauty. At his feet are the dwarves who had previously succumbed to the powers of evil. They are sitting in a circle arguing, apparently unable to see the wonders around them. In fact, it seems that they are still sitting in the dark evil hut, caught up in their selfish plans and fearful pettiness. No matter how vociferously the hero calls to them, they are oblivious to his presence and his world. "Victory," it turns out, is a matter of what one sees and this is, in turn, the fruit of abiding in courageous love rather than fear. The battle is not won but left behind, at least for those who have courageously embraced the struggle out of love. A voice calls, "Move up, move higher," and every time the hero steps through a doorway in the wood he enters the same forest, only more "real," more "there." The colors deepen, the sounds are more vibrant, the smells more luscious, everything becomes more "solid." Again and again, this entreaty occurs, again and again, the hero enters a new world that is the same but "more" than the last. Evil is overcome, victory has been won, not through domination but by transformation, and this transformation involves an eternity of wonderful discoveries that land one, in an entirely new way, in the same place one has always been.

46. On dialectical oppositions in relation to physical suffering and mind/body dualisms, see Smith, "Chronic Pain," 172.

47. This is not to say, of course, that this opposition is always obvious or simple to discern. Our lives are intricate mixtures of healing and oppression, wounds and gifts: we live within the social surd of moral evils that sin has produced. The process of overcoming evil (domination and suffering) with good (healing and forgiveness) is a very messy one. This is why *discernment* and trusted communities of discernment are so vital to resistance and surrender. But it is precisely because

of the opposition of good and evil that such discernment is needed. One, or one's community, needs to discover the excluded middle in order to claim transformative action and not mistake it for capitulation or domination.

48. In the interests of this latter option, several recent works have sought to retrieve the Greek notion of tragedy, for example, Farley, *Tragic Vision,* and Sands, *Escape.* I think that this appeal to tragedy is a valid attempt to highlight the ambiguity involved in dealing with evil in the world, and to offset a simplistic domination worldview in which good conquers evil through violent power. However, I don't see how one can adopt tragedy as a paradigm for dealing with God, good, and evil, without at the same time incorporating the assumption that tragedy and fate are inextricably bound to "being." The best of the Christian tradition sees the surd of sin as a symptom of evil, which is the deprivation of the good, creation being essentially good and not ultimately tragic. To make tragedy, as essential to being and creation, the central motif in the drama of evil in the world is to reduce God to hapless Fate and to undercut the transcendent power that is precisely what is needed to break cycles of alienation. See related comments in n. 13 above in nn. 49 and 51 below.

49. Clearly, the issue here is one's definition of power, and this is a topic that I do not directly address here. Many feminists find that, in order to retrieve the Judeo-Christian God at all, one must redefine power as "power with" rather than "power over." These distinctions are absolutely essential to the position I take in this book. My main point here is that I prefer to retrieve a very powerful God and carefully exegete the meaning of "power" rather than make power and therefore an omnipotent God the enemy. See Heyward, *Redemption of God,* 41–44; and Sally B. Purvis, *The Power of the Cross: Foundations for a Christian Feminist Ethic of Community* (Nashville: Abingdon Press, 1993).

50. Having spent the winter months—while writing this book—in the heart of Benedictine life, at St. John's University in Collegeville, Minnesota, I can't help but reflect on the power of *praxis,* in this case the praxis of daily morning and evening prayer. These are services in which the Psalms and prophets (in translations palatable to the feminist ear) resonate with the power and righteousness of God. The lived life of prayer, surrounded by images of a powerful yet loving, embracing God, yields a vision of omnipotence radically different from the omnipotent God of whom Welch is so eager to rid us.

51. The position I take here is directly opposed to the position that Sharon Welch arrives at in the final chapters of *A Feminist Ethic of Risk.* She does not believe that the idea of an omnipotent God is recoverable. She reviews and critiques a host of Christian theologians to show that even those who say they are reinterpreting power are really just reinforcing traditional and destructive images of God. I do not find her case convincing. First, it is not clear to me that she has accurately interpreted some of her sources, for example, Paul Tillich. She quotes him making refinements to notions of power and God's omnipotence but then con-

cludes that he didn't really mean what he said and was actually endorsing a valorization of power (see pp. 116–22, 160). This kind of hermeneutic seems to me to have an infinite regress: maybe Welch doesn't really mean what she is saying and is implicitly valorizing feminine power. A case for "inner hidden deeper secret meanings" has to be made and I do not think she makes the case with many of her sources. Second, she ends up with the "Beloved Community" in which God is immanent and love provides the energy and vision for resistance (see chap. 8). This is a wonderful image and resource but, I think, needs a transcendent referent if it is not to revert to a community caught in its own cycles of despair and distortion. Something has to garner and transform our energies and love and, unless that something is truly an Other that can abide without our assistance, we are stuck within an idolatry and faith of our own creating. I suspect that my differences with Welch are, at base, epistemological rather than theological, but that issue will have to be left to another time and space. Third, given her extensive use of African American literature, I am surprised that Welch does not pick up on the centrality of an omnipotent God in African American theology and praxis. For example, see Major J. Jones, *The Color of God in Afro-American Thought* (Macon, Ga.: Mercer University Press, 1987), and the discussion of God's omnipotence in Smith, "Chronic Pain," 176–78.

52. Welch, *Ethic of Risk,* 33–36.

53. Ibid., 33; cf. 43.

54. Wink, *Engaging,* 71.

55. Ibid.

56. Welch, *Ethic of Risk,* 106 (for further works on contemporary eschatology and the "eschatological reservation" see chap. 6 n. 12).

57. Welch cites Johann Baptist Metz as discussing an "eschatological proviso" in *Theology of the World,* trans. William Glen-Doepel (New York: Seabury Press, 1969), 153. She quotes Juan Luis Segundo as challenging such reservations in *The Liberation of Theology,* trans. John Drury (Maryknoll, N.Y.: Orbis Books, 1976), 145. Another critique of liberation theology along these lines is Dennis McCann, *Christian Realism and Liberation Theology: Practical Theologies in Conflict* (Maryknoll, N.Y.: Orbis Books, 1981). See Welch's discussion of all this, *Ethic of Risk,* 106–11.

58. Gerald May, *The Awakened Heart: Living Beyond Addiction* (San Francisco: HarperCollins, 1991), 80–81.

59. See Peter Phan, "Woman and the Last Things: A Feminist Eschatology," in *In the Embrace of God: Feminist Approaches to Theological Anthropology,* ed. Ann O'Hara Graff (Maryknoll, N.Y.: Orbis Books, 1995), 206–28. He notes the lack of engagement of feminist theology with eschatology, reviews two exceptions to this (Rosemary R. Ruether and Sally McFague), and then offers some further questions. He lists other works on contemporary eschatology in n. 4. On the communion of saints, see Elizabeth A. Johnson, *Friends of God and Prophets: A Feminist Theological Reading of the Communion of Saints* (New York: Continuum, 1998).

60. M. Shawn Copeland, "Toward a Critical Feminist Theology of Solidarity," in *Women and Theology*, ed. Mary Ann Hinsdale and Phyllis H. Kaminski (Maryknoll, N.Y.: Orbis Books, 1995), 3–38, at 11.

61. Ibid., 15.

62. Wink, *Engaging*, 205.

63. On this topic Shawn Copeland cites Jeanne Perrault, "White Feminist Guilt, Abject Scripts, and (Other) Transformative Necessities," *West Coast Line*, 13/14 (Spring–Fall): 226–38. See also Barbara H. Andolsen, *Daughters of Jefferson, Daughters of Bootblacks: Racism and American Feminism* (Macon, Ga.: Mercer University Press, 1986).

64. This is what Sharon Welch is doing in using the narratives of African American women to illumine white middle-class cynicism. See her comment on this in *Ethic of Risk*, 129.

65. Copeland, "Solidarity," in *Women and Theology*, ed. Hinsdale and Kaminski, 25.

66. Ibid. In the *next* sentence, however, Copeland again cautions: "Yet those who have so enjoyed the fruits of privilege ought not quickly seize the silence." Though she sees these roles as reversible, she is cautious that this reversibility not be seen as a reinforcement of traditional boundaries of discourse.

CHAPTER 4

GAINING A VOICE: THE DISCOVERY OF DISCOVERY

1. See William Gibson, *The Miracle Worker* (New York: Alfred A. Knopf, 1976); and *The Miracle Worker*, directed by Arthur Penn, United Artists, 1962. For Bernard Lonergan's discussion of Helen Keller, see *Method in Theology* (New York: Seabury Press, 1979), 70.

2. Walter Conn, *Christian Conversion: A Developmental Interpretation of Autonomy and Surrender* (New York: Paulist Press, 1986), 122. Conn is relying on Frank Deford, "Problem Solving Can Be Beautiful," *Sports Illustrated*, May 10, 1976, pp. 83–96.

3. Deford, "Problem Solving," 93, as quoted in Conn, *Christian Conversion*, 122.

4. Ibid.

5. For a review of women's studies as they developed in the 1970s and 1980s, see Anne E. Carr, *Transforming Grace: Christian Tradition and Women's Experience* (San Francisco: Harper & Row, 1988), 63–94. For other historical overviews of feminist theory and of feminist theology, see Mary Ann Zimmer, "Stepping Stones in Feminist Theory," and Mary Ann Hinsdale, "Heeding the Voices: An Historical Overview," in *In the Embrace of God: Feminist Approaches to Theological Anthropology*, ed. Ann O'Hara Graff (Maryknoll, N.Y.: Orbis Books, 1995).

6. Carol Gilligan, *In a Different Voice: Psychological Theory and Women's Development* (Cambridge, Mass.: Harvard University Press, 1982).

7. For a review of the ethics of care and responses to Gilligan's work, see Cynthia S. W. Crysdale, "Gilligan and the Ethics of Care: An Update," *Religious Studies Review* 20 (1994): 21–28. Several works that arose in response to Gilligan's work include a special issue on *Women and Morality* in *Social Research* 50 (1983) and *Women and Moral Theory*, ed. Eva Feder Kittay and Diana T. Meyers (Lanham, Md.: Rowman & Littlefield, 1987).

8. Elizabeth A. Morelli, "Women's Intuition: A Lonerganian Analysis," in *Lonergan and Feminism*, ed. Cynthia S. W. Crysdale (Toronto: University of Toronto Press, 1994), 74.

9. Lorraine Code, "Responsibility and the Epistemic Community: Woman's Place," *Social Research* 50 (1983): 537–55.

10. George W. F. Hegel, *Philosophy of Right*, trans. T. M. Knox (New York: Oxford University Press, 1973), 263. See discussion in Morelli, "Women's Intuition," 74. See also Carol McMillan, *Women, Reason, and Nature* (Princeton, N.J.: Princeton University Press, 1982), 8.

11. Arthur Schopenhauer, *On the Basis of Morality* (Indianapolis: Bobbs-Merrill, 1965), 151. See Morelli, "Women's Intuition," 75; and McMillan, *Women, Reason, and Nature*, 11.

12. Hegel, *Philosophy of Right*, 263. See Morelli, "Women's Intuition," 75.

13. See Mary F. Belenky, Blythe M. Clinchy, Nancy R. Goldberger, and Jill M. Tarule, *Women's Ways of Knowing: The Development of Self, Voice, and Mind* (New York: Basic Books, 1986), 7. They refer to Rosalind Rosenberg, *Beyond Separate Spheres: Intellectual Roots of Modern Feminism* (New Haven, Conn.: Yale University Press, 1982).

14. As quoted in Rosemary R. Ruether, "Home and Work: Women's Roles and the Transformation of Values," in *Perspectives on Marriage: A Reader*, ed. Kieren Scott and Michael Warren (New York: Oxford University Press, 1993), 288.

15. Thomas Aquinas, *Summa Theologica*, Pt. 1, Q. 95, Ar. 1.

16. For a more thorough review, see Rosemary R. Ruether, *Women and Redemption: A Theological History* (Minneapolis: Fortress Press, 1998).

17. On the legal status of women in Western history, see Rosemary R. Ruether, "The Western Religious Tradition and Violence Against Women in the Home," in *Christianity, Patriarchy, and Abuse: A Feminist Critique*, ed. Joanne C. Brown and Carole R. Bohn (Cleveland, Oh.: Pilgrim Press, 1989), 31–42, esp. 31. On gossip, see William H. Willimon, "Heard about the Pastor Who . . . ? Gossip as an Ethical Activity," *The Christian Century*, Oct. 31. 1990, pp. 994–96. Willimon discusses Patricia M. Spacks, author of *Gossip* (Chicago: University of Chicago Press, 1986), who "speculates that one reason gossip became associated with the conversation of women was that early usages of the word referred to the speech of women who attended at childbirth. To be present at so intimate an occasion was to be privy to

some very personal information. Male envy at being excluded from the mystery of childbirth may have contributed to the negative assessments of the speech of those who were present" (Willimon, "Heard about the Pastor Who?" 995). On credibility, see Lorraine Code, "Credibility: A Double Standard," in *Feminist Perspectives: Philosophical Essays on Method and Morals,* ed. Lorraine Code, Sheila Mullett, and Christine Overall (Toronto: University of Toronto Press, 1988), 64–88; and Dale Spender, *Women of Ideas (and What Men Have Done to Them)* (Boston: ARK Paperbacks, 1983).

18. Ruether, "Violence against Women," in *Patriarchy*, ed. Brown and Bohn, 36.

19. See ibid. Ruether refers to Barbara Ehrenreich and Deirdre English, *Witches, Midwives and Nurses* (New York: Feminist Press, 1973).

20. *Malleus Maleficarum*, trans. Montague Summers (London: J. Rodker, 1928), pt. 1, sec. 6, as quoted in Ruether, "Violence against Women," in *Patriarchy*, ed. Brown and Bohn, 37.

21. See Elisabeth Schüssler Fiorenza, "Breaking the Silence—Becoming Visible," in *The Power of Naming: A Concilium Reader in Feminist Liberation Theology*, ed. Elisabeth Schüssler Fiorenza (Maryknoll, N.Y.: Orbis Books, 1996), esp. 161ff.

22. See Thomas More, *English Works,* 1187, as cited in George G. Coulton, *Life in the Middle Ages* (New York: Cambridge University Press, 1931), 3:165–67. Discussed in Ruether, "Violence against Women," in *Patriarchy*, ed. Brown and Bohn, 35.

23. Ruether, "Violence against Women," 35. She refers to Roger Thompson, *Women in Stuart England and America* (London: Routledge & Kegan Paul, 1974), 10.

24. Miriam T. Winter, Adair Lummis, and Allison Stokes, *Defecting in Place: Women Claiming Responsibility for Their Own Spiritual Lives* (New York: Crossroad, 1995), 37. This quotation demonstrates the double bind that women find themselves in when they speak or lead with conviction. On the one hand, this parishioner wants strong leadership. On the other hand, when a woman pastor demonstrates such leadership, she is "pushy."

25. See Ruether, "Home and Work," in *Perspectives on Marriage*, ed. Scott and Warren. See also Maxine B. Zinn and D. Stanley Eitzen, *Diversity in Families*, 4th ed. (New York: HarperCollins, 1996), 59–64. Note that the ideal of women at home in the private sphere functioned as a middle-class ideal. Poor women and women of color did not have the luxury of staying at home but had to become wage earners themselves. In fact, there existed a double layer of women's work in the nineteenth century, whereby immigrant women (the Irish in Boston) or women of color (slaves in the South) served as domestic servants in order for white middle- and upperclass women to fulfill the "cult of domesticity." On black women's experience of servanthood, see Jacquelyn Grant, "The Sin of Servanthood and the Deliverance of Discipleship," in *A Troubling in My Soul: Womanist Perspectives on Evil and Suffering*, ed. Emilie Townes (Maryknoll, N.Y.: Orbis Books, 1993), 199–218.

26. Code, "Responsibility," 545. Code cites the women of Jane Austin's novels as exemplars of this trend.

27. *N.Y. Globe,* June 22, 1911 (Documents of the Catholic Bishops against Women's Suffrage, 1910-1920; Sophia Smith Collection, Smith College), as quoted in Ruether, "Home and Work," in *Perspectives on Marriage,* ed. Scott and Warren, 291.

28. Several examples from African American literature come to mind. See Mildred D. Taylor, *Roll of Thunder, Hear My Cry* (New York: Penguin Books, 1976), esp. p. 84, and Maya Angelou, *I Know Why the Caged Bird Sings* (New York: Bantam Books, 1969), esp. chap. 23.

29. This denigration of certain persons can be attributed to a culture at large and need not be blamed on any one individual, nor even on a single (male) gender. In recounting the poor record of Christian history in this regard, we need to distinguish between malevolence and ignorance. In most cases, though not all, the distorted view and harsh treatment of women came as part of an unenlightened culture. More culpability could be ascribed to certain persons and institutions today, for whom the equal capabilities of men and women have been clearly delineated. In this case, continued misogynist practices are more obviously a case of bias and prejudice, in which the persons involved willfully refuse to confront all the relevant questions.

30. Belenky et al., *Women's Ways of Knowing.*

31. For a further discussion of the sample used and the coding system devised, see ibid., 11-16. While they present these perspectives in order, and record how some subjects seemed to develop from one perspective to another, the researchers disavow any claims that these are stages in a developmental sequence. Their work takes place in response to the earlier work of William Perry (*Women's Ways of Knowing,* 9-10; cf. William Perry, *Forms of Intellectual and Ethical Development in the College Years* [New York: Holt, Rinehart, & Winston, 1970]).

32. To facilitate this review I have inserted relevant page references in parentheses in the text. Much of this discussion comes from a previously published article of my own: "Women and the Social Construction of the Self-Appropriation," in *Lonergan and Feminism,* ed. Cynthia S. W. Crysdale (Toronto: University of Toronto Press, 1994), 88-113.

33. Though language is available to these women, the lack of representational thought stands out (pp. 25-26). A lack of play in childhood seems tied to this absence of symbolic images.

34. On fear of success in women, see Matina S. Horner, "Towards an Understanding of Achievement-Related Conflicts in Women," *Journal of Social Issues* 28 (1972): 157-76. See also Georgia Sassen, "Success Anxiety in Women: A Constructivist Interpretation of Its Source and Its Significance," *Harvard Educational Review* 50 (1980): 13-24.

35. Belenky et al. have a further section in the chapter on received knowing,

comparing their findings about [female] "received knowers" with Perry's elite [male] sample of what he calls "dualists." The most interesting comparison lies in the conception of authority. While for both groups authorities are the source of truth, Perry's male subjects tend to identify with these authorities and dichotomize "the familiar world of Authority-right-we as against the alien world of illegitimate-wrong-others" (Perry, *Forms of Intellectual and Ethical Development,* 59, as quoted in Belenky et al., *Women's Ways of Knowing,* 43). The women studied by Belenky et al. tend to describe these authorities *as* "other." They are awed by authority but do not identify with it; rather, they see it as "authority-right-they."

36. Belenky et al. note that there remains an implicit dualism in many of these subjectivists: "In fact, subjectivism is dualistic in the sense that there is still the con-viction that there are right answers; the fountain of truth simply has shifted locale. Truth now resides within the person and can negate answers that the outside world supplies" (*Women's Ways of Knowing,* 54). That the "subjectivism" labeled by Belenky et al. is a single, discrete epistemological position seems doubtful. Rather, as they themselves admit (p. 55), it is a loosely defined term, a kind of "catch-all" label that links a group of women together. Likewise, just what these women mean, and what these researchers mean, by "intuition" remains vague. A footnote on p. 55 refers to the philosophical tradition of intuitivism, but just how the common-sense usage of it here relates to this tradition is not made clear. See Morelli, "Women's Intuition," in *Lonergan and Feminism,* ed. Crysdale, esp. 79ff.

37. Again, the authors compare their female "subjectivists" with Perry's male subjects at the stage that he calls "multiplists." These male college students exhib-ited the traditional relativistic and rebellious stance of many young adults leaving a homogenous home environment. Belenky et al. found that their middle-class and upper-class women in college fit neatly into Perry's category. The *difference* they found between Perry's men and their women lay in the confidence with which their subjects asserted their new-found perspective. Whereas the male subjects would brazenly insist on their views over against parents, teachers, and adminis-trators, the women "hidden multiplists" were often lonely and reticent to express their quiet but passionate differences with authority. This difference is best sum-marized in the oft-repeated phrase of the men, "I have a *right* to my own opinion," in contrast to the more common female version, "It's *just* my opinion." See pp. 62–68.

38. Belenky et al. point out that there is a negative side to the emphasis on pro-cedure. The form of an argument ends up taking precedence over the content, such that one student insists: "It does not matter . . . whether you decide to have your baby or abort it. It matters only that you think the decision through thor-oughly" (p. 95). This emphasis on method can verge on what Mary Daly labels "methodolatry." Acceptable procedures within a certain institution can limit women's access to the knowledge they need. An ideology of methodology can assert that only certain types of arguments are acceptable, and when women or other minorities do not easily adopt these methods, they are left out of the sphere

of acceptable knowledge (see ibid., pp. 95–96). See also Mary Daly, *Beyond God the Father* (Boston: Beacon Press, 1973).

39. Note especially the footnote on p. 59 of Belenky et al. indicating the many other studies that confirm their findings. The two works that they cite the most are Judith Herman, *Father-Daughter Incest* (Cambridge, Mass.: Harvard University Press, 1981); and Diana E. H. Russell, *The Secret Trauma: Incest in the Lives of Girls and Women* (New York: Basic Books, 1986). See also Juidth Herman, *Trauma and Recovery* (New York: Basic Books, 1992).

40. Carole R. Bohn, "Dominion to Rule: The Roots and Consequences of a Theology of Ownership," in *Patriarchy*, ed. Brown and Bohn, 111 (emphasis added).

41. Polly Young-Eisendrath and Demaris Wehr, "The Fallacy of Individualism and Reasonable Violence Against Women," in *Patriarchy*, ed. Brown and Bohn, 119.

42. Code, "Responsibility," 547.

43. Ibid., 550. It is interesting to note that Bernard J. F. Lonergan discusses "intellectual conversion" (what I am—loosely—calling the "discovery of discovery") as a correction of the myth that "knowing is like looking." *Women's Ways of Knowing* and observations such as Code's, quoted here, indicate that the "myth" that women need to overcome is not so much that "knowing is like looking" as that "knowing is merely hearing." See Crysdale, "Self-Appropriation," 99. On intellectual conversion, see Lonergan, *Method in Theology*, 238, and my own discussion of it in chapter 6 below.

44. See Alison Moore's study of the relation between basic social and material resources and women's conception of themselves as moral agents: "Moral Agency of Women in a Battered Women's Shelter," *The Annual of the Society of Christian Ethics* (1990): 131–47. See also Young-Eisendrath and Wehr, "Fallacy of Individualism."

45. For more extended discussions of the resurrection accounts, see Pheme Perkins, *Resurrection: New Testament Witness and Contemporary Reflection* (New York: Doubleday, 1984); Gerald O'Collins, *Interpreting the Resurrection: Examining The Major Problems in the Stories of Jesus' Resurrection* (New York: Paulist Press, 1988); and Raymond Brown, "The Resurrection of Jesus," in *The New Jerome Biblical Commentary*, ed. Raymond Brown, Joseph Fitzmyer, and Roland Murphy (Englewood Cliffs, N.J.: Prentice Hall, 1990); and John Galvin, "The Resurrection of Jesus in Catholic Systematics," *Heythrop Journal* 20 (1979): 123–45.

46. See my discussion of solidarity, with reference to Shawn Copeland's work, in chapter 3 above.

47. On the community level I think of a book such as *Roots*, which took many decades out of one man's life, but came to fruition after generations of suffering under slavery. On the personal level, I think of a student who told me of her experience of being assaulted in the middle of the night while at home in her bed. She said that she intuitively began praying and quickly was filled with a sense of peace;

she knew that everything would be all right no matter what happened. But it has taken her several years of spiritual direction, therapy, writing, and courses in self-defense to understand and explain just what that experience was all about.

48. Unfortunately, the church itself—either on the official institutional level or in small communities—is often the agent of this distortion of voice. Then salvation can mean resistant action against the dominant modes of speech in our own communities of faith. Some people work within their inherited religious communions, attempting to retell or retrieve gospel meanings. Others find that they must leave these inherited faiths and reclaim voice in alternative settings.

49. This is perhaps one of the earliest "creeds" recorded in the Christian tradition. Creeds are, in a sense, the codified "stories" that the church has told about the meaning of the Christ event. Older statements of faith from the Hebrew tradition recount the story of the exodus as the action of God in history (see Deut. 26:5: "A wandering Aramean was my father . . ."). While these "creeds" are narrative in form, later Christian creeds move to nonbiblical language and more systematic statements of sets of truths (doctrines)—hence the "I believe" formulation of most creeds with which we are familiar.

It is interesting to note that Paul's narrative of the cross and resurrection appearances (in contrast to the Gospel versions) neglects to mention any of the women. Appearances of the Risen Lord are central to Paul's point here (which is that he too saw the Risen Lord, making him a valid apostle, albeit "the least"). Yet appearances to Kephas and the Twelve are front and center while Mary Magdalene, the other Mary, and other women mentioned in Gospel accounts are left out entirely.

50. Note that for these Corinthian Christians, as for many in the early church, speaking up and telling their story, that is, proclaiming the gospel, was risky business. By becoming Christians many ran the danger of disinheritance, of losing public respect, if not of losing their lives. As the weak and the foolish, as those not part of the learned elite, their confession of faith would likely be taken as nonsense. Thus, Code's earlier allusion to the courage necessary to claim one's voice "in the face of pervasive and infectious feeling on every side that one is bound not to succeed in one's enterprise" ("Responsibility," 550) can be applied to these Corinthians as well as to many contemporary women.

51. Elisabeth Schüssler Fiorenza, ed., *The Power of Naming: A Concilium Reader in Feminist Liberation Theology* (Maryknoll, N.Y.: Orbis Books, 1996). The subsections follow this theme of "voice": Part I: Claiming Our Own Theological Voices; Part II: Naming the Structures of Women's Oppression; Part III: The Theological Construction of Women's Oppression; Part IV: Changing Theological Discourses.

52. Mary John Mananzan, "Education to Femininity or Education to Feminism?" in *Power of Naming*, ed. Schüssler Fiorenza, 187–97.

53. Eileen J. Stenzel, "Maria Goretti: Rape and the Politics of Sainthood," in *Power of Naming*, ed. Schüssler Fiorenza, 224–31. Pertinent to the discussion of redemption from the side of the victims, Stenzel says:

Prior to the development of feminist perspectives on rape in the late 1960s, societal definitions of rape excluded the victim's experience of rape and insisted that rape was a form of sexual deviance, often precipitated by its victims. . . . Feminist scholars have viewed rape in the context of patriarchal culture and defined it in terms of victims' accounts of their experience of rape. . . . There is general agreement that violence against women rises from a systemic cultural acceptance of power and control as a means of affection and defining human relationships. (p. 225)

She cites the following: Patricia L. N. Donat and John D'Emilio, "A Feminist Redefinition of Rape and Sexual Assault: Historical Foundations and Change," *Journal of Social Issues* 48 (1992): 9–22; D. Herman, "The Rape Culture," in *Women: A Feminist Perspective*, ed. Jo Freeman, 2nd ed. (Mountain View, Calif.: Mayfield Publishing, 1975). On Maria Goretti, see Sheila A. Redmond, "Christian 'Virtues' and Recovery from Sexual Abuse," in *Patriarchy*, ed. Brown and Bohn, 70–88.

54. Diane Neu, "Our Name is Church: Catholic-Christian Feminist Liturgies," in *Power of Naming*, ed. Schüssler Fiorenza, 259–72.

55. Janet Walton, "Ecclesiastical and Feminist Blessing," in *Power of Naming*, ed. Schüssler Fiorenza, 284–91.

56. See Ann O'Hara Graff, "The Struggle to Name Women's Experience," in *Embrace*, ed. Graff, 71–89, esp. 75–77. See also Schüssler Fiorenza, "Breaking the Silence," in *Power of Naming*, ed. Schüssler Fiorenza, 169–70; and Nelle Morton, "The Rising Woman Consciousness in a Male Language Structure," in *The Journey is Home*, ed. Nelle Morton (Boston: Beacon Press, 1985).

57. Willimon, "Heard about the Pastor Who," 995. This first came up when I presented this material in lecture form at St. Paul University in Ottawa. Someone asked afterward "What is the white middle-class woman's counterpart to 'sass'?" At the time I could not think of a response but later came to think that "gossip" might be the answer. The degree to which gossip is an activity of resistance or simply a passive-aggressive way of getting around the system remains to be explored. Gossip certainly can be a way of building community and even of re-structuring the meaning of a community. Still, one would have to work out the criteria of authentic versus harmful gossip.

58. It is interesting to think of the episode on the road to Emmaus as an instance of gossip. Jesus joins some people walking along the road and asks them what they are discussing. They look at him in shock and say, in effect: How can you possibly not know what is going on? When he asks them to elaborate, they tell a long tale about how "this happened" and then "that happened" and how "we had hoped . . . , but" and then "some women have claimed . . ." and "now we don't know what to think!!" Jesus takes the bait and gives them his spin on the affair. There is, of course, something different about his version of the story: his understanding of it warms their hearts, but the penny doesn't drop until he breaks bread with them. Still, the walk along the road, and the opportunity for "gossip" pro-

vided them with an occasion to discover new meanings to what they had experienced.

59. James H. Cone, "An African-American Perspective on the Cross and Suffering," in *The Scandal of a Crucified World: Perspectives on the Cross and Suffering*, ed. Yacob Tesfai (Maryknoll, N.Y.: Orbis Books, 1994), 50. See also Cheryl Kirk-Duggan, "African-American Spirituals: Confronting and Exorcising Evil through Song," and Karen B. Fletcher "'Soprano Obligato': The Voices of Black Women and American Conflict in the Thought of Anna Julia Cooper," in *Troubling*, ed. Townes. See also, Cheryl Kirk-Duggan, *Exorcizing Evil: A Womanist Perspective on the Spirituals* (Maryknoll, N.Y.: Orbis Books, 1997).

60. Cone, "An African-American Perspective," in *Scandal*, ed. Tesfai, 58.

61. Jean Marc Ela, "The Memory of the African People and the Cross of Christ," in *Scandal*, ed. Tesfai, 21.

62. Andreas A. Yewangoe, "An Asian Perspective on the Cross and Suffering," in *Scandal*, ed. Tesfai, 70. See also Byung-Mu Ahn, "Jesus and People (Minjung)," in *Asian Faces of Jesus*, ed. Rasiah S. Sugirtharajah (Maryknoll, N.Y.: Orbis Books), 1993.

63. Yewangoe, "An Asian Perspective," in *Scandal*, ed. Tesfai, 70. He goes on to show how this particularly involves the *minjung* relating to Jesus as the crucified. He also notes how the image of the exodus has become a paradigm used in *minjung* theology. Compare this with Cone's discussion of the exodus theme in black theology in "An African-American Perspective," in *Scandal*, ed. Tesfai, 51.

64. Gustavo Gutiérrez, *The Power of the Poor in History* (Maryknoll, N.Y.: Orbis Books, 1983), 80; as quoted in Ada Maria Isasi-Diaz, "Elements of a *Mujerista* Anthropology," in *Embrace*, ed. Graff, 93.

65. Isasi-Diaz, "Elements," 95–96.

66. Dorothy Soelle, *Suffering*, trans. Everett R. Kalin (Philadelphia: Fortress, 1975), 70. She goes on to delineate a further phase of action, in which one makes changes in order to alleviate the named suffering.

67. Ibid., 76.

CHAPTER 5
REDEEMING REDEMPTION: TRANSFORMING THE TRADITION

1. From Peggy Halsey, *Abuse in the Family: Breaking the Church's Silence* (New York: Office of Ministries with Women, General Board of Global Ministry, United Methodist Church, 1982), 4–5; as quoted in Carole R. Bohn, "Dominion to Rule: The Roots and Consequences of a Theology of Ownership," in *Christianity, Patriarchy, and Abuse: A Feminist Critique*, ed. Joanne C. Brown and Carole R. Bohn (Cleveland, Oh.: Pilgrim Press, 1989), 107.

2. Halsey, *Abuse*, 4–5, as quoted in Bohn, "Dominion to Rule," in *Patriarchy*, ed. Brown and Bohn, 108.

3. Sheila A. Redmond, "Christian 'Virtues' and Recovery from Child Sexual Abuse," in *Patriarchy*, ed. Brown and Bohn, 70–88, at 77. The speaker is Roxanne Yesu, who made the comment on the Phil Donahue show, Sept. 1986.

4. From Susan B. Thistlethwaite, "Every Two Minutes: Battered Women and Feminist Interpretation," in *Weaving the Visions: New Patterns in Feminist Spirituality*, ed. Judith Plaskow and Carol Christ (San Francisco: Harper & Row, 1989), 311. This is discussed in Regina A. Boisclair, "Amnesia in the Catholic Sunday Lectionary: Women—Silenced from the Memories of Salvation History," in *Women and Theology*, ed. Mary Ann Hinsdale and Phyllis H. Kaminski (Maryknoll, N.Y.: Orbis Books, 1995), 109–35, at 116.

5. Caucasian woman in her thirties, Church of the Latter Day Saints, West Coast, as quoted in *Defecting in Place: Women Claiming Responsibility for Their Own Spiritual Lives*, ed. Miriam T. Winter, Adair Lummis, and Allison Stokes (New York: Crossroad, 1994), 27.

6. Ibid., 38, caucasian woman in her thirties, Mennonite, in the Southwest.

7. Ibid., 25, caucasian woman in her fifties, Congregationalist, in New England.

8. Ibid., 28, caucasian woman over sixty, Episcopal, in the South.

9. Ibid., 80, caucasian woman in her forties, now United Church of Christ, in New England.

10. Ibid., 96, caucasian woman in her fifties, Roman Catholic, in the Midwest.

11. Ibid., 14, caucasian women in her thirties, United Methodist, in the central region.

12. Bohn, "Dominion to Rule," in *Patriarchy*, ed. Brown and Bohn, 107. Note that these comments are not necessarily representative of Christian pastoral practice today. Many pastors and priests are well versed about the power differentials that exist in families and in society, and about the vulnerability of certain kinds of persons to injustice and abuse. This list is simply an illustration of the kind of counseling many women have received throughout the centuries.

13. A lot of ink has been spilled recently over these passages and their interpretation. Many today reread these passages in terms of God establishing mutuality between the genders, with both men and women being created in the image of God. (This interpretation arises in light of Gen. 1:26–27, in which "man"—as both male and female—is created in the image of God.) Nevertheless, whatever the correct interpretation of these passages, the tradition that has accepted (1) a hierarchical view of men and women, and (2) the greater propensity of women for sin, has been long-standing and deeply influential in the hearts and minds of believers. A good representative article examining these issues is Elisabeth Gossmann, "The Construction of Women's Difference," in *The Power of Naming: A Concilium Reader in Feminist Liberation Theology*, ed. Elisabeth Schüssler Fiorenza (Maryknoll, N.Y.: Orbis Books, 1996), 198–207. On interpretations of Genesis, see Rosemary R.

Ruether, *Women and Redemption: A Theological History* (Minneapolis: Fortress, 1998), 24–30.

14. Again, much has been written over this controversial passage in light of the raising of women's consciousness. A good rendition of a feminist interpretation of the passage can be found in Sally B. Purvis, *The Power of the Cross: Foundations for a Christian Feminist Ethic of Community* (Nashville: Abingdon Press, 1993), chap. 1. See also Ruether, *Women and Redemption*, 30–33.

15. To be fair, there is here, as in many of Paul's more seemingly outrageous passages, a hint of mutuality. The next verses say: "Woman is not independent of man or man of woman in the Lord. For just as woman came from man, so man is born of woman; but all things are from God" (vv. 11–12).

16. For a closer examination of biblical passages regarding women, see the following: Elisabeth Schüssler Fiorenza, *In Memory of Her: A Feminist Theological Reconstruction of Christian Origins* (New York: Crossroad, 1984), chaps. 6 and 7; Virginia Mollenkott, *Women, Men and the Bible* (New York: Crossroad, 1989), esp. chap. 5; Robin Scroggs, "Paul and the Eschatological Woman," *Journal of the American Academy of Religion* 40 (1972): 283–303; Robert Jewett, "The Sexual Liberation of the Apostle Paul," *Journal of the American Academy of Religion Supplements* 47 (1979): 55–87; William Walker, "1 Corinthians 11:2–16 and Paul's View Regarding Women," *Journal of Biblical Literature* 94 (1975): 94–110.

17. A useful definition of "patriarchy" comes from a committee of the Roman Catholic Bishops in Quebec: "Patriarchy is a social system which supports and authenticates the predominance of men, brings about a concentration of power and privilege in the hands of men, and, consequently, leads to the control and subordination of women, generating social inequality between the sexes" (Social Affairs Committee of the Assembly of Quebec Bishops, *A Heritage of Violence* [Montreal, 1989], 48, as discussed and quoted in Mary J. Mananzan, "Feminine Socialization: Women as Victims and Collaborators, in *Violence against Women*, ed. Elisabeth Schüssler Fiorenza and M. Shawn Copeland, *Concilium* 1994/1 [Maryknoll, N.Y.: Orbis Books, 1994], 44–52, at 47). All the articles in this volume are useful in making the connections between Christian theologies, as traditionally practiced, and violence against women. On the retreat of the Christian church to patriarchal patterns in the early centuries, see Schüssler Fiorenza, *In Memory of Her*, chap. 8.

18. For a more thorough historical review, see Ruether, *Women and Redemption*.

19. Tertullian, *De Cultu Fem.* 1.1. See Mananzan, "Feminine Socialization," 51.

20. Juan Luis Vives, *Instrucción de la mujer cristiana*, book 2, chap. 9, in *Obras Completas*, trans. L. Riber (Madrid, 1947), 1094, as quoted in Felisa Elizondo, "Strategies of Resistance and Sources of Healing in Christianity," in *Violence*, ed. Schüssler Fiorenza and Copeland, 102.

21. See Mary P. Engel, "Evil, Sin, and Violation of the Vulnerable," in *Lift Every Voice and Sing: Constructing Christian Theologies from the Underside*, ed. Susan B. Thistlethwaite and Mary P. Engel (San Francisco: HarperCollins, 1990), 152–64.

Engel discusses both sides of these notions of sin, recognizing that, for victims of abuse, even the feminist suggestions for alternative views of sin (e.g., moral callousness, lack of trust, overdependency) can be harmful. She gives a very nuanced reading of how sin must be interpreted in light of both victims and perpetrators. See also Sally McReynolds and Ann O'Hara Graff, "Sin: When Women are the Context," in *In the Embrace of God: Feminist Approaches to Theological Anthropology*, ed. Ann O'Hara Graff (Maryknoll, N.Y.: Orbis Books, 1995), 161–72.

22. Engel, "Evil, Sin, and Violation," 157.

23. Tracy Nagurski, "To Daddy," in *Voices in the Night: Women Speaking About Incest*, ed. Toni A. H. McNaron and Yarrow Morgan (Pittsburgh, Penn.: Cleis, 1982), 146, as quoted in Engel, "Evil, Sin, and Violation," in *Lift Every Voice*, ed. Thistlethwaite and Engel, 159. On critiques of sin as pride, see discussion in chapter 1 above, and citations there, n. 9.

24. Redmond, "Christian 'Virtues,'" in *Patriarchy*, ed. Brown and Bohn, 77.

25. See ibid. See also Elizondo, "Strategies of Resistance," 105ff., and Patricia Wismer, "For Women in Pain: A Feminist Theology of Suffering," in *Embrace*, ed. Graff, 138–58, at 153.

26. This need for sexual purity and the virtue of forgiveness are illustrated by the story of a twentieth-century saint, Maria Goretti. Maria refused the sexual advances of a nineteen-year-old relative and, in turn, was stabbed by him fourteen times. She died within a few days, but not before she had time to forgive her attacker. She was canonized in 1950, and has been heralded as an exemplar for young women and children, first, because she was willing to die rather than be "defiled" and, second, because she forgave her murderer on her deathbed. For an example of how her suffering has been idealized, see John Carr, *Saint Maria Goretti: Martyr for Purity* (Dublin: Clonmore & Reynolds, 1950 [1948]). For critiques of this idealization, see Redmond, "Christian 'Virtues,'" in *Patriarchy*, ed. Brown and Bohn, 74ff.; and Eileen Stenzel, "Maria Goretti: Rape and the Politics of Sainthood," in *Power of Naming*, ed. Schüssler Fiorenza, 224–31.

27. Of course, the racism involved here was not really a matter of color at all. As many have pointed out, race is a social construct, in which—undoubtedly—color is one factor. But in some ways the issue of color was secondary in colonialism to the hegemony of culture. The indigenous peoples were "black" or "yellow" or "red" simply because they were not Europeans. An excellent revisitation of the effects of colonization and evangelization on the Americas can be found in Leonardo Boff and Virgil Elizondo, eds., *1492–1992: The Voice of the Victims, Concilium* 1990/6 (London: SCM Press, 1990).

28. Yacob Tesfai, "Introduction," in *The Scandal of a Crucified World: Perspectives on the Cross and Suffering*, ed. Yacob Tesfai (Maryknoll, N.Y.: Orbis Books, 1994), 4, quoting Regis Debray, *Christoph Colomb: Le visiteur de l'aube* (Paris: La Difference, 1991), 36.

29. Walter Altmann, "A Latin American Perspective on the Cross and Suffering," in *Scandal*, ed. Tesfai, 76–77. See also Dom Pedro Casadaliga, "The 'Cruci-

fied' Indians—A Case of Anonymous Collective Martyrdom," in *Martyrdom Today*, ed. Johannes Baptist Metz and Edward Schillebeeckx, *Concilium* 163 (New York: Seabury Press, 1983), 48–52.

30. Jon Sobrino, "The Crucified Peoples: Yahweh's Suffering Servant Today," in *Voice of the Victims*, ed. Boff and Elizondo, 120–29, at 121.

31. Altmann, "A Latin American Perspective," 79.

32. Ibid., 82.

33. Simon S. Maimela, "The Suffering of Human Divisions and the Cross," in *Scandal*, ed. Tesfai, 36–47, at 43.

34. Floris A. van Jaarsveld, *The Afrikaner's Interpretation of South African History* (Cape Town: Simondium Publishers, 1964), 25. See also Maimela, "Human Divisions," 45.

35. Maimela, "Human Divisions," in *Scandal*, ed. Tesfai, 37.

36. Ibid., quoting Jürgen Moltmann, *The Crucified God: The Cross of Christ as the Foundation and Criticism of Christian Theology* (New York: Harper & Row, 1974), 49.

37. Andreas A. Yewangoe, "An Asian Perspective on the Cross and Suffering," in *Scandal*, ed. Tesfai, 61–74, at 62.

38. Edward Joesting, *Hawaii, an Uncommon History* (New York: W. W. Norton, 1972), 76–77. See also Jill Raitt, "Christianity, Inc.," in *Broken and Whole: Essays on Religion and the Body*, ed. Maureen A. Tilley and Susan A. Ross (Lanham, Md.: University Press of America, 1995), 99–113, at 100–101.

39. Archibald W. Murray, *Forty Years' Mission Work in Polynesia and New Guinea from 1835 to 1875* (London: James Nisbet, 1876), 10. See also Raitt, "Christianity, Inc.," in *Broken and Whole*, ed. Tilley and Ross, 101.

40. Hiram Bingham, *A residence of twenty one years in the Sandwich Islands; or the civil, religious, and political history of those islands*, 2nd ed. (Hartford, Conn.: H. Huntington, 1948), 107, as quoted in Raitt, "Christianity, Inc.," in *Broken and Whole*, ed. Tilley and Ross, 102.

41. Tesfai, "Introduction," in *Scandal*, ed Tesfai, 5. Note the double hierarchy, of race/culture *and* of gender, that put women of non-European descent in a position of double jeopardy. Not only were they subject to cultural prejudice and treated as "savages"; they were considered even more depraved than their male counterparts. The hierarchy of gender was inculcated into converts so that, even when they were "civilised," gender discrimination continued *within* the nondominant cultural sphere. For more on this double discrimination, see Frances E. Wood, "'Take My Yoke Upon You'—The Role of the Church in the Oppression of African-American Women," in *A Troubling in My Soul: Womanist Perspectives on Evil and Suffering*, ed. Emilie M. Townes (Maryknoll, N.Y.: Orbis Books, 1993), 37–47, esp. 39.

42. Gilles Danroc, "Haiti ou la question retournée," in *Le rendezvous de Saint-Domingue: Enjeu d'un anniversaire 1492-1992*, ed. Ignace Berten and René Luneau

(Paris: Editions du Centurion, 1991), 225, as quoted in Tesfai, "Introduction," in *Scandal,* ed Tesfai, 5.

43. This review of ideas is, I admit, skewed in that the purpose of the review is to trace how certain distortions of the good news became entrenched. This certainly does not tell the whole story of Christian faith throughout the ages, and it leaves out, in particular, the many ways in which people came to experience resurrection in their lives. For a more thorough review of theologies of the cross, see Ruether, *Women and Redemption;* and Gerard S. Sloyan, *The Crucifixion of Jesus* (Minneapolis: Fortress, 1995).

44. Elizabeth A. Johnson, "Jesus and Salvation," *Proceedings, Forty-Ninth Annual Convention of The Catholic Theology Society of America* 49 (1994): 1–18, at 3. This plenary lecture briefly reviews traditional interpretations of salvation but also gives an astute perspective on issues in reinterpreting salvation today in light of historical consciousness. For further discussion of the early disciples' interpretation of their experience of Jesus, Johnson cites the following: Edward Schillebeeckx, *Jesus: An Experiment in Christology,* trans. Hubert Hoskins (New York: Seabury Press, 1979); idem, *Christ: The Experience of Jesus as Lord,* trans. John Bowden (New York: Seabury Press, 1980).

45. On the origins and meaning of atonement, see Herbert A. Hodges, *The Pattern of Atonement* (London: SCM Press, 1955), 9. Atonement seems to be the category of choice in twentieth-century writings, given numerous book titles. See, e.g., Don Browning, *Atonement and Psychotherapy* (Philadelphia: Westminster Press, 1966); John Goldingay, ed., *Atonement Today* (London: SPCK, 1995); John Driver, *Understanding the Atonement for the Mission of the Church* (Scottdale, Penn.: Herald Press, 1986).

46. Johnson ("Jesus and Salvation," 4) cites Irenaeus's recapitulation theory and Athanasius's divinization theology as examples of this trend.

47. Here Johnson ("Jesus and Salvation," 4) refers to Tertullian's satisfaction theory and Augustine's sacrificial theory. For more on patristic approaches to salvation, see Joseph F. Mitros, "Patristic Views of Christ's Salvific Work," *Thought* 42 (1967): 415–47. See also Sloyan, *Crucifixion,* chap. 3; and Ruether, *Women and Redemption,* chap. 2.

48. The designation of these three approaches is attributed to Gustav Aulen, *Christus Victor* (New York: Macmillan, 1969). See also Driver, *Atonement,* chap. 2; and Joanne C. Brown and Rebecca Parker, "For God so Loved the World?" in *Patriarchy,* ed. Brown and Bohn, 1–30, esp. 4–13.

49. In some versions God actually deceived Satan, tricked him outright. The notion that there is a law of the universe by which the evil powers have a right to a death for an infraction is illustrated in C. S. Lewis's *The Loin, the Witch, and the Wardrobe.* Aslan suffers this death in place of the guilty one. Still, there is a deeper law by which Aslan is resurrected.

50. For a discussion of Anselm's method, see William P. Loewe, "Method in

the *Cur Deus Homo:* Concept, Performance and the Question of Rationalism," in *Ethnicity, Nationality, and Religious Experience,* ed. Peter Phan (Lanham, Md.: University Press of America, 1995), 73–83. For modern interpretations of Anselm, see John McIntyre, *St. Anselm and His Critics* (Edinburgh/London: Oliver & Boyd, 1953); Gillian R. Evans, *Anselm and Talking about God* (Oxford: Clarendon Press, 1974); and Charles Hefling, "A Perhaps Permanently Valid Achievement: Lonergan on Christ's Satisfaction," *Method: Journal of Lonergan Studies* 10 (1992): 51–76.

51. Johnson, "Jesus and Salvation," 5.

52. Driver, *Understanding the Atonement,* 50. An important element that the Reformers retrieved was that the salvation won by Christ comes to the believer as a free gift rather than as a reward for penitential acts. The element of grace, and to this extent the original gospel message, was rightly recovered in the Protestant Reformation. Nevertheless, the backdrop for this recovery was a worldview that presumed that judgment by a wrathful God was the problem to be solved. In other words, it took on the basic premises that Anselm had incorporated into his theory: an all-powerful God who by his very nature demanded payment for an offense. Thus, Protestantism incorporated implicitly a certain "theological sadism." For more on this, see Dorothy Soelle, *Suffering* (Philadelphia: Fortress, 1975), chap. 1. esp. 22–25. See also Hodges, *Atonement,* chap 4, esp. 67–68.

53. See Johnson, "Jesus and Salvation," 5–6.

54. See Driver, *Atonement,* 50–64.

55. For a somewhat dated but nevertheless astute outline of the problems with a "penal substitutionary" view of the atonement, see Hodges, *Atonement,* chap. 3.

56. Maimela, "Human Divisions," in *Scandal,* ed. Tesfai, 41.

57. See Schüssler Fiorenza, *In Memory of Her,* chaps. 7 and 8.

58. See Maimela, "Human Divisions," in Scandal, ed. Tesfai, 42.

59. Beverly W. Harrison and Carter Heyward, "Pain and Pleasure: Avoiding the Confusions of Christian Tradition in Feminist Theory," in *Patriarchy,* ed. Brown and Bohn, 148–73, at 151–52.

60. Ibid., 152.

61. See Soelle, *Suffering,* 24.

62. Alice Miller's seminal work on child abuse is entitled *For Your Own Good: Hidden Cruelty in Child-rearing and the Roots of Violence,* trans. Hildegarde and Hunter Hannum (New York: Farrar, Straus, & Giroux, 1983/1985).

63. In reference to the biblical tradition, Walter Brueggemann speaks of two trajectories evident throughout. He calls these the "royal trajectory," which protects the "trusted memory" and the "liberation trajectory," which instigates the "faithful voice." The first is "universalistic in intention, socially conservative, and emphasizes God's glory and holiness." The second "is more concrete and historically minded in perspective, socially revolutionary and transformative, and focuses on God's justice and righteousness." These trajectories in the biblical narratives reflect a bipolar aspect of faith itself. There is in both individual lives and in the development of traditions an extant dialectic between the familiar, the trusted, the

status quo, and the transformative, the risky, and the creative. See Walter Brueggemann, *The Bible Makes Sense* (Atlanta: John Knox Press, 1977), 150; idem, "A Shape for Old Testament Theology I: Structure Legitimation," *Catholic Biblical Quarterly* 47 (1985); idem, "A Shape for Old Testament Theology, II: Embrace of Pain," *Catholic Biblical Quarterly* 47 (1985). See also the chapter on Brueggemann in Lucien Richard, *What Are They Saying about the Theology of Suffering?* (New York: Paulist Press, 1992).

64. Rosemary Haughton, *The Transformation of Man* (1967; reprint, Springfield, Ill.: Templegate, 1980). An excerpt from this book is reprinted as "Formation and Transformation," in *Conversion: Perspectives on Personal and Social Transformation*, ed. Walter E. Conn (New York: Alba House, 1978), 23–26.

65. Haughton, *Transformation*, 31–32. Haughton goes on to use examples from Christian history that emphasize one element or the other. She uses the early Puritans (late sixteenth and early seventeenth centuries) as an example of a "community of the transformed" (chap. 6). She then discusses the early Benedictines (sixth through ninth centuries) as a "formation community" (chap. 7). In both cases, leaning to one extreme forces, eventually, a return to the other pole.

66. The possibility arises, as with the Puritan community that Haughton discusses, that conversional experiences can become an element into which one is socialized. Then transformation becomes an aspect of formation, and conversion is "programmed." See Walter E. Oates, "Conversion: Sacred and Secular," in *Conversion*, ed. Conn, 149–68, esp. 163–64.

67. See Bernard J. F. Lonergan, *Insight: A Study of Human Understanding*, ed. Frederick E. Crowe and Robert M. Doran (1957; reprint, Toronto: University of Toronto Press, 1992), 242.

68. Frederick E. Crowe, *Old Things and New: A Strategy for Education* (Atlanta, Ga.: Scholars Press, 1985), x.

69. See Bernard J. F. Lonergan, *Method in Theology* (New York: Seabury Press, 1972), 41–47; idem, *Insight*, 725–40; idem, "Natural Right and Historical Mindedness," in *A Third Collection: Papers by Bernard J.F. Lonergan, S.J.*, ed. Frederick E. Crowe (New York: Paulist Press, 1985), 180–81.

70. Note that there are certain times in life during which the tension between "belief" and "discovery" becomes particularly salient, for example, during adolescence. See Cynthia S. W. Crysdale, "Development, Conversion, and Religious Education," *Horizons* 17 (1990): 30–46, esp. 43ff.

71. Sally B. Purvis speaks of the need for "resocialization," and claims that this is what Paul was up to in his missionary work—resocializing converts and communities into new life under the power of the cross. See *Power of the Cross*, 49, 70ff.

72. On idolatry and the elusive nature of the ultimate, see Paul Tillich, *The Dynamics of Faith* (New York: Harper & Row, 1957); and H. Richard Niebuhr, *Radical Monotheism and Western Culture* (Louisville, Ky.: Westminster/John Knox, 1960).

73. On the interaction of truth and interpretation in various contexts, see

Winston D. Persaud, "The Cross, the Unity of the Church, and Human Suffering," in *Scandal*, ed. Tesfai, 111–29. On authentic subjectivity, see Lonergan, *Method*, 265, 292. On authenticity with regard to the tradition, see ibid., 80, 162, 299. See also Cynthia S. W. Crysdale, "Reason, Faith, and Authentic Religion," in *The Struggle Over the Past: Fundamentalism in the Modern World*, ed. William Shea (New York: University Press of America, 1993), 157–80.

74. See Cynthia S. W. Crysdale, "Feminist Theology: Ideology, Authenticity, and the Cross," *Église et Théologie* 28 (1997): 245–63.

75. In its most general interpretation, this is simply what the Roman Catholic doctrine of infallibility is all about: faith that God will protect the church in truth and preserve the truth in the church. This broad understanding of infallibility can incorporate the notion that the church can and does get skewed in its practice and its theology. The faith is that God will never allow such deviations to ultimately destroy the gospel, but will revive and renew the church as necessary. This is infallibility in a dialectical and developmental view. Narrower interpretations locate the agency of truth in the magisterium of the Roman Catholic Church, specifically the papal office, and reject the possibility that the church might ever deviate from the truth.

76. See Hodges, *Atonement*, chap. 3; Johnson, "Jesus and Salvation," 5–6; and Tesfai, "Introduction," in *Scandal*, ed Tesfai, 5–6.

77. See Purvis, *Power of the Cross;* she distinguishes controlling power from life-giving power and relies on Paul's New Testament writings to support the latter. See also Gossmann, "Difference"; she juxtaposes every critique of the tradition with evidence from Christian history of countertraditions that affirm women.

78. See Rita Brock, "And a Little Child Shall Lead Us: Christology and Child Abuse," in *Patriarchy*, ed. Brown and Bohn, 42–61.

79. See Sobrino, "Crucified Peoples." He dedicates this article to Ignacio Ellacuria, a modern martyr, who first elaborated on the idea of a "crucified people" (in contrast to Moltmann's *Crucified God*). See Ignacio Ellacuria, "El Pueblo crucifado: Ensayo de soterología histórica," *Revista Latinoamerica de Teología* 18 (1989): 305–33; idem, "Discernir 'el signo' de los tiempos," *Diakonia* 17 (1981): 57–59. See also Altmann, "A Latin American Perspective."

80. See James Cone, "An African-American Perspective on the Cross and Suffering," in *Scandal*, ed. Tesfai, 48–60. See also Cone, *The Spirituals and the Blues* (Maryknoll, N.Y.: Orbis Books, 1991); Albert Raboteau, *Slave Religion* (New York: Oxford University Press, 1978); Vincent Harding, *There Is a River* (New York: Harcourt Brace Jovanovich, 1981); Gayrand S. Wilmore, *Black Religion and Black Radicalism* (Maryknoll, N.Y.: Orbis Books, 1983); and Cheryl Kirk-Duggan, *Exorcizing Evil: A Womanist Perspective on the Spirituals* (Maryknoll, N.Y.: Orbis Books, 1997).

81. See Jean-Marc Ela, "The Memory of the African People and the Cross of Christ," in *Scandal*, ed. Tesfai, 17–35. See also Maimela, "Human Divisions," in *Scandal*, ed. Tesfai.

82. See Ada Maria Isasi-Diaz, "Elements of a *Mujerista* Anthropology," in *Embrace,* ed. Graff, 90–102, esp. 91.

83. See Elisabeth Moltmann-Wendel, "Is There a Feminist Theology of the Cross? in *Scandal,* ed. Tesfai, 87–98; Wismer, "Women in Pain"; Pamela A. Smith, "Chronic Pain and Creative Possibility: A Psychological Phenomenon Confronts Theologies of Suffering," in *Broken and Whole,* ed. Tilley and Ross, 159–87; and Soelle, *Suffering.*

84. See Andreas A. Yewangoe, "An Asian Perspective on the Cross and Suffering," in *Scandal,* ed. Tesfai, 61–74; and Choan S. Song, "Christian Mission Toward Abolition of the Cross," in *Scandal,* ed. Tesfai, 130–48. See also Kwok Pui-Lan, "Emergent Feminist Theology from Asia," in *Women and Theology,* ed. Hinsdale and Kaminski, 93–98; and Mary Rattigan, "Korean Women Theologians: An Observer's Appreciation," in *Women and Theology,* ed. Hinsdale and Kaminski, 156–74.

85. See Raitt, "Christianity, Inc.," in *Broken and Whole,* ed. Tilley and Ross, esp. 104, where she discusses her own efforts to reconcile her Christian faith with its oppressive past.

Other examples of communal repentance and requests for forgiveness have occurred over the last decade. These include, for example, the following: (1) The Anglican Church of Canada has officially recognized the personal and cultural abuse that Anglican missions brought to Canadian aboriginal peoples, especially with regard to residential schools established for indigenous children in northern and western Canada. (2) The Canadian government has officially apologized to all Japanese-Canadians and their families who were incarcerated during World War II without due cause or opportunity for appeal. (3) The Southern Baptist Convention in the United States has acknowledged publicly that its founding as a denomination was grounded in large part on opposition to abolitionists of the North during the Civil War era. It has acknowledged, with regret, the racism inherent in its origins.

CHAPTER 6

A THEOLOGICAL MODEL:
GRACE, CONVERSION, AND THE LAW OF THE CROSS

1. One of my first ecumenical encounters occurred in the context of this class. The group of people taking this course consisted of fifteen: six Protestants (including Dutch Reformed, Mennonite, United Church of Canada, and Anglican communions), eight Roman Catholics (including religious and layfolk, all from a variety of contexts), and one "Moonie." When we discussed the "mediation of revelation through Scripture" I went into high gear with questions about the author-

ity of the Bible. My Roman Catholic friends were baffled at my concerns. However, when we got to the "mediation of revelation through the Magisterium," chaos broke out on the Catholic front. It soon became clear that we all had the same questions regarding authority, only mine surfaced with regard to the Bible and those of my Roman Catholic friends emerged with regard to the church. The issues were the same, just located differently.

2. In fact, this course was taught at St. Michael's College in Toronto, and this observation was made by Margaret O'Gara, who followed it up immediately with the advice: "I think you should have a talk with my husband." Her husband is, of course, Michael Vertin, with whom I did, indeed, have many a further talk. He ended up directing my dissertation, and both of them have continued to be influential mentors for my work.

3. On the usefulness of models, see Bernard J. F. Lonergan, *Method in Theology* (New York: Seabury Press, 1972), xii.

4. As each of the previous chapters relies on one or two key resources, so also this chapter has its facilitators. In this case I rely on the work of Bernard Lonergan, his basic position on knowing, his transcendental method, and its implications for religious life. I draw also on Robert Doran's development of Lonergan's work in relation to the psychic/sensitive aspect of our lives, as well as his explication of the "law of limitation and transcendence." As in other chapters, my primary aim is not to present the ideas of these authors but to use their insights and categories to help make my points.

See Bernard J. F. Lonergan, *Insight: A Study of Human Understanding* (Toronto: University of Toronto Press, 1992) and *Method.* For works pertaining specifically to the topic of this chapter, see Lonergan, "The Redemption," in *Philosophical and Theological Papers, 1958–1964,* ed. Robert C. Croken, Frederick E. Crowe, and Robert M. Doran (Toronto: University of Toronto Press, 1996), 3–28; idem, "Healing and Creating in History," in *A Third Collection,* ed. Frederick E. Crowe (New York: Paulist Press, 1985), 100–109. See also Robert M. Doran, *Theology and the Dialectics of History* (Toronto: University of Toronto Press, 1990).

5. On essential and effective freedom, see Lonergan, *Insight,* 643–47.

6. This is what Lonergan calls the "principle of limitation and transcendence" and Doran discusses as the "dialectic of the subject." See Lonergan, *Insight,* 497–99, 501–2; and Doran, *Dialectics,* chaps. 3 (sec. 4) and 7.

7. See Lonergan on "scotosis" and "dramatic bias," in *Insight,* 214–15.

8. See references cited in n. 6 above.

9. On basic sin and moral evils, as well as physical evils, see Lonergan, *Insight,* 689.

10. See Elizabeth A. Morelli, "Women's Intuition: A Lonerganian Analysis," in *Lonergan and Feminism,* ed. Cynthia S. W. Crysdale (Toronto: University of Toronto Press, 1994), 72–87.

11. In the colonial south this was illustrated by the conflict over Christian missions to slaves. The problem was that baptizing slaves and making them Christian

meant acknowledging that slaves had souls (= a transcendent orientation), which implicitly destroyed the entire framework of the slave system. For this reason, slave masters were consistently ambivalent about Christian missions to their slaves. See Albert J. Raboteau, *Slave Religion: The "Invisible Institution" in the Antebellum South* (New York: Oxford University Press, 1978), chap. 3.

12. In this regard, Doran places his analysis of this "dialectic of the subject" within two further and interrelated dialectics: that of *community* and that of *culture.* See Doran, *Dialectics,* chap. 4 and pp. 521–24.

13. Richard M. Gula sums up the meaning of original sin along these lines: "Original sin is the theological code word for the human condition of living in a world where we are influenced by more evil than what we do ourselves" (*Reason Informed by Faith: Foundations of Catholic Morality* [New York: Paulist Press, 1989], 106).

14. See Rom. 7:24: "Wretched man that I am! Who will save me from this body of death?" Paul's dilemma, as he presents it in Romans 7, is one expression of the vicious cycle I have been describing here. Paul puts it in terms of the "law" and ponders the strange fact that the Judaic law has been unable to free him from the cycle of sin and death.

15. On Aquinas and theological virtues, see Reginald Garrigou-Lagrange, *The Theological Virtues,* trans. T. Reilly (London: B. Herder, 1965). On love, hope, and faith as part of the solution to the problem of evil, see Lonergan, *Insight,* 720–25, 741–42.

16. On operative and cooperative grace, see Lonergan, *Method,* 107, 241. See also the discussion above in chapter 2.

17. Lonergan, *Method,* 240. The latter phrase, of course, he takes from Paul Tillich (see p. 106).

18. Ibid., 105–6.

19. For brief accounts of these peoples' conversions, see Hugh T. Kerr and John M. Mulder, eds., *Conversions: The Christian Experience* (Grand Rapids: Eerdmans, 1983).

20. See Roberta C. Bondi, *Memories of God: Theological Reflections on a Life* (Nashville: Abingdon Press, 1995).

21. Lonergan, *Method,* 32–33.

22. There are, of course, many further qualifications that could be added to this presentation of religious love. First and foremost is that such religious love is the inner experience that is expressed in religious beliefs, in worship, song, art, and many other forms. Lonergan speaks of the experience of religious love as the "inner word" and the expressions of this love as the "outer word." While one may claim, as Lonergan does, that the inner experience of an other-worldly falling in love is a universal potential of human consciousness, one cannot get at this underlying commonality without its embodiment in religious traditions, so one is thrown necessarily into issues of cross-cultural and interreligious dialogue. See *Method,* chap. 4.

23. Jean Piaget and Lawrence Kohlberg have documented these shifts in their theories of moral development. See Jean Piaget, *The Moral Judgment of the Child* (New York: Free Press, 1965); and Lawrence Kohlberg, *The Psychology of Moral Development* (San Francisco: Harper & Row, 1984). For a review of these theories in light of Lonergan's notion of conversion, see Walter E. Conn, *Conscience: Development and Self-Transcendence* (Birmingham, Ala.: Religious Education Press, 1981). See also idem, *Christian Conversion: A Developmental Interpretation of Autonomy and Surrender* (New York: Paulist Press, 1986).

24. Lonergan, *Method,* 240. Note that this shift in criterion from satisfaction to value in no way implies that the two are never co-extensive. Moral conversion does not involve the notion that something must be painful in order to be good. There are choices for value that can be immensely pleasurable. The point is not that value and satisfaction never coexist but that satisfaction, if it serves as the *sole* criterion of decision making, will not guarantee the creation of value.

25. Ibid.

26. "Intellectual conversion" is the name Lonergan gives to a very specific insight into how one comes to know truth. Though the insight itself is into one's own operating rather than into epistemological theories, Lonergan's discussion partners are philosophers of knowledge, and so his explanation of intellectual conversion has to do with taking a particular position regarding knowing, objectivity, and the real. That such a pivotal insight has implications for knowing value as well as truth is recognized by Michael Vertin, who prefers, for this reason, to use the term "cognitional conversion." Walter Conn notes that such a transformational grasp of one's critical role in knowing and deciding is not limited to an explicitly formulated position, and so uses the more general "cognitive conversion." I am certainly discussing these expanded versions of intellectual conversion here, but prefer to use Lonergan's term rather than to generate new categories. See Michael Vertin, "Gender, Science, and Cognitional Conversion," in *Lonergan and Feminism,* ed. Crysdale, 49–71; and Conn, *Christian Conversion,* 116–28.

27. Lonergan, *Method,* 238.

28. Ibid.

29. This is not to say that every single judgment and decision come to a definitive term. Some judgments are merely probable, meaning that they are heading toward a firm conclusion but that all the evidence is not yet in. Likewise, some decisions are provisional until further evidence, in the situation or in one's discernment of value, comes forward. The point is that, even in these situations, when one is not entirely sure, it is the notion of truth or of value toward which one is oriented that allows one to realize that one has not yet arrived. See Lonergan, *Insight,* 308–12 (on the "virtually unconditioned" as the criteria of true judgments) and 324–29 (on probable judgments).

30. See my discussion earlier (chapter 4, esp. n. 43) of women as "receivers" of knowledge who believe that truth is whatever others tell them.

31. On authentic subjectivity, see Lonergan, *Method*, 265, 292.

32. One aspect of the corruption of power is the false premise that one can create and/or control truth. This is evident in political scandals such as Watergate or in the more recent Clinton–Lewinsky affair. It also appears in the work of propaganda, when governments create the interpretations they wish the populace to receive. Investigative journalism unveils *evidence* and in so doing reveals truth to be a matter of true judgment and not the will to power. It is for this reason that corrupt powers in government, church, and the marketplace are so repressive of information and so suspicious of the media. On the relation between authority and authenticity, see Bernard J. F. Lonergan, "Dialectic of Authority," in *Third Collection*, ed. Crowe, 2–12.

33. In his discussion of conversion Lonergan speaks of intellectual conversion first, then moral conversion, then religious conversion. Still, from a chronological point of view, religious conversion usually comes first. It is the occasion for posing further questions about one's knowing and deciding, which can then lead to moral and intellectual conversions. See *Method*, 241–43.

34. My primary resource here is the already cited Doran, *Theology and the Dialectics of History;* see also idem, *Psychic Conversion and Theological Foundations: Toward a Reorientation of the Human Sciences* (Atlanta: Scholars Press, 1981); and idem, "Psychic Conversion," in *The Thomist* 41 (1977): 200–236.

35. For a discussion of the important distinction between consciousness and knowing, see Doran, *Dialectics*, 22, 25, 68–69.

36. Ibid., 46.

37. Ibid., 665. For a discussion of the differences between Jung's and Lonergan's understanding of the unconscious, see ibid., 305, 664–65, and chap. 3 n. 4. Cf. Lonergan, *Method*, 34 n. 5.

38. Doran, *Dialectics*, 665.

39. Ibid., 61–62.

40. Ibid., 59.

41. Ibid., 248.

42. Ibid. The classic mode of negotiating such complexes, as presented in depth psychology, is through dream analysis. Dreams can indeed reveal images that can be liberating, though not without interpretation (i.e., not without insights). Still, dreams are not the only resource for psychic liberation. For example, African American slaves used spirituals, "shouting" and other rituals by which liberating symbols emerged. Prayer, spiritual direction, autobiographical writing, poetry: all these can be media for negotiating feeling complexes and embracing the darkness of travail. The key is to allow such images and symbols their "upward mobility" and to address them with *intentional* discernment so that their potential is realized in consciousness through a control of meaning and a greater awareness of choice.

43. Ibid., 246.

44. Doran discusses these two kinds of opposition as a "dialectic of contradictories" (an unreconcilable polarity) and a "dialectic of contraries" (that can be integrated). See *Dialectics,* 9–10, 68, 71. For his development of Lonergan's principle of limitation and transcendence in reference to these, see pp. 71–77. With regard to his understanding of these in relation to Jungian thought, see Robert M. Doran, "Jungian Psychology and Christian Spirituality, I, II, and III," in *Carl Jung and Christian Spirituality,* ed. Robert L. Moore (New York: Paulist Press, 1988), 66–108; on good and evil as irreconcilable, see pp. 94–96, 102–7.

45. A comment on "complementarity" is necessary here. There has been in recent years much defensive rhetoric about the "complementarity" of the sexes and of gender roles in Christian circles. This is not necessarily what I am advocating. As long as this "complementarity" lies on a presumption of the contradictory nature of the mind/body dualism it is doomed to become a hierarchy. So far from restoring the necessary balance within a nonoppositional dialectic, such talk of complementarity becomes a cover story for a hierarchal and patriarchal worldview. Unless the underlying mistake—of conceiving mind and body, and therefore men and women, to be contradictory opposites—is corrected, appeals to "complementarity" are misguided. True complementarity would involve *something like* what Frederick E. Crowe discusses (picking up a clue from Lonergan) as "mutual self-mediation" and "encounter." See Frederick E. Crowe, "The Genus 'Lonergan and . . .' and Feminism," in *Lonergan and Feminism,* ed. Crysdale, 13–32, esp. 23–27.

46. Note that even though this choice is "either/or" it is not "once only." Because of the historical nature of human existence, conversion can be "lost," healing/elevating grace must be accepted over and over again, and its acceptance is incremental and gradual. Thus, in addition to an initial choice for salvation, there is what the Christian tradition has called "sanctification."

47. Lonergan, *Insight,* 690.

48. Examples of the never-ending quest to "set the record straight" abound: in Ireland, the Middle East, Bosnia, etc. Though retaliation is undertaken (supposedly) in order to correct the situation, the record can never be set straight since there was never any intelligibility to the initial act of sin in the first place, even if such could be identified. Attempts to create intelligibility where there is none simply perpetuate the nonsense; hence the "senseless" acts of violence that are often entailed in such situations.

49. This is illustrated by *Dead Man Walking,* the book and movie discussed in chapter 3 above. There simply was no rational explanation for the horrible rape and murders done by the death-row inmate and his accomplice. They were acts that revealed a lack of reason and a failure of will. To try to make sense of them is a misguided task. For the perpetrator this "making sense" is "rationalization," making sense when there is none. For the victims, in this case the families of the slain, demanding the death penalty was an attempt to grant intelligibility to an

unintelligible set of actions. Neither resolution of the "non-sense" works. The only way out of the non-sense for the perpetrator is to admit his failure and repent. The only way out of the non-sense for the victims' families is to face the irrationality of the situation and forgive. Both of these will involve the reversal of conversion—and embracing travail—rather than the logic of retributive justice.

50. Lonergan, *Insight*, 44.

51. The most common responses to the problem of evil can be caricatured by two alternatives here. On the one hand, people insist on finding intelligibility where there is none; this is most often manifested in finding an agent to blame and then retaliating. On the other hand, those who have an inverse insight and realize that there is no intelligibility to be grasped can highlight the absurdity of life. World process and human aspiration come to be seen, then, as one big cosmic joke, in which the punch line is that there isn't a punch line. Still, persons cannot live long without meaning, and the alternative of absurdity cannot sustain one in life; its ultimate and logical consequence is suicide. Both responses to evil ultimately fail to resolve the problem of evil, the one by making sense when there is none, the other grasping the non-sense but failing to grasp a higher viewpoint from which evil can make sense.

52. This lack of intelligibility at the strictly human level may account for some of the anti-intellectualism of certain strands of modern Christian practice. Faith can be appealed to over against reason because, at one level, there is no "reasonable" grasp of the nature of salvation. The mistake is to assume that there is therefore *no* intelligibility to God's act of salvation in Jesus, and that salvation comes as a matter of denying reason in favor of faith. In this interpretation, seeking to make sense of salvation becomes an enemy in itself, to be shunned by a faith that is inherently irrational.

53. From Lonergan, *De Verbo Incarnato* (Rome: Gregorian University Press, 1964), 552, as translated by William P. Loewe, "Toward a Responsible Contemporary Soteriology," in *Creativity and Method: Essays in Honor of Bernard Lonergan*, ed. Matthew Lamb (Milwaukee: Marquette University Press, 1981), 216. Quoted in Doran, *Dialectics*, 203.

54. Lonergan, *Insight*, 721–22.

55. I would add that the obverse is also true: one cannot have an effective ethic of risk without a higher synthesis. This is where I differ with Sharon Welch in her rejection of God's omnipotence, as discussed in chapter 3. I think that perhaps Welch functions with such a "higher synthesis," but her theology is not, to my mind, consistent with such a practice.

56. This clearly has implications for eschatology. The "already" is the permanence of the new conditions of possibility. The "not yet" recognizes that these are just *conditions* and not yet complete *fulfillment* of the possibilities for transformation.

EPILOGUE: REDEMPTION REVISITED

1. Robert M. Doran claims that this "soteriological principle" was first recognized in the religion of Israel, in the proclamations of Deutero-Isaiah about the Suffering Servant. See *Theology and the Dialectics of History* (Toronto: University of Toronto Press, 1990): 108–35, 203–6.

2. On the *inner word* of religious experience and the *outer word* of religious expression, see Bernard J. F. Lonergan, *Method in Theology* (New York: Seabury Press, 1972), 108–9, 112–15.

3. Bernard J. F. Lonergan, "The Redemption," in *Philosophical and Theological Papers, 1958–1964*, ed. Robert C. Croken, Frederick E. Crowe, and Robert M. Doran (Toronto: University of Toronto Press, 1996): 5–6. On the reference to Newman, see ibid., n. 13.

4. Lonergan, "Redemption," 22–23.

5. First and last verses, as found in *The Hymnal, 1982* (New York: The Church Hymnal Corporation, 1985), no. 458. Attributed to Dean Samuel Crossman, 1664.

Index of Names

Abelard, 110
  Moral Influence Theory of, 110
Ahn, Byung-Mu, 180n. 62
Alsford, Sally, 159n. 9
Altmann, Walter, 183n. 29, 184nn. 31, 32, 188n. 79
Andolsen, Barbara H., 172n. 63
Angelou, Maya, 6, 53, 64, 89, 158n. 5, 168n. 32, 175n. 28
Anselm, 110–12, 115, 153, 185n. 50, 186n. 52
  satisfaction theory of atonement and, 110
Aristotle, 72, 75, 114
Athanasius, 185n. 46
Augustine, 185n. 47
Aulen, Gustav, 185n. 48
Austin, Jane, 175n. 26

Belenky, Mary F., 77, 79, 85, 173n. 13, 175nn. 30, 31, 35, 176nn. 35–38, 177n. 39
Benedict, St., 119
Bingham, Hiram, 107, 184n. 40
Boff, Leonardo, 183n. 27
Bohn, Carole R., 6, 98–99, 158n. 7, 177n. 40, 180n. 1, 181nn. 2, 12

Boisclair, Regina A., 181n. 4
Bondi, Roberta, 6–7, 131, 136, 158n. 8, 191n. 20
Braden, Vic, 69–71
Brent, Linda, 167n. 30
Brock, Rita, 188n. 78
Brown, Joanne Carlson, 6, 158n. 7, 185n. 48
Brown, Raymond E., 177n. 45
Browning, Don, 185n. 45
Brueggemann, Walter, 186–87n. 63

Cahoy, William J., 159n. 9
Carr, Anne E., 172n. 5
Carr, John, 183n. 26
Casadaliga, Pedro, 183n. 29
Clinchy, Blythe M., 77, 173n. 13
Code, Lorraine, 72, 75, 84, 85, 173n. 9, 174n. 17, 175nn. 26, 27, 177n. 42, 178n. 50
Colson, Charles, 131, 132
Columbus, Christopher, 104
Cone, James H., 92–93, 180nn. 59, 60, 63, 188n. 80
Conn, Walter, 69, 172n. 2, 192nn. 23, 26
Constantine, 113

197

Index of Subjects